Terror Disrupted

Terrorism and organized violence are crucially reliant on adequate sources of funding. Blocking those sources has thus become a key goal of national security services in most countries throughout the world. *Terror Disrupted* is the first book to provide an insider's account of how national security services have worked to understand how terrorist groups and organizations are financed and what the best ways are to block such financing. It goes beyond banks to examine the private sector and cryptocurrency forensic firms that are on the front lines of countering terrorist access to new forms of value, like cryptocurrency. Investigating the ways the US and other governments have struggled to tackle the financing of terrorism by the radical right, it describes the various ways in which governments and the private sector can counter terrorist access to finance and fight the financing of groups like ISIS and al-Qa'ida.

JASON BLAZAKIS is Professor of Global Studies at the Middlebury Institute of International Studies (MIIS). He is also the Executive Director of MIIS's Center on Terrorism, Extremism, and Counterterrorism. He served as the Director of the Counterterrorism Finance and Designations Office, Bureau of Counterterrorism, US Department of State. He has published articles in the *Wall Street Journal, Washington Post, Los Angeles Times, USA Today, Time Magazine, Foreign Affairs, The Hill, Philadelphia Inquirer, Lawfare*, and other publications.

Terror Disrupted
Countering the Financing of Terrorism

JASON BLAZAKIS
Middlebury Institute of International Studies

Shaftesbury Road, Cambridge CB2 8EA, United Kingdom

One Liberty Plaza, 20th Floor, New York, NY 10006, USA

477 Williamstown Road, Port Melbourne, VIC 3207, Australia

314–321, 3rd Floor, Plot 3, Splendor Forum, Jasola District Centre, New Delhi – 110025, India

103 Penang Road, #05–06/07, Visioncrest Commercial, Singapore 238467

Cambridge University Press is part of Cambridge University Press & Assessment, a department of the University of Cambridge.

We share the University's mission to contribute to society through the pursuit of education, learning and research at the highest international levels of excellence.

www.cambridge.org
Information on this title: www.cambridge.org/9781009232845

DOI: 10.1017/9781009232838

© Jason Blazakis 2026

This publication is in copyright. Subject to statutory exception and to the provisions of relevant collective licensing agreements, no reproduction of any part may take place without the written permission of Cambridge University Press & Assessment.

When citing this work, please include a reference to the DOI 10.1017/9781009232838

First published 2026

Cover image: bubaone / Getty Images

A catalogue record for this publication is available from the British Library

A Cataloging-in-Publication data record for this book is available from the Library of Congress

ISBN 978-1-009-23282-1 Hardback
ISBN 978-1-009-23284-5 Paperback

Cambridge University Press & Assessment has no responsibility for the persistence or accuracy of URLs for external or third-party internet websites referred to in this publication and does not guarantee that any content on such websites is, or will remain, accurate or appropriate.

For EU product safety concerns, contact us at Calle de José Abascal, 56, 1°, 28003 Madrid, Spain, or email eugpsr@cambridge.org

Contents

	Preface	*page* vii
	Acknowledgments	viii
1	Why Does Terrorist Finance Matter?	1
2	Terrorist Finance, What Is It?	11
3	The Financing of the Radical Right – And Why Countering Isn't Working	27
4	The Financing of ISIS and How It Was Countered – A Template for Success?	42
5	Intelligence and the Countering of Terrorist Financing	59
6	Terrorist Designations – An Inside Look at the United States Department of State's Process to Sanction Terrorists	84
7	Countering State Sponsors of Terrorism	128
8	Multilateral Approaches to Countering Terrorist Access to Finance: A Look at the Roles Played by the Financial Action Task Force and the United Nations	140
9	The Role of the Private Sector in Countering Terrorist Financing and the Importance of Public–Private Partnerships	167

10 Cryptocurrency: Key Source of Terrorist Finance or
   Much Ado about Nothing? 188

11 Conclusion 212

   Bibliography 220
   Index 239

Preface

This book is shaped by my direct experiences of working against terrorist access to finance while I was a government employee, where the bulk of my career was dedicated to countering terrorism. In particular, Chapter 6 is a reflection of my hands-on experiences of running a government office that sanctioned terrorists pursuant to US law. After government, I joined Middlebury College's graduate school as a full-time professor. There I teach a course on terrorism financing. In addition to my work at Middlebury, I've continued working with governments and multilateral institutions to counter bad actor access to finance, whether criminal groups, terrorist organizations, or countries trying to finance their Weapons of Mass Destruction (WMD) programs. My experience of working in the US Intelligence Community allowed me to shape Chapter 5, which explores how intelligence is used to counter terrorist access to funding. All this to say, this book is very much the work of a practitioner, and any failings are those of the author.

Acknowledgments

The author would like to thank MIIS for funding several graduate research assistants over the course of this book project. I am thankful for the research, citation, and bibliographic work carried out by Eli Drachman, Sam Kostopulos, Arthur Churchwell, Michael Burton, Michael Hamby, and Allison Owen. I would like to thank Cambridge University Press, especially editor Philip Good, for the patience they showed me. This book project began before the COVID-19 pandemic. I am grateful for the willingness of John Jefferies, Ari Redbord, Ron Hendren, and Shaun McLeary to be interviewed for this book.

I Why Does Terrorist Finance Matter?

"Modern terrorists do not live by enthusiasm alone; they need a great deal of money."

– Walter Laqueur, A History of Terrorism

The quote above, written by the late Walter Laqueur in 1977, still holds true today. Carrying out an act of terrorism not only requires intent but also a steadfast determination to collect the finance to further violent political ends. Like any walk of life, having intentions, no matter if they are good or bad, is not sufficient in achieving a goal. A terrorist with bad intentions will not succeed unless they also have the capacity to act. The essence of Laqueur's thinking is this, without money, terrorism is extremely difficult to sustain.

The resonance of Laqueur's words is, however, somewhat diminished with the inclusion of the clause, "A great deal of money." This phrase is misleading to the nonterrorism finance expert since it paints an image of a terrorist organization needing extravagant financial sources to carry out an attack. However, this is not always the case. With that said, the term "great deal" is, of course, also very subjective. What may not be a "great deal of money" to ISIS, the richest terrorist group to walk the earth, may be a great deal to the US-based neo-Nazi Atomwaffen Division. Similarly, "a great deal of money" can go much further in purchasing the components of a bomb in Pakistan than it would in the United States.[1] Fifty kilograms of calcium ammonium nitrate fertilizer, which can be boiled to separate the calcium from the explosive component, ammonium nitrate, and mixed with fuel oil to create two to four bombs, can be purchased in Pakistan for around $5, whereas in the United States, the same

---

[1] Laqueur, Walter. *A History of Terrorism*. 1st ed. New York: Little, Brown and Company, 1977.

amount of ammonium nitrate fertilizer goes for around $31, albeit sold only in 1-ton (1,000-kilogram) bags.[2]

As you'll read in this chapter, terrorist operations have not always required a significant amount of funding to succeed. On the other hand, a terrorist attack successfully being carried out can be costly to the government.

The nineteenth-century anarchist-based Russian organization known as Narodnaya Volya, or more formally known by the English translation as the People's Will, ran its operations on a small budget. Despite a lack of resources, the People's Will remains one of the few terrorist organizations in history to successfully assassinate the leader of a country. On the day of the attack, the Tsar of Russia, Alexander II, planned to travel along Malaya Sadovaya Street[3] to Mikhailovsky Manege, a riding school in Saint Petersburg.[4] The People's Will was acutely aware of the tsar's routine to attend roll call here every Sunday, thus not needing to spend additional costs on bribing the tsar's Cossack guards for further details. Along the route, the terrorist organization planned to blow up the Sadovaya Street tunnel and throw bombs at the tsar's carriage. However, Alexander II, upon advice from his second wife, decided to take an alternative route. Without hesitation, the People's Will adapted to the alteration and deployed four individuals, each carrying a bomb, along the Catherine Canal to wait for his return from the riding school. As the tsar's carriage appeared in the distance, the assassins got into position to carry out the attack. When given the signal, the first assassin lobbed his bomb at the tsar's carriage, failing to meet the intended goal, but nonetheless halting the convoy. By doing so, it provided ample opportunity for the second assassin

---

[2] "Pakistani fertilizer fuels Afghan bombs." Karachi: *Dawn News*, August 31, 2011. www.dawn.com/news/655920/pakistani-fertilizer-fuels-afghan-bombs. Accessed February 18, 2021.

[3] Gérard, Chaliand, & Blin, Arnaud. *The History of Terrorism: From Antiquity to Al Qaeda*. 1st ed. Berkeley: University of California Press, 2007.

[4] Yarmolinsky, Avrahm. *Road to Revolution: A Century of Russian Radicalism*. Springfield: Collier Books, 1962.

to successfully carry out the attack, consequently killing himself along with the tsar.

March 13, 1881, the day of the assassination based on the Gregorian calendar, provides valuable information about the cost of terrorist attacks. In dissecting this attack, one can divine that the People's Will's attack did not require significant funding. The People's Will devoted minimal resources to the attack, and despite the group being ravaged to the brink of dissolution by the tsar's repressive counterterrorism tactics, the group successfully assassinated Alexander II. The anarchists did not pay its members, and the cost of the bombs, probably nothing more than dynamite,[5] was also minimal. Due to the carriage route of the tsar being well-known, the People's Will did not have the extra cost of bribing crooked government or police officials for information.

The success of the People's Will in this case inspired revolutionaries and nascent anarchists everywhere. With limited financing, the organizations' deeds lived on despite the group's death shortly after the tsar's execution. The People's Will did not have the resources of the Russian Empire, yet it was able to strike the heart of the empire. Terrorist groups, with few exceptions, do not have the capability of states and therefore, logically, must do more with less. In the case of the People's Will, human resources were used to strike a blow against tsarist Russia. This dependence on a human's willingness to sacrifice everything for a cause has yet to diminish over the last century.

This concept is reinforced by Ramadan Shalah of the Palestinian Islamic Jihad (PIJ), who starkly noted, "our enemy possesses the most sophisticated weapons in the world and its army is trained to a very high standard. We have nothing with which to repel the killing except the weapons of martyrdom."[6] Shalah is not only lamenting the power of its adversary but speaking to PIJ's own capability. Shalah's point is this, despite the PIJ's lack of technical and financial resources,

---

[5] Gérard, Chaliand, & Blin, Arnaud. *The History of Terrorism: From Antiquity to Al Qaeda*. 1st ed. Berkeley: University of California Press, 2007.

[6] Hoffman, Bruce. *Inside Terrorism*. New York: Columbia University Press, 2017.

limited financing is needed to carry out an uncomplicated suicide attack. Simply put, the cost, in terms of material needs, is not great. The cost of martyrdom is often little more than the willingness to take one's own life.

In *Countering the Financing of Terrorism*, Susan Eckert and Tom Bierstecker provide essential details regarding the cost of higher-profile attacks carried out over the past few decades. According to their research, the first attempt to bomb the World Trade Center in 1993 by al-Gama'a al-Islamiyya only cost 18,000 USD. To finance the attack, most of the funds were derived from a combination of credit and check fraud, along with charitable donations.[7]

Eckert and Bierstecker also examined al-Qa'ida's bombing of the US Embassies in Kenya and Tanzania and found that it cost less than 50,000 USD.[8] In later research, the costs associated with the financing of that attack were further reduced following a Central Intelligence Agency analysis, as cited by Bruce Hoffman, to less than 10,000 USD.[9] While it may seem shocking that it can cost so little to kill 301 people and wound more than 5,000, the price of that attack goes beyond the immediate death toll and the true long-term impact is difficult to calculate. Al-Qa'ida's 1998 attacks would change the way the United States would carry out its foreign policy mission. Prior to the attacks in Dar es Salaam and Nairobi, diplomats abroad worked inside buildings with little fortification near city centers. After 1998, US embassies would move and become less accessible, and this resulted in diplomatic business being carried out in isolated parts of capital cities within hardened fortresses. The increasing isolation of these embassies, along with the battery of security protocols visitors must clear before meeting with US foreign service officers to secure a visa; or to discuss possible commercial partnerships, is incalculable. Al-Qa'ida, in one attack, single-handedly changed the

---

[7] Biersteker, Thomas J., and Eckert, Sue T. *Countering the Financing of Terrorism*. 1st ed. Oxon: Routledge, 2008.
[8] Ibid.
[9] Hoffman, Bruce. *Inside Terrorism*. New York: Columbia University Press, 2017.

way US embassies operate and are fortified for a fraction of the cost of those fortifications.

Only a few years after the 1998 embassy attacks, in 2000, al-Qa'ida successfully carried out a maritime operation against the USS Cole in the Gulf of Aden for a cost of no more than 10,000 USD, according to Rifa'i Ahmad Taha.[10] With this funding, the organization purchased C4 explosives and a boat with a specially outfitted motor. Although the equipment was sparse, the attack resulted in the death of 17 sailors and more than 250 million USD worth of repairs on the Arleigh Burke class destroyer.[11]

Non-US targets, of course, have also been the focus of terrorist vitriol. The October 12, 2002, bombings on the Indonesian island of Bali reportedly cost between 20,000 and 35,000 USD.[12] The attack, carried out by Jemaah Islamiyah (JI), resulted in the death of more than 200 people. Three years later, on July 7, four men detonated fertilizer bombs on the London transport system, killing fifty-two people and injuring several hundred others.[13] Following the attack, the United Kingdom House of Commons investigated the variables involved in carrying out the terrorist attack to determine the cost and method of financing used. Accounting for transportation, the equipment used to make the bomb, rent, and car hire, the United Kingdom reported the overall cost to be no greater than $14,000.[14] When looking into how the operatives financed the attack, the analysis showed that one of the bombers, Mohammad Sidique Khan, defaulted on his personal loan repayments and overdrew on his bank accounts.

---

[10] Ibid.
[11] Ibid.
[12] Biersteker, Thomas J., and Sue T. Eckert. *Countering the Financing of Terrorism*. 1st ed. Oxon: Routledge, 2008.
[13] "Could 7/7 Have Been Prevented? Review of the Intelligence on the London Terrorist Attacks on 7 July 2005." London: *Intelligence and Security Committee*, 2009. https://fas.org/irp/world/uk/july7review.pdf. Accessed February 15, 2021.
[14] United Kingdom House of Commons. "Report of the Official Account of the Bombings in London on 7th July 2005." London: *Her Majesty Stationary Office*, HMSO, 2006. https://assets.publishing.service.gov.uk/government/uploads/system/uploads/attachment_data/file/228837/1087.pdf. Accessed February 18, 2021.

Another bomber, Jermaine Lindsay, used checks to purchase items within the weeks prior to the attack.[15]

Like many of the attacks previously cited, the funding of al-Qa'ida's 9/11 attack was relatively inexpensive, albeit it cost more than all of the other attacks combined. According to the findings of the staff monograph on terrorist financing of the National Commission's report on Terrorist Attacks Upon the United States, the 9/11 attack cost al-Qa'ida between 400,000 and 500,000 USD. Of that amount, 300,000 USD passed through the formal financial system of the United States.[16] Al-Qa'ida operatives had US bank accounts, made wire transfers and ATM transactions, used traveler's checks and credit cards to move and spend money. Much of that was used for nonoperational costs, like to pay for general living expenses and flight training in the United States. Al-Qa'ida abused the US financial system and the group built its wealth, according to the 9/11 Staff Monograph, by diverting money from Islamic charities primarily based in the Persian Gulf. The other significant finding was that the financiers in the Gulf and in Germany facilitated the movement of money. As you'll read in Chapter 2, successful terrorist organizations must diversify income streams if they are going to remain stable. This funding is necessary to support recruitment, train members, establish bases and safe houses, pay for transportation, and acquire supplies, in addition to weapons and explosives. Remarkably, in 2003, the Australian commonwealth of Director of Public prosecutions estimated that Al-Qa'ida only used 10 percent of its income on operations. The other 90 percent went to the cost of administering and maintaining the organization, including the cost of operating training camps and maintaining an international network of cells.[17] Due to the diverse range of needs and overhead costs,

---

[15] Ibid.

[16] Roth, John, Douglas Greenburg, and Wille, Serena B. "Monograph on Terrorist Financing: Staff Report to the Commission." Washington, DC: *National Commission on Terrorist Attacks upon the United States*, 2004. Internet resource.

[17] Biersteker, Thomas J., and Eckert, Sue T. *Countering the Financing of Terrorism*. 1st ed. Oxon: Routledge, 2008.

terrorists will use legitimate businesses and manipulate unwitting nongovernmental organizations to raise funds, as well as engage in criminal activity, such as the drug trade, weapons smuggling, fraud, kidnapping for ransom, extortion, and theft.

COST-EFFECTIVENESS

Another important aspect of terrorist financing is how terrorists think about the costs related to their attacks. After 9/11, Usama bin Laden lauded the cost-effectiveness of the attacks in a videotaped message released in 2004.[18] Estimates of the costs of 9/11 to the United States vary widely, but the lowest estimate is 500 billion USD. Bin Laden noted in his 2004 video that "every dollar of al-Qa'ida defeated a million US Government dollars." Bin Laden had a reputation for taking credit for budget-deficit problems and job losses.

Bin Laden is not the only terrorist to laud the cost-effectiveness of his attacks. On October 20, 2010, two bombers were found in toner cartridges on two separate cargo planes. These cartridges were filled with military-grade explosives similar to that found in the underwear of Abdulmutallab, a member of al-Qa'ida in the Arabian Peninsula (AQAP), who tried to detonate a bomb on a US commercial aircraft on December 25, 2009. In a separate case that occurred in 2010, AQAP attempted to down cargo planes and lauded the cost of the operation in ITS online publication named *Inspire*. AQAP claimed that the attack cost 4,200 USD to carry out and that its intent was to disrupt global air cargo systems. AQAP dubbed the attempted attack, "Operation Hemorrhage" and cataloged the cost of the operation as follows: two Nokia phones at 250 USD each, two HP printers at 300 USD each plus shipping, along with transportation and other miscellaneous expenses that add up to a total bill of 4,200 USD.[19]

---

[18] Hoffman, Bruce. *Inside Terrorism*. New York: Columbia University Press, 2017.

[19] Gartenstein-Ross, Daveed. "Death by a Thousand Cuts." *Foreign Policy*, November 23, 2010. https://foreignpolicy.com/2010/11/23/death-by-a-thousand-cuts-2/. Accessed February 2, 2021.

AQAP went further and noted that the attempt reflected its new strategy of low-cost attacks designed to inflict broad economic damage, noting that it did not need to carry out a 9/11 like attack to destroy the United States, but rather would destroy it by a death of a thousand cuts.

The leaders of terrorist groups think deeply about the cost-effectiveness of their attacks and the lasting impact an even failed act of terrorism can have on society. The AQAP attack changed the way the world screens commercial cargo – increasing the costs of doing business for governments and the private sector. At the same time, the costs of successful attacks are severe. The 9/11 attack changed the way the US government structured itself to counter not just terrorist financing but counterterrorism as a whole. New bureaucracies were created, to include the creation of the Office of the Director of National Intelligence, the National Counterterrorism Center, the Department of Homeland Security, and many other government agencies. At the same time, simple things people took for granted, such as going to the airport, have inalterably changed. The Transportation Security Agency relentlessly screens for bad actors trying to evade aviation security protocols. Privacy, by virtue of walking through body-scatters to better detect anomalies that may be indicative of a terrorist smuggling box cutters onto an aircraft, at the airport no longer exists. Society, privacy, commercial enterprise, and how governments organize themselves are on the minds of terrorist operators and financiers. That's not going to change. Yet, the study of how terrorists finance themselves and how governments counter that financing remains important.

HOW THIS BOOK IS ORGANIZED

This book is a natural evolution of my career. I spent nearly twenty years in the US government, the bulk of which my time was spent on countering the financial activities of terrorist groups. The bulk of this book is devoted to the manner in which governments, such as the United States Government, private sector, and the multilateral community, such as the United Nations (UN), counter the financial activities of nefarious actors. First, though, Chapter 2 is devoted to defining the phrase "Terrorist finance," and the methods terrorist groups accrue wealth. Chapter 2 also examines how terrorists generally move, use, and store wealth. Chapter 3 examines how the surging threat posed by violent extremist radical right actors fund their activities. The challenge of a growing transnational set of violent right-wing actors became the focal point of the world's attention because of the January 6, 2021 insurrection that threatened to usurp US democracy. Chapter 3 also examines the range of licit and illicit activities far-right actors engage in to fund themselves and some of the difficulties governments have encountered in challenging far-right financing. Chapter 4 looks at the financing of the terrorist group ISIS, and how the United States and international community responded to its significant fundraising activities. Chapter 5, among other things, examines the key programs and types of intelligence collection, such as financial intelligence, that inform the decisions to be taken to counter illicit activity associated with terrorist groups. Chapter 6 examines the oft-most used tool in the counterterrorism financing arsenal, targeted financial sanctions. Based on the author's direct experience of leading the State Department's office charged with sanctioning terrorist groups under the Secretary of State's legal authorities, Chapter 6 attempts to demystify the terrorist designations process by examining several controversial terrorist designations that took place between 2008 and 2018. Chapter 7 reviews the role state's place in providing support to terrorism and how governments, such as the United States and Canadian governments, use broad-base sanctions to penalize rogue country's support to terrorism. Chapter 8 looks at the world of multilateral counterterrorism financing, specifically the roles the United Nations and the Financial Action Task Force (FATF) play to counter terrorism financing. Chapter 9 examines the importance of the private sector, such as banks, money service businesses, and designated nonfinancial businesses and professions, in countering illicit financing. Chapter 9 also examines how the public and private sectors can cooperate to counter terrorist financing and money laundering. Chapter 10 explores the world of virtual assets, such as cryptocurrency. Chapter 10 also looks at how governments are working with the private sector to counter illicit actor use of virtual assets. Finally, Chapter 11 concludes with a recap and look toward the future of terrorist financing. With the Trump Administration rapidly changing laws and interrogating the utility of regulations, the enforcement environment is going to rapidly change. What could that mean for terrorist financing?

2 Terrorist Finance, What Is It?

Defining the term terrorism is notoriously sticky. There is no universally agreed-upon definition of the term. Nonetheless, defining what terrorist financing is, whether countries are criminalizing the financing of terrorism or not, slightly less controversial. Multiple international bodies have achieved some level of consensus in getting member-states of the body to come to an agreement on defining terrorist financing. Nevertheless, various international bodies define terrorist financing differently. The United Nations Office of Drugs and Crime (UNODC) defines terrorist financing as encompassing "the means and methods used by terrorist organizations to finance their activities."[1] The UNODC definition focuses on "groups" and, of course, this is limiting since, especially as you'll read in Chapter 3, individuals, or so-called lone-wolf actors, can finance their misdeeds without a need for organizational backing. In October 2001, the Financial Action Task Force (FATF), the international body that sets the counterterrorist financing and anti-money laundering (CFT/AML) recommendations for governments to adhere to, defined terrorist financing as "any person, group, undertaking, or other entity that provides or collects by any means, directly or indirectly, funds or other assets that may be used, in full or part, to facilitate the commission of terrorist acts..."[2] The FATF definition is more comprehensive than the UNODC's in that it broadens the aperture to include a

---

[1] United Nations Office of Drugs and Crime. "Combatting Terrorist Financing." www.unodc.org/unodc/en/terrorism/expertise/combating-terrorist-financing .html#:~:text=Terrorist%20financing%20encompasses%20the%20means,drugs%20 or%20people%2C%20or%20kidnapping.

[2] The Financial Action Task Force (FATF). "FATF IX Special Recommendations." October 2001. Page 10.

broader set of actors, including individuals, who may try to accumulate wealth for violent purposes. The International Monetary Fund (IMF) defines the financing of terrorism as, "the collection or provision of funds for terrorist purposes."[3] Three major organizations – all charged with countering terrorist financing, UNODC, FATF, and the IMF – have three different definitions of the term. It wouldn't take long to dig deeper and see that other international bodies, governments, and agencies within governments would all take a slightly different approach to defining terrorist financing. Definitions always matter, because the way governments define terms shapes the manner in which they counter the actions of individuals and groups engaged in furthering their political objectives through the use of violence. For the purposes of this book, terrorist financing is defined as the way groups, individuals, or entities raise funds, or other assets, for the purposes of terrorism. The author defines terrorism as carrying out acts of violence, or threats thereof, against civilians for the purpose of creating an atmosphere of fear, with the objective of achieving political or social change. This chapter examines terrorist financing through the lens of these definitions. It also examines the terrorist financing cycle. Terrorist financing is not just about fundraising. Understanding the various phases that allow for terrorist financing to occur is vitally important for governments, international bodies, and the private sector to comprehend if they are to successfully counter the financial objectives of terrorists.

Perhaps more important than the definition of terrorist financing is its multiphase funding cycle. Figure 2.1 depicts the four stages of the terrorist financing cycle. The process of financing cycle, however, should not be seen as something static that must always happen in a specific sequence. Nevertheless, it is simpler to understand the elements of terrorist financing by conceptualizing them in a step-by-step process. Stage one, however, is generally understood as the

---

[3] The International Monetary Fund (IMF). "Anti-Money Laundering/Combatting the Financing of Terrorism (AML/CFT)." www.imf.org/external/np/leg/amlcft/eng/aml1.htm

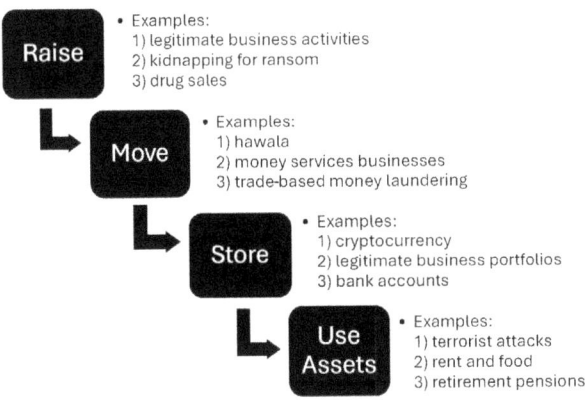

FIGURE 2.1 Flowchart that demonstrates the steps used by terrorists to finance their terrorism.

process in which terrorists raise funds. Stage two is the process in which terrorists may move their assets. Stage three is how terrorists store their assets. Finally, the fourth stage is how terrorists use their assets.

RAISING ASSETS

Terrorists raise their funds from both licit and illicit means. The range of licit activities terrorists have leveraged to accrue wealth is significant, but it is outside the scope of this book to provide an exhaustive list of such methods. Instead, a few examples should provide a glimpse into the creative minds of the terrorist financiers. Among the most important methods the Irish Republican Army (IRA) used to finance its misdeeds throughout the 1970s, 1980s, and 1990s was the use of legitimate businesses.

Running a legitimate business operation allows a terrorist group to do several things. First, the group may accrue some profit by running the business. Second, the business can serve as a place to launder money associated with any illegal fundraising activities. The legitimate enterprise can obscure the source of the illegal funds and allow the organization to place the illegitimate funds into the formal financial system. Third, the business can serve as a front to employ terrorist group members to make it look like they have a legitimate job. Fourth, the legitimate business can be one way the terrorist group can deepen its roots with the local community.

The IRA recognized all of these benefits, and in among the best examinations of IRA financing, author James Adams provides important examples of how the IRA was able to utilize legitimate businesses to further its political objectives in Northern Ireland.[4] Adams explains how in the 1970s, the IRA created a taxi company, drinking club, and breweries in an effort to supplement its illegal means of income, such as through extortion. The group also needed to establish legitimate cash-intensive businesses in an effort to recirculate its money made from illegal endeavors. The IRA understood that in the 1970s, taxi companies and bars were cash-intensive businesses. The taxi company, in particular, became a source of revenue because the IRA took over not only the taxi companies but it also carried out a significant bombing operation against Belfast's city-run bus system. The bus bombings pushed people to the IRA's taxicabs because of fears they'd die in a bus bombing. This maneuver gave the IRA a monopoly over transportation in much of Belfast. Between January and June 1972, after only six months of running the taxicab company, which consisted of 600 cab cars, the IRA had more than 1.5 million US dollars.[5]

The IRA, for a span of nearly two decades, received the bulk of its funding from a US-based organization known as Irish Northern Aid (better known by its acronym NORAID). NORAID's formation happened to align with the uptick in the IRA's operational activity. Formed in 1969 by an Irish American by the name of Michael Flannery, NORAID would become the primary conduit of funds for the IRA until the late 1980s. NORAID operated like a legitimate charitable organization. Based in Bronx, New York,

---

[4] Adams, James. "The Financing of Terror." Simon and Schuster. New York. 1986. Pages 156–187.
[5] Ibid. Page 173.

at its zenith NORAID had more than ninety chapters across the United States with a membership base that comprised more than 5,000 people. The organization's modest beginnings, according to James Adams, began when Flannery cut a 5,000-dollar check for the IRA in 1969. The organization quickly expanded, and at its height in the 1970s, it was providing IRA more than half of its overall budget. At this time NORAID was funneling annually more than $7 million per year to the IRA.[6] Expatriates who had emigrated to the United States from Ireland from all walks of life provided a great deal of money back to the homeland to further the IRA's cause. Adams notes that NORAID's supporters ranged from longshoremen to the glitterati of Washington, DC. Adams notes the black-tie affairs that were attended by US congressman, such as Peter Rodino, the chair of the House of Representatives Judiciary Committee.[7]

The scale of NORAID's support to the IRA was astonishing, particularly when one examines the shift in the IRA's capability from the 1960s to the 1980s. In 1969, the IRA was fighting with World War II vintage rifles or guns that would be more appropriately used by Al Capone in the 1930s. In less than three years, the IRA transitioned from its cache of antiquated arms to AR-16 and AR-18 rifles, as well as M-60 heavy machine guns. Many of these arms were provided courtesy of NORAID. In 1976, armed robberies of military facilities, which resulted in the theft of more than 100 M-16 rifles and at least 8 heavy machine guns, were funneled to Ireland via NORAID contacts. Although the arms and ammunition were seized, the scale of NORAID's activity to support the IRA cause was significant.[8] The improved IRA arsenal boosted the organization's morale. Further, the support of powerful American politicians for the cause gave the IRA a great deal of legitimacy.

---

[6] Ibid. Pages 135–136.
[7] Ibid. Page 137.
[8] Ibid. Page 144.

The IRA began to lose a great amount of its US based financial support when it went too far and assassinated Lord Mountbatten in 1979. Two children were collaterally killed in the attack, and the British government used the deaths as leverage to request that the US government look more seriously at the sources of IRA funding. Shortly after the Mountbatten attack, the FBI formed a small team to follow the money from the United States to Ireland. At the same time, the FBI also successfully carried out several sting operations, which ultimately led to the successful prosecution of NORAID in 1981. Nevertheless, the damage was done at the point. NORAID, a legitimate charity based in the United States, fueled the IRA's terrorist activity.

NORAID's story is particularly interesting when considering that al-Qa'ida infiltrated and abused, or outrightly ran charities, which were instrumental to the funding behind the September 11, 2001, attacks. Of course, NORAID operated[9] during a different place and time than al-Qa'ida. Regardless, the United States did not learn from the missteps it made during the height of NORAID, nearly forty years before al-Qa'ida's rapid rise, which was bankrolled by making more than $30 million per year from its worldwide network of charities.[10]

Just as there are several ways that terrorists can accumulate wealth by legitimate means, they can engage in a wide range of illicit activity to fatten their wallets. These types of illegal activities can range from engaging in fraud, extortion, and kidnapping for ransom to weapons, human, natural resources, and drug trafficking.

Moving Assets

The worlds of licit and illicit finance often merge, especially when it becomes time to move assets. There is a myriad of ways in which terrorists can move money, but this section will examine just a few so the

---

[9] Interestingly, NORAID still exists today and remains a legal charity based in New York City. It is a supporter of the Good Friday Agreements.

[10] National Commission on Terrorist Attacks upon the United States. "Monograph on Terrorist Financing." 2004. Page 7.

reader can become acquainted with the enormity of the challenge governments and the private sector face when countering terrorist movement of funds. This becomes no more evident than examining the activities of the IRA's most sophisticated terrorist financier – Thomas Murphy, also known as Slab. Slab ran a farm that every year profited the IRA at least 250,000 dollars. Slab, through his ability to manipulate currency and customs regulations, would take advantage of subsidies offered by the European Economic Community (EEC). Slab knew that there was a twelve-dollar per animal subsidy paid by the EEC to farmers of southern Ireland that exported pigs to the United Kingdom (of which Northern Ireland is a part). Slab would ferry the pigs back and forth between Ulster and Newry to avoid tax penalties and reap the benefit of the tax subsidy. When authorities amended the regulations that provided the subsidy, Slab diversified and converted his operation to grain, and then to cattle. Slab's ingenuity provided the IRA a stable source of funding. Slab's ingenuity was both a source of income for the IRA and provided it the ability to move funds in and out of the EEC.

Perhaps the most common way bad actors, whether terrorist groups or criminal organizations, move money is through money laundering. Very simply, money laundering is the movement of funds for the purpose of concealing the true source, ownership, or use of the funds. The money laundering process has three stages. Figure 2.2 visually depicts the money laundering process.

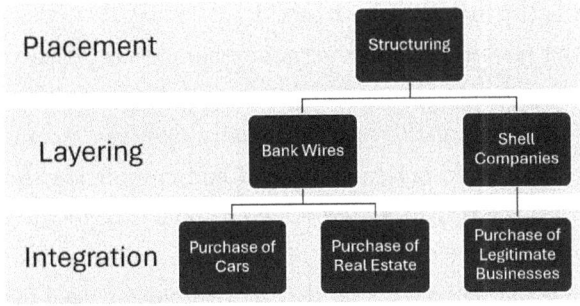

FIGURE 2.2 Flowchart that demonstrates the money laundering process.

Placement is the first and most vulnerable stage of laundering money. During this stage of the process, the terrorist group or criminal organization is often dealing with bulk cash – often acquired through the proceeds of crime, such as money made by the sale of illicit drugs. The objective of the terrorist financier and money launderer is to "place" the funds into the financial system without attracting the attention of law enforcement. The launderer does not want to raise any red flags, such as current transaction reports (CTRs) or suspicious activity reports (SARs) containing information to tie the funds to the owner or launderer of the monies. Placement techniques include structuring, commingling, smuggling, inaccurate, or falsified Bank Secrecy Act reports, and causing Bank Secrecy Act reports not to be filed.

How can a money launderer or terrorist financier place cash into the financial system? There are a number of methods: (1) deposit to a bank account; (2) purchase of cashier's checks or other monetary instruments such as money orders; (3) the wiring of cash to another person to be paid out in the form of a check; (4) the purchase of travel tickets for cash, followed by the cancellation of the trip and request for the refund in the form of a check; and (5) purchase of a large insurance policy with a cash premium under $10,000 and quickly cancel the policy and request the refunded premium in a check. This is legitimately allowed in some US jurisdictions (states) under what's called "first look," which is a sort of right of rescission for insurance policies after reading the fine print, so to speak.

Layering is the second stage of the money laundering process. This involves moving funds around in the financial system after they are placed. This stage of the process usually involves a complex series of transactions to create confusion and complicate the paper trail. What does layering look like? One example is depositing a refund check from a canceled vacation or insurance policy. A second example could be a cashier's check that has been exchanged for other cashier's checks, larger or smaller, adding additional cash or other monetary instruments. A third example would be the wiring of funds numerous times to various accounts and various persons and business entities, particularly through banking secrecy havens, such as Switzerland.

Once the funds are in the financial system and insulated through the layering process, the integration phase is used to create the appearance of legality through additional transactions such as loans and real estate deals. These transactions provide the terrorist financier a plausible explanation as to where funds came from to purchase assets and shield the terrorist from any type of recorded connection to the funds.

What kinds of schemes do terrorists or criminals deploy to integrate illegal funds into society? Integration is often the most difficult aspect of money laundering to understand. Thus, it is critical to examine a few practical examples to help explain this process.

First, import/export and invoicing schemes are common for integration. A terrorist can set up an import/export business that ships empty or highly overvalued containers to a purchaser who then pays phony invoices for the nonexistent or overvalued goods. Payment is made with funds that have been previously placed and layered through the financial system. For example, the bad actor can ship bottles of cheap wine but invoice for bottles of expensive wine.

Second, trade-based money laundering uses such schemes with actual commodities and goods and can be used to move money while having the cover of a legitimate business transaction. Simply by manipulating invoices, money can be moved in this fashion. For example, if you wanted to move $50,000 to the US from Country X, you could ship $200,000 worth of textiles to the US, but only invoice $150,000. Sales of the imported textiles net the receiver an additional $50,000. There is a limitless variety of such transactions a creative terrorist financier or money launderer can devise. However, this has often been achieved via the trade of gold. To a very large extent, money laundering in the Arabian Gulf and the Indian subcontinent is governed by what is loosely called trade-based money laundering. The area historically is a region of brokers and traders who have developed close business ties and trading routes that seek to avoid taxes, tariffs, customs duties, and government scrutiny. Many of the trade systems ignore in whole or part traditional financial institutions.

Third, schemes have been identified where gold bullion is bought and sold between entities. In actuality, the bullion is a gold-plated lead bar, which is later melted, and the lead is discarded. However, all entities involved have purchase and sale agreements and paid receipts, thereby effectively laundering the funds. Again, payment is made with funds that have been previously placed and layered through the financial system. These schemes differ from trade-based laundering schemes in that fraudulent gold bullion is used instead of the actual commodity.

Fourth, a terrorist could create a foreign trust, perhaps in a secrecy haven, which is funded by illegal proceeds. The original owner of the dirty money is made the beneficiary of the trust, which was created by a supposed wealthy relative abroad. When the trust is paid to the terrorist as beneficiary, he then has use of what appears to be legitimately obtained wealth in the inheritance.

A terrorist can also loan himself his own money. One would need to set up a corporation that appeared to be independent of the actual owner through an attorney or a straw party or through an offshore entity. The corporation is funded by dirty money. After setting up a relationship with a financial institution, a loan is negotiated using corporate receivables as collateral. The receivables appear to be legitimate but are not supported by any real goods. Now the terrorist has his illegal money and the proceeds of the loan. After the corporation appears to sell the goods, the financial institution is paid off on the loan. The terrorist ends up with what looks like legitimate profits. Although the financial institution is used to facilitate the scheme, it is not damaged and does not suffer a loss.

A terrorist could also involve a financial institution in a scheme using a hypothecation. One could set up an account or multiple accounts funded with dirty money or using securities previously purchased with dirty money and offer the accounts and securities as collateral on a hypothecation. The terrorist can simply default on the loan, at which time the financial institution will take ownership of the accounts or negotiate and sell the securities. Again, the financial institution unwittingly facilitates the laundering process but is not damaged.

Groups like the FATF, a key focus of Chapter 8, and various financial intelligence units have long identified use of front companies in terrorist financing schemes. Front companies established by terrorists and terrorist financiers can accomplish one of several purposes, or a combination of objectives. For example, theoretically a detained Malaysian leader and former Malaysian military officer/ biochemistry student can establish a pharmaceuticals company. Not only did this front company permit them to generate legitimate profits that they could rechannel into terrorist activities, but it also served as a cover for the ordering of ammonium nitrate – raw material often used in truck bombs. Additionally, such companies can be used to employ other terrorists or terrorist sympathizers, which provides cover.

If unchecked, money laundering can undermine the integrity of financial institutions and the entire social, economic, and political structure of a society. Illegally financed businesses stifle competition. For instance, legitimate businesses don't have extensive sources of revenue like illegal ones for start-up and overhead. Moreover, money laundering increases the tax burden on the general public. For example, laundered funds do not generate revenue and therefore provide no benefit to society or the public. Laundered monies also finance terrorist attacks and related activities such as arms purchases or kidnapping.

Money laundering can be very difficult to detect for financial institutions. Criminals and terrorists are often very creative and change their behavior – as law enforcement prevents methods of money laundering, terrorists invent new ones. Enhancements in laws and regulations combined with increased levels of compliance by financial institutions and intensified efforts by law enforcement have forced terrorists to adapt their conduct. Terrorists have modified their behavior to remain unnoticed as part of an effort to not raise any "red flags." One example of avoiding detection is by making smaller transaction amounts and using numerous financial accounts.

Money laundering is also difficult to detect because it is masked by the large volume of legitimate financial activity. Simply put, money laundering is a large problem in absolute terms but is still a very small amount of money moving illicitly in comparison to the total dollar volume of legitimate business transactions. Money laundering is generally disguised to look like legitimate business, such as the taxi cabs and bars the IRA had a knack for running, and therefore identifying it can be much like looking for the proverbial needle in the haystack.

A money laundering scheme might involve many people, businesses, and accounts at numerous financial institutions over a period of time. The sheer number of entities that can be involved in a money laundering operation can be enormous. One of the most significant examples globally of such a large-scale money laundering operation was carried out by Lebanese Hizballah (LH). LH's scheme became subject of a multiagency law enforcement investigation led by the US Drug Enforcement Administration (DEA). The investigation, which would become known by the name Operation Pegasus (aka Cassandra), uncovered an LH money laundering activity spanning multiple years. The DEA's operation spanned a multiyear period between 2007 and 2011. The scheme had multiple steps. First, LH would buy used cars in the United States and ship them to West Africa. These cars are then sold in West Africa. Second, at the same time, LH operatives would send cocaine to Africa from Latin America and eventually route it to Europe for sale. Third, the drug profits from the sale in Europe would then be sent back to West Africa and intermingled with the legitimate money from the sale of cars, which were purchased in the United States and sent to West Africa. The commingling of the used cars sales and proceeds of crime (the drug sales) is how LH made the funds to look legitimate or clean. Finally, the aggregate washed profits derived from the car sales and drugs were then sent to the Lebanese Canadian Bank (LCB) via exchange houses. At this time some of the money is then sent to LH. The other profits are then sent to either Asia or back to the United States (for the purchase of more used cars). The money in Asia was used to purchase consumer products, which were then shipped to Latin America to help pay off the cocaine suppliers. This LH money laundering cycle would repeat over and over again and would become a lynchpin to its financial success for so many years because of LH's ability to influence a seemingly legitimate bank, LCB, to facilitate transactions. The moral of this story is that terrorist groups want to use the formal financial system to give their dirty money an appearance of legitimacy. In this case, it took five continents for LH to achieve that objective. According to the DEA, more than $329 million of LH funds passed through the US formal financial system. When it comes to protecting profit, formal financial institutions are critical to the successful storing of funds by terrorist groups.

STORING ASSETS

Terrorists, like anybody else, must store their assets. There are several methods of storage that bad actors can avail themselves of. First, storing funds in a formal financial institution, like Lebanese Hizballah did by maintaining accounts in the LCB during its massive five-continent money laundering scheme that became the subject of the USG's Operation Cassandra. Keeping assets in bank accounts, however, is not without risk since large compliance sections within banks carry out comprehensive customer due diligence to remain in the good graces of government regulation. For instance, banks, depending on where they are based in the world, will file suspicious transaction reports (STRs) or SARs when they observe potential money laundering or terrorist financing acts. Further, any deposit in a bank that exceeds more than 10,000 USD automatically generates a CTR. Since the 1970s, with the passage of the Bank Secrecy Act (BSA), formal financial institutions, like banks, have been on the frontlines of the battle against illicit financing. As such, criminal actors, like terrorists, have taken creative steps to manage their wealth – often looking outside of banks to maintain the value of their assets.

One group that has been especially creative in storing its wealth has been the Afghanistan-based Haqqani Network (HQN). In her comprehensive study of illicit financing in Afghanistan, Gretchen Peters explains that HQN moved money made in Afghanistan and Pakistan via illegal activities, such as via its involvement in the illicit drug trade, to the Persian Gulf, where the group invested its funds in real estate.[11] Managing wealth by investing it real estate, such as commercial or residential property, is often a sound strategy for building wealth. HQN, in storing its profits like this, is building equity and at the same time making it more difficult for law enforcement to detect their financial misdeeds. Realtors and other businesses adjacent to transactions in the real estate sector are considered "Designated Non-financial Businesses and Professions (DNFBPs)." DNFBPs, an area of focus in Chapter 8, have historically been late to the game in terms of protecting against financial abuse by illicit actors. As a consequence, FATF issued multiple recommendations, such as Recommendation 22, that requires DNFBPs to adopt measures similar to banks, such as the issuance of STRS/SARS. Further, FATF has pushed "countries to … ensure that DNFBPs are subject to effective systems for monitoring and ensuring compliance with AML/CFT requirements."[12]

Like real estate, precious stones and metals are another asset in which terrorists can store wealth. Following the 9/11 attack, there was speculation that al-Qa'ida partially stored its wealth and benefited

---

[11] Gretchen Peters, *Haqqani Network Financing: The Evolution of an Industry*, Harmony Program, the Combating Terrorism Center at West Point, 21 (July 2012) [Report].

[12] The Financial Action Task Force (FATF). "FATF IX Special Recommendations." October 2001. Page 24.

from the trade of precious stones. In the aftermath of 9/11, it was explained by scholars such as Douglas Farah that al-Qa'ida benefitted from its access to diamond mines in Liberia.[13] The 9/11 report, however, found that it was inconclusive whether al-Qa'ida benefited from the diamond trade. Nonetheless, precious stones like diamonds and gold are an important source of stored wealth for illicit actors. For example, precious stones like diamonds can retain value because they are often a sought-after commodity. Further, an asset like a diamond, because it is small, is more difficult to detect by government agencies when bad actors cross borders. It's much easier to move a diamond through an airport than bulk cash and it is this portability that terrorist financiers and money launderers prize. FATF has also recognized that precious stones and metals are a source of concern, and as a consequence, in its interpretative note of Recommendation 22, it explains, "dealers in precious metals and dealers in precious stones when engaged in cash transactions of 15,000 USD/EUR" ... should file reports with regulatory authorities.[14] Like those engaged in the real estate industry, precious stones and metal dealers are considered a DNFBP and are still in the early years of implementing protective measures like banks have been doing for the past fifty years since the passage of the BSA.

Storing and managing assets or funds is a critical component of the terrorist financing lifecycle. Without the successful storing of funds so they can be later tapped into, terrorist groups cannot retain a long-term capability to carry out attacks.

USING ASSETS

The final stage in the terrorist financing cycle is the use of funds. As detailed in Chapter 1, carrying out a terrorist attack doesn't require a

---

[13] Douglas, F. *Blood from Stones: The Secret Financial Network of Terror*. Broadway Books, 2004.
[14] The Financial Action Task Force (FATF). "FATF IX Special Recommendations." October 2001. Page 90.

lot of money. For example, the most catastrophic attack carried out in history, 9/11, cost approximately 500,000 USD, and it is also the most expensive in recent memory. However, most funds are used for mundane purposes – to buy food, clothes, and secure housing. This book isn't focused on how terrorists accrue wealth, however.[15] The bulk of this book's focus is on countering the financing of terrorism. Nonetheless, the Chapters 3 and 4 will explore terrorist financing through specific case studies – with Chapter 3 examining the phenomenon of far-right financing and the Chapter 4 examining the financing of ISIS. In examining the far-right and ISIS, the reader will become attuned to the effectiveness of illicit actor financing. Further, the reader will begin to comprehend the difficulty governments have in countering terrorist financing. Following the money trail isn't easy and terrorist groups and extremist movements are creative and adept at obfuscation.

---

[15] For readers interested in comprehensive examination of the terrorist financing lifecycle, check out Jessica Davis's book: "Illicit Money: Terrorist Financing in the 21st Century," and Colin Clarke's book, "Terror Inc."

3 The Financing of the Radical Right – And Why Countering Isn't Working

Radical right[1] wing forms of terrorism and extremism have been on the rise, especially in the United States. This case study of far-right financing is particularly important given the challenges in countering this form of extremism in the United States due to constitutional protections, such as the first amendment. This chapter will first discuss the methods used, historically and currently, by the radical right. Following that, there will be an examination of how the international community, including the United States, has tried to counter right-wing financing.

In the lead-up to the January 6, 2021, insurrection in the United States, there was a significant spike in forms of violence animated by right-wing ideology. CSIS, a Washington, DC based think tank, noted that during the previous decade (ten years prior to 2018) right-wing acts of terrorism had quadrupled.[2] In 2019, the most significant act of terrorism targeting Jews in the United States was carried out by Robert Bowers, a far-right figure, who attacked the Tree of Life Synagogue resulting in eleven deaths.

Of course, right-wing forms of extremism are not new. In the United States, the bombing of the Oklahoma City federal building in

---

[1] This chapter will use the terms "radical right" and "far right" interchangeably. The United States Government, however, uses the term "racially and ethnically motivated violent extremism" when discussing the phenomenon of "right-wing" extremism due to the political sensitivities of right-wing ideologues within the Republican party who believe any use of the phrase "radical right" or "far right" is a politically driven smear. European governments, in contrast, and because of their historical experience of fighting against Nazism during WWII have been less bashful about affixing using terms like "far-right" when discussing ideological-driven forms of violence.

[2] Jones, S. G., "The Rise of Far-right Extremism in the United States," Center for Strategic and International Studies, 2018. www.csis.org/analysis/rise-far-right-extremism-united-states

1995, which killed 168 people, remains the deadliest far-right attack on US soil. Additionally, the United States has been a fertile ground for right-wing racists, with sizable organizations like the KKK operating in the pre- and post civil war period.

Nor are right-wing forms of extremism a threat specific to the United States. Europe has suffered at the hands of violent far-right extremists. Today, these groups tend to be catalyzed by issues like the migration of individuals to Europe. Anders Breivik, a terrorist who carried out a deadly multi-prong 2011 attack in Norway that killed nearly 80 people, explicitly pointed to multiculturalism and the changing of European demographics because of the surge of immigration.

These attacks, in Oslo, Oklahoma City, and Washington, DC, were funded in various ways, and groups like the KKK also sourced their finances creatively. The KKK established commercialized pathways for funding its activities – not unlike more contemporary far-right groups. In using licit methods to finance their activities, these far-right groups can target a wider range of interested individuals, often with paraphernalia for purchase. At the same time, these groups are able to avoid the heat of government law enforcement action.

Often there are two fundamental reasons why far-right groups have nimbly avoided the net of law enforcement, especially in the United States. First, the use of licit tactics to fundraise is not inherently illegal because of the second reason. Second, in the United States, one of the primary tools to counter the financing of terrorism, terrorist designations, is difficult to use by the United States. In fact, terrorist designations,[3] as of late 2024, have been deployed by the US government against only two radical-right groups, the Russian Imperial Movement (RIM) and the Nordic Resistance Front. The challenge is further compounded by the fact that the US government does not have the legal authority to designate US based groups.

---

[3] See Chapter 6 for more content on terrorist designations.

LICIT FUNDRAISING

Merchandise

The KKK, a forerunner among white supremacist groups based in the United States, was heavily involved in the sale of a range of merchandise, including belt buckles, apparel, and jewelry. Today's iteration of the KKK follows the same bloody footsteps, selling dozens of different types of hats, flags, mundane household items, like mugs, and much more.[4] Interestingly, the KKK cannot accept credit cards for purchases and requests sympathizers to pay with check or money order. This difficulty in processing payments is not surprising since credit card companies and financial institutions have derisked from relationships with radical right-wing groups with white supremacist tendencies. For example, credit card companies and banks denying financial services to radical right-wing groups have pushed the far-right to adopt new payment methods, such as the use of cryptocurrency, the topic of Chapter 10. This KKK group, however, relied on outdated forms of money transfer methods, such as checks, which created an inefficiency in the group's ability to accumulate wealth quickly.

The KKK has company when it comes to securing finance through the sale of merchandise. During the mid/late 2010s, far-right movements like QAnon, Proud Boys, and Boogaloo Bois[5] merchandise were readily available on Etsy and Pinterest despite those platforms announcing that these far-right groups, specifically QAnon, would no longer be allowed to use their platforms. In some cases, a simple search for QAnon or Boogaloo might take you right to pages that are still selling t-shirts, hats, pins, stickers, and flags. In other cases, the search might yield nothing and display a message

---

[4] "The Knights Party – the American Heritage Store." https://web.archive.org/web/20200217012846/http://americanheritagecommittee.com/main/product-category/clothing-apparel/hats/

[5] The Boogaloo Bois were an anti-authority group, the Proud Boys a nationalist far-right group, and QAnon was a far-right conspiracy theory-oriented movement.

concerning a terms of service (TOS) violation. In that case, coded language comes into play, which might be just as simple as utilizing a different spelling of QAnon or Boogaloo (a persistent shopper could use phrases like: "C U E," or "Big Luau"). The deployment of alternative search terms would often result in the far-right merchandise being on full display – even if Boogaloo Boi t-shirt or patch is interspersed between legitimate luau party gear. This simple example highlights the ease in which groups can sell merchandise even after platforms try to counter their access. All it takes is a new name, a new spelling of that name, or a new email address that acts as a front for a previously banned individual or group.

These forms of "wearable hate,"[6] as scholar Cynthia Miller-Idriss labels it, not only provide these groups a source of important, and legal, finance, but it also allow the groups to spread their message in often innocuous ways – spurring recruitment to grow the far-right movement.

Selling "merch" isn't the only method the radical right has effectively deployed. Often, freebies are as important of a source of financing, with radical right groups being highly effective in securing donations from private citizens via a range of methods, through their own highly curated websites or via crowdfunding platforms.

Crowdfunding

Crowdfunding is the process of funding projects by gaining the interest of multiple individuals who see value in the project and decide to contribute small amounts of money to it. Often individuals or organizations seeking funding from large groups of people will source their audience by advertising needs over social media outlets. Once an interested donor clicks on the social media link advertising the need for finance, they could be taken to the group's website or to a crowdfunding platform, such as GoFundMe, Kickstarter, and

---

[6] Miller-Idriss, C., *Hate in the Homeland: The New Global Far Right*. 1st ed. Princeton University Press, 2020, Page 78.

Patreon – these three are among the most popular on the internet. US based white supremacists and anti-authority groups, like militias, have been particularly adept at crowdfunding initiatives. As Blazakis et al. wrote in the 2019 Soufan Center's report on the transnational white supremacy movement, several radical right-wing figures organized financing by establishing a significant audience over platforms like YouTube. Laura Southern, a prominent identitarian, who once had a massive following on YouTube before her channel was removed, would push viewers to Patreon to provide her funding – she would make nearly $5,000 per month via the crowdfunding platform during the late 2010s.[7] A prominent UK based white supremacist, Tommy Robinson, who founded the so-called English Defense league, became the subject of multiple UK based prosecutions. Robinson would receive donations for his legal defense by seeking donations over the US based crowdfunding platform, Donorbox.[8]

Just as banks derisked in their relationships with notorious white supremacist groups like the KKK, mainstream crowdfunding platforms also began severing their relationships with far-right individuals and groups in the late 2010s. As a result, a new universe of crowdfunding platforms that catered to hate groups would spring up – often overnight and with short-lived shelf lives. The venerable UK-based think tank, the Royal United Services Institute (RUSI) would document in a 2019 report that one such crowdfunding platform with an anti-Semitic name, GoyFundMe, would collect approximately $25,000 per month on behalf of white-supremacy enterprises.[9] Among the most prominent examples of radical right-wing groups leveraging alternative crowdfunding platforms occurred in the lead-up and the aftermath of the January 6, 2021, insurrection. As

---

[7] Blazakis, J., "White Supremacy Extremism: The Transnational Rise of the Violent White Supremacist Movement," *The Soufan Center*, 2019.

[8] Taylor, Matthew, & Wainwright, Martin. "English Defence League Supporters Attack Police at Bradford Rally," *The Guardian*, August 28, 2010, www.theguardian.com/uk/2010/aug/28/english-defence-league-bradford-demonstrations

[9] Keatinge, Tom, & Izenman, Kayla. *Fundraising for Right-Wing Extremist Movements*. Royal United Services Institute, 2019, May.

Blazakis wrote in the Global Center on Cooperative Security's report on far-right financing, prominent Proud Boy members financed their travel using the right-wing crowdfunding platform GiveSendGo. Further, insurrectionists associated with groups like the Proud Boys, Oathkeepers, and Three Percenters would fund their legal defense via GiveSendGo following their arrest for the violence they perpetrated on January 6.[10] Alternative platforms have become critical to sustaining US domestic based far-right actor administrative functionality during the aftermath of major law enforcement crackdowns in the aftermath of January 6, 2021. Without platforms like Give SendGo, the radical right would be less effective in accruing wealth via charitable giving.

Donations

Just as donations via crowdfunding platforms have been a lucrative source of financing, prominent white supremacists have also successfully received significant funds via their websites. Andrew Anglin, a notorious neo-Nazi propagandist, has made millions via donations made through his website, the Daily Stormer.[11] Anglin specifically has sought donations made in the form of cryptocurrency, like Bitcoin. In seeking these donations, Anglin has appealed to donors that virtual currency would allow him to avoid censorship and tracking by governments. The common combination of donations and propaganda allowed Anglin to motivate his followers to target a Jewish woman, Tanya Gersh, in Montana, who was going to sell a property owned by the mother of prominent white supremacist, Richard Spencer.[12] Gersh and her family feared for their lives and because they became the subject of abuse, they would ultimately sue

---

[10] Blazakis, J., *Far-Right Online Financing and How to Counter It*. Global Center, 2022, August.
[11] Ibid.
[12] Rosenberg, M., & Weiser, M. "How a Nazi Rally in Whitefish Led to a Deadly Attack in Charlottesville." *The New York Times*, September 5, 2021. www.nytimes.com/2021/09/05/us/politics/nazi-whitefish-charlottesville.html

Anglin and win a judgment in court.[13] The Gersh case represents the intersection of finance, cryptocurrency, propaganda, and far-right ideology. Spencer, like Anglin, was a keen advocate of Bitcoin, famously saying that "Bitcoin was the currency of the alt-right."[14]

Cryptocurrency, like Bitcoin, is not only a source of finance, often received via donations by the radical right, but it is also a form of stored value. Indeed, a savvy terrorist financier may invest in virtual assets like Bitcoin with an eye toward hoping the value of Bitcoin increases. According to Investopedia, the value of one Bitcoin in October 2010 was less than ten cents. As of November 19, 2024, following the reelection of President Trump, one Bitcoin was valued at more than 93,000 USD.[15] Further, virtual assets, like cryptocurrency, have an appeal to extremist actors, like Andrew Anglin, because they are pseudonymous. Additionally, many governments do not have sufficient regulation or law enforcement capabilities in place to track the exchange of crypto assets. As such, the radical right, like other types of terrorist groups, will continue to seek donations in the form of cryptocurrency and they will continue to see Bitcoin as an investment that can be stored and then deployed later to augment a group's operational or administrative activity.

Legitimate Businesses (Music Labels and More)

Like the sale of merchandize, important cultural and social elements of society, like music, have been both weaponized for recruitment and financial purposes by a range of extremist actors, to include those on the far-right. The music genre known as fascist wave, also known as fashwave, is a subversion of popular electronic music that was particularly popular in the 2010s. One of the key figures behind

---

[13] Blazakis, J. "Far-right Online Financing and How to Counter It." Global Center, 2022.
[14] Hinnant, Lindsay, & Kinetz, Emma. "White Dissidents Raise Millions in Cryptocurrency," *Frontline*, September 7, 2021. https://apnews.com/article/cryptocurrency-coronavirus-pandemic-technology-business-europe-f7f754fc2c68b0eb0d712239323f26c3
[15] Edwards, John. "Bitcoin's Price History," *Investopia*, www.investopedia.com/articles/forex/121815/bitcoins-price-history.asp

fashwave was Andrew Anglin, the neo-Nazi propagandist.[16] Anglin created a "Fashwave Friday" segment for his website, the Daily Stormer.[17] Anglin would seek to provide content, such as music, over the Daily Stormer as part of an effort to push propaganda, but also to seek funding. Not only did Daily Stormer readers access the written words of far-right figures, but they'd also have the capability to listen to music of their favorite far-right musicians. The exposure provided by the Daily Stormer on behalf of these musicians would increase their audience base and thus increase the chances of CD or streaming-related sales.

Far-right music groups, like neo-Nazis and Skinheads, have been making money via legitimate music sales that predates the fashwave movement. The neo-Nazi music group led by Ian Stuart Donaldson, Skrewdriver, was active in the UK punk scene in the 1970s and had a large following.[18] Skrewdriver would set the stage for the many far-right neo-Nazi and fascist music groups and labels that would seek to push propaganda via the airwaves. In the United States, during the 1990s, the white-power music scene was dominated by Skinhead groups like the Hammerskins, who pushed their neo-Nazi worldview by creating musical lyrics inspired by hatred. Another far-right group based in the UK, Blood & Honor, like Skrewdriver and the Hammerskins, made money by charging event fees to attend live concerts.[19] Blood & Honor, which would be designated by the Canadian government as a terrorist group pursuant to Canadian law, in addition to harvesting the hardcore neo-Nazi music scene by staging live

---

[16] Macnair, Liam. "Understanding Fashwave: The Alt-Right's Ever-Evolving Media Strategy," *GNET*, June 28, 2023. https://gnet-research.org/2023/06/28/understanding-fashwave-the-alt-rights-ever-evolving-media-strategy/

[17] Ibid.

[18] Furtell, Robert, Simi, Pete, Gottschalk, Simon. "Understanding Music in Movements: The White Power Music Scene," *The Sociological Quarterly: Official Journal of the Midwest Sociological Society*, March 31, 2006.

[19] Blood and Honour. "B & H Calendar – B & H Worldwide," 2019. https://url.avanan.click/v2/r02/___www.bloodandhonourworldwide.co.uk/bhww/b-h-calendar/ Last accessed September 2019.

events, would also create a music label and serve as a zine publisher for far-right music groups.[20]

The global far-right movement has also made money by profiting from the creation of travel businesses. For instance, one Italian neo-fascist group, Forza Nuova, profited by creating multiple travel companies catering to students.[21] Entertainment is big business and an inroad to young recruits who can carry a movement forward. Establishing a legitimate travel company gave Forza Nuova access to young people, which is key to the development of movements, while at the same time providing the right-wing organization access to wealth to push forward its agenda. Like leveraging the travel business, extremist far-right groups have also been adept at monetizing sports.

Events – From Fight Clubs to Bake Sales

Active Clubs (AC) have become a critical node within the extreme far-right movement by touting the health benefits of taking part in warrior culture by engaging in extreme fighting. ACs have a global network that has particularly been successful at recruiting young white men. Geographically, ACs have been especially successful in recruiting in the United States and the United Kingdom. In the UK, where they first sprouted up in 2023, extremist expert Nigel Bromage told the BBC that the clubs are getting fit to prepare for a "mythical race war."[22] In the United States, well-known far-right extremist Robert Rundo was among the first to leverage fight clubs for profit. Rundo, one of the perpetrators behind the violence at the 2017 Unite the Right Rally in Charlottesville, Virginia, was on the lam from US federal law enforcement for multiple years before his arrest in 2023.

---

[20] Worley, M., & Copsey, N. "White youth in tomorrow belongs to us: The British far right since 1967," *Routledge*. Pages 112–131; 114, 2007.

[21] Palladino, Andrea, Giovanni Tizian, & Stefano Vergine. "The Italian Far-Right Money," *L'Espresso*, November 8, 2017. http://espresso.repubblica.it/inchieste/2017/11/06/news/the-italian-far-right-money-1.313568

[22] O'Donoghue, D., "Far-Right Group Using Sports to Build Militia, Experts Warn." *BBC News*. www.bbc.com/news/articles/c5ydnqdq38wo.

Rundo, the founder of the Rise Above Movement (RAM), organized multiple mixed martial arts (MMA) events in Ukraine (prior to the Russia invasion). In addition to securing much-needed funding, the MMA events also provided a forum for white supremacists from different countries to meet and organize.[23]

The ticket sales for organized fighting events, whether a one-time MMA event or membership dues secured by running an Active Club, generate an important source of finance while promoting a warrior culture that touts the importance of being in shape for the next battle. On the opposite side of the spectrum, far-right figures have also tried to promote, and profit, from a softer image – an old-school femininity where white women are demur and happy to play the traditional role of housewife. The image often left is one over social media where these women, who are part of what is now called the tradwife movement, gain significant funding by promoting their cooking prowess. Each click they receive over YouTube or TikTok is the equivalent of the old-school ching of a cash register. In a Johns Hopkins University look at the tradwife industry, it is conservatively estimated that a tradwife production can bring in $400 per video.[24] Like fight clubs that typecast men in a traditional gender role, man as a fighter, the funding from promoting traditional stereotypes, a woman as nurturer and homemaker is important for establishing footholds for far-right cultures within mainstream social media. More clicks and views help grow the radical right movement by reaching people in online spaces – meeting people where they are at. Further, the profit made through in-person ticket sales and online clicks allows for the creation of additional events and videos – creating a cycle of profit, recruitment, and cultural immersion that creates momentum for a movement of millions.

---

[23] Blazakis, J. "White Supremacy Extremism: The Transnational Rise of the Violent White Supremacist Movement." *The Soufan Center*, 2019.

[24] Madruga, I. "An Incel's Fantasy: Into the World of Tradwives. The Johns Hopkins News-Letter." April 12, 2024. www.jhunewsletter.com/article/2024/04/an-incels-fantasy-into-the-world-of-tradwives.

Self-Funding

While the radical right is a global transnational movement that has made money by creating social activities that bring people together through culture, food, and music, there are countless examples of violent far-right individuals who have eschewed social camaraderie to carry out terrorist attacks that were self-funded. Indeed, in the Financial Action Task Force (FATF) Report that examined the sourcing of far-right financing explained, "right-wing terrorist attacks are perpetrated by self-funded lone actors."[25] Among those highlighted briefly in the FATF report was Anders Breivik, the culprit behind the 2011 multi-pronged attack that killed nearly eighty people in Utoya and Oslo, Norway.

Breivik detailed in exhaustive detail the methods in which he financed his deadly attack. His manifesto and trial not only illuminated the methods in which he financed his terror but also pointed to the difficulty law enforcement and regulators have in countering lone-actor (aka, lone wolf) funding. Breivik used a range of licit methods to self-fund his attack. Among the strategies adopted by Breivik was the creation of multiple companies, some of which were founded nearly a decade prior to the 2011 attack. While some of his businesses failed, one was lucrative – a diploma mill that provided fake academic credentials and reportedly brought in more than six figures during its operations.[26] The FATF report on far-right financing further explained that Breivik's diploma business engaged in money laundering operation that leveraged multiple Baltic banks and several Caribbean businesses to facilitate the conduct of his business.[27]

---

[25] Financial Action Task Force (FATF). "Ethnically or Racially Motivated Terrorism Financing." *FATF*, 2021. Page 3. www.fatf-gafi.org/publications/methodsandtrends/documents/ethnically-racially-motivatedterrorism-financing.html

[26] Center, C. T., "A post-trial profile of Anders Behring Breivik. Combating Terrorism Center at West Point. Reference 7." 2021, Page 29. https://ctc.westpoint.edu/a-post-trial-profile-of-anders-behring-breivik/.

[27] The Financial Action Task Force (FATF). "Ethnically or Racially Motivated Terrorism Financing." FATF, Paris, France, 2021, Page 22. https://url.avanan.click/v2/r02/___www.fatf-gafi.org/content/dam/fatf-gafi/reports/Ethnically-or-racially-motivated-terrorism-financing.pdf.coredownload.inline.pdf.

When Breivik ran his businesses into the ground, and as he neared the day of his planned attack, he pivoted to maxing out multiple credit cards that he legally acquired.[28]

Since Breivik's deadly attack, several other self-funded lone actor attacks have been carried out in cities like Christchurch, New Zealand; Halle, Germany; and Buffalo, New York. In these attacks, not unlike Breivik those attackers left a financial trail – one in which the deadly weapons were acquired through legitimate funding sources. Countering self-funded lone actors' access to finance is extremely difficult, especially because they often are not part of a broader network and because they are using licit methods of finance. As the FATF explains in its far-right financing report, "self-funded attacks can be challenging for Financial Institutions and Designated Non-Financial Businesses and Professions can be difficult to identify."[29] This challenge will remain a persistent challenge for countering far-right actors, but the challenge of extremist far-right financing also extends to illegal methods.

Illicit Activity

While licit means of financing for violent far-right actors have been a key source of financing, illicit means have also been deployed by violent far-right groups to fund their misdeeds. In the United States, during the 1980s, a neo-Nazi group known as the Order engaged in a crime spree that included a wide range of illicit fundraising techniques. Among the Order's financial feats was the brazen 1984 robbery of Brink's armored car. The group stole, in less than twenty minutes, $3.6 million and at the time the crime was the most successful

---

[28] Taylor, M. "Norway Gunman Claims He Had Nine-Year Plan to Finance Attacks," *The Guardian*, July 25, 2011. https://url.avanan.click/v2/r02/___www.theguardian.com/world/2011/jul/25/norway-gunman-attack-funding-claim.

[29] The Financial Action Task Force (FATF). "Ethnically or Racially Motivated Terrorism Financing." FATF, Paris, France, 2021, Page 8. https://url.avanan.click/v2/r02/___www.fatf-gafi.org/content/dam/fatf-gafi/reports/Ethnically-or-racially-motivated-terrorism-financing.pdf.coredownload.inline.pdf.

overland robbery in the United States.[30] The Order remains among the most successful violent far-right groups in raising funds in the United States, but the Brink's robbery was not the group's only illicit fundraising success. The Order also engaged in a sophisticated operation to counterfeit US dollars. Bruce Pierce, a member of the Order, would lead the group's effort in counterfeiting up to nearly $500,000 in 1983.[31] In a short span, the Order would raise more than $4 million to push forward its violent far-right agenda.

Today's violent far-right continues to read the Order's playbook. The RAM, which engaged in a wide array of licit activities, also conducted multiple robberies according to investigations carried out by ProPublica.[32] The German-based National Socialist Underground (NSU), a neo-Nazi group, primarily funded its operations by carrying out armed robberies, which resulted in the arrest of key leaders and the diminishment of the group.[33] The FATF would also highlight the NSU's robberies in its 2021 report and would explain that the proceeds of its crime sprees would be used for living costs, such as food, rent, and clothing.[34] Like the Order before it, the NSU's illicit activity would be its undoing.

The Order's demise in the mid 1980s occurred in tandem with the methods in which the US Department of Justice utilized the

---

[30] Hamm, M. S. "Crimes Committed by Terrorist Groups: Theory, Research, and Prevention," Final Report, Criminology Department, Indiana State University, Terre Haute, IN, 2005, Page 162. www.ojp.gov/pdffiles1/nij/grants/211203.pdf.

[31] King, W. "1983 Arrest an Elusive Clue to Neo-Nazi Group's Plans," *The New York Times*, September 29, 1985. www.nytimes.com/1985/09/29/us/1983-arrest-an-elusive-clue-to-neo-nazi-group-s-plans.html.

[32] Bond, Graham, Thompson, A. C., & Winston, Ali. "Racist, Violent, Unpunished: A White Hate Group's Campaign of Menace." *ProPublica*, October 19, 2017. www.propublica.org/article/white-hate-group-campaign-of-menace-rise-above-movement.

[33] Melzer, Ralf, & Serafin, Sebastian (eds.), "Right-Wing Extremism in Europe: Country Analyses, Counter-Strategies and Labor-Market Oriented Exit Strategies," Friedrich-Ebert-Stiftung Project, 2013, Page 194. https://library.fes.de/pdf-files/dialog/10031.pdf.

[34] The Financial Action Task Force (FATF). "Ethnically or Racially Motivated Terrorism Financing," FATF, Paris, France, 2021, Page 19. www.fatf-gafi.org/content/dam/fatf-gafi/reports/Ethnically-or-racially-motivated-terrorism-financing.pdf.coredownload.inline.pdf.

legal system. Namely, the Justice Department prosecuted members of the Order pursuant to the Racketeer-Influenced and Corrupt Organizations (RICO) law, which was passed in Congress in the 1970s as part of an effort to stem the tide against organized crime from corrupting businesses with money gained illegally.[35] Among the bevy of Federal crimes the group faced under RICO and other criminal statutes included the financial crimes of counterfeiting and robbery. The successful dissolvement of far-right groups like the Order by deploying non-terrorism specific legal measures remains the predominant method for US federal law enforcement to counter violent far-right groups. Indeed, there is a lack of domestic terrorism charges that US federal law enforcement can utilize to counter the violent far right and a consequence. Unlike dealing with individuals linked to groups like the so-called Islamic State in Iraq and Syria (ISIS) where, as discussed in Chapter 4, there are a wide range of terrorism-specific legal tools that can be deployed against it. Against the violent far-right, the Department of Justice and the Federal Bureau of Investigation must be more creative, leaning on RICO or other laws to counter the financing and operational capacity of violent far-right groups, such as those that stormed the US Capitol building on January 6, 2021.

The challenge of countering the violent far-right in the United States is further compounded by the fact that one of the most important tools in countering terrorists, the deployment of terrorist designations, is little used against far-right actors. Consequently, especially in the United States, inherently far-right violent groups are not banned – allowing them to fundraise via licit means. When groups, such as RAM, which isn't designated as a terrorist entity pursuant to US law, dabble in robberies and murder, just as the Order did forty years before it, only then can the long hand of US federal

---

[35] King, W. "Indictment of 24 Neo-Nazis Expected under U.S. Racketeering Law." *The New York Times*, April 12, 1985. https://url.avanan.click/v2/r02/___www.nytimes.com/1985/04/12/us/indictment-of-24-neo-nazis-expected-under-u-s-racketeering-law.html___

law enforcement act. As detailed by Blazakis and Rennebaum in a Soufan Center 2022 report, "the United States, the most prolific country in the world in dispensing terrorist designations against transnational terrorist actors, has used its legal authorities very sparingly against violent far-right terrorists."[36] This stands in contrast to the US government's pursuant of groups like ISIS vis-à-vis terrorist designations but also in comparison to the United States' so-called Five-Eye (FVEYE) partner countries of the United Kingdom, New Zealand, Australia, and Canada – the latter of which designated the Proud Boys, one of the perpetrators of the January 6 insurrection, as a terrorist group pursuant to its 2001 Anti-terrorism Act (ATA).[37] US FVEYE allies do not have the First Amendment considerations to navigate like the United States when it comes to the use of sanctions against violent far-right actors.

However, the United States is not alone in its inaction against the violent far-right's financial activities. Beyond the FATF's 2021 report on far-right financing, FATF has done little to emphasize the importance of countering the financial activities associated with groups or lone actors perpetrating acts of violence. Additionally, as will be discussed in Chapter 8, multilateral bodies like the United Nations have done little to counter the violent far-right. Indeed, the United Nations, as will be outlined later in more detail, has one sanctions regime that counters the finances of terrorist groups, and that UN body, known as the UN 1267 Committee, only tackles groups like al-Qa'ida, ISIS, and their associates.

---

[36] Blazakis, J., & Rennebaum, M. "Deterrence and Denial: The Impact of Sanctions and Designations on Violent Far-Right Groups: Comparing Violent Far-Right Terrorist Designations among Five Eyes Countries." July, 2022. Page 1. https://thesoufancenter.org/research/comparing-violent-far-right-terrorist-designations-among-five-eyes-countries/.

[37] *Security Legislation Amendment (Terrorism) Act 2002*. https://classic.austlii.edu.au/au/legis/cth/num_act/slaa2002451/sch1.html.

4 The Financing of ISIS and How It Was Countered – A Template for Success?

In modern times, and likely all-time, there has been no better financed terrorist group than ISIS. This fact is all the more remarkable because ISIS was able to take over portions of Iraq and Syria approximately the size of Great Britain in less than two decades after al-Qa'ida's deadly 9/11 attack. Among the results of the September 11 attack was an increased focus by the international community on countering terrorists and their financing. Yet, set against the backdrop of a post 9/11 world of more domestic regulations and laws, as well as international organizational approaches by groups like the United Nations and FATF to counter terrorist access to finance, ISIS was able to eclipse al-Qa'ida's capacity to raise finance. ISIS's approach to finance also deviated from the al-Qa'ida financial model, which relied on funding through nonprofit organizations and the contributions of wealthy donors. ISIS's diversification of funding streams would provide the international community and the United States a new opportunity to deploy laws, regulations, sanctions, and military operations to counter the world's deadliest terrorist group. Lessons learned from 9/11, especially the need to coordinate internationally and share information between agencies, would be critical to counter the ISIS's finances – which would be key to uprooting the group from its territorial caliphate. This chapter will briefly examine the sources of ISIS's financing and then will look at the tools the United States and the international community deployed to counter the financing of ISIS. The story of ISIS's finances and the countering of it provides a case study of how all the tools of intelligence, military, and economic warfare can be harnessed effectively. It also is a story that cannot be applied across the board to all forms of extremism. What was used to defeat ISIS's financing, in other words, will be difficult to use, especially the United States, against violent far-right groups. The chapter will conclude by examining why this is the case.

THE FINANCING OF ISIS

ISIS's access to wealth allows it to publish glossy magazines, like Dabiq, and other polished propaganda pieces that were vitally important to recruiting members to join ISIS in the fight to establish a caliphate. The wealth that the group would accrue would not only help pay the salaries of ISIS's foreign fighters but also help entice skilled workers, like doctors or engineers, who would operate and maintain equipment related to ISIS's exploitation of natural resources, like oil. The money ISIS would make would allow it to purchase weapons for its fighters and give the group a capacity to carry out attacks that were requisite for the conquest of territory. Finally, and perhaps most importantly, the Islamic State had to govern. Unlike al-Qa'ida, which never held territory like the huge tracts of land ISIS would acquire, ISIS also had an obligation to govern the people in the land it controlled. ISIS had to provide the citizens of the fledgling pseudo-state basic services like medical care, sanitation pickup, water, and salaries for the skilled and unskilled workforce that comprised the caliphate. The costs of governance are expensive, and therefore ISIS would have to diversify its income streams.

Arguably, the most lucrative source of revenue for ISIS came from its access to oil fields in Syria and Iraq. The group has captured these fields while taking over territory. In addition to ISIS's access to established oil refineries and wells, the group also took measures to create makeshift wells to extract natural resources. ISIS, however, could not profit from its newfound riches without moving its products outside of Syria and Iraq. The group has used both licit and illicit means to move this oil through northern Iraq and Syria and into Turkey. By working through mature smuggling networks, some of which have existed since the days of the Saddam Hussein regime, the organization made, according to some estimates,[1] hundreds of millions on the sale of oil. The sale of oil would become such an important revenue source for the group that it tailored its propaganda messages to encourage recruits with petroleum engineering and technical backgrounds to migrate to ISIS's caliphate. It is very rare for a terrorist group to profit by gaining access to natural resources, much less at the scale ISIS did, because terrorist groups often lack the bureaucratic structure to hold, govern, and maintain territory.

While gaining access to territory, ISIS gained access to the citizens of Iraq and Syria. ISIS would be ruthless in exploiting its captive audience, which the group would extort and tax. ISIS would make money by taxing store shop owners who were selling goods in the territory it controlled. As detailed by an FATF 2015 report that detailed the various methods ISIS financed its operations, the group would also tax the salaries of employees of the governments of Iraq and Syria. Within ISIS-controlled territory, Iraqi and Syrian civil servants were still receiving salary from their governments while they were held captive by ISIS. ISIS would allow the civil servants to drive out of ISIS-controlled territory so they could access their government salaries at the nearest city controlled by the government of Iraq or Syria. When the civil servants came back home, ISIS would take a cut of the salary when they passed through ISIS controlled checkpoints. Some experts contend that the extortion, or taxation as ISIS tried to justify it, of the captive population may have exceeded the profits made by the sale of oil. The costs borne by those held captive by ISIS were significant, but for many there would be other terrible ways the group would profit by gaining, often by force, access to people.[2]

At ISIS's zenith, another, perhaps unsurprising, significant source of revenue for the group was kidnapping people and then ransoming them off to governments, family members, or companies.

---

[1] Estimates vary considerably among sources regarding the scale in which ISIS profited from the extraction of oil.
[2] The Financial Action Task Force. "Financing of the Terrorist Organisation Islamic State in Iraq and the Levant (ISIL)." February 2015.

A November 2014 UN report, for example, estimated that the Islamic State may have made anywhere from 35 to 45 million US dollars by engaging in kidnapping for ransom operations.[3] ISIS would take hostages from Europe, Asia, the Middle East, and North America. Although the group is well known to have viciously beheaded many of its hostages in pulp fiction like videos, the group took advantage of its access to people by ransoming off many of its kidnapped victims. This revenue stream was not consistent and slowed as the conflict in Syria became more gruesome and beheading videos circulated globally. Supply, simply put, would dry up, as journalists and nonprofit workers made decisions to refrain from travelling to ISIS-controlled territory in Syria and Iraq.

While ISIS did not tap into the wallets of wealthy donors like al-Qa'ida historically did, ISIS still has received donations, by some estimates up to 40 million US dollars per year in 2013 and 2014, from wealthy supporters. For the most part, ISIS's wealthy donors were based in the Gulf States of Saudi Arabia, Kuwait, Qatar, and the United Arab Emirates. The group, especially at its zenith, was attractive to wealthy donors because it accrued significant power, gained large swaths of territory, and could influence the destiny of both Syria and Iraq. The group's interest in rekindling a religious caliphate was another significant draw for donors who believed the ruling monarchies in the Gulf States had lost their way by not embracing the austere form of Islam ISIS promised.

While less prevalent as a source of finance than the group's profits derived by tapping into natural resources and the wallets of captive Iraqis and Syrians, ISIS made money by selling cultural antiquities. As ISIS gained control over large swaths of land in Iraq and Syria, the group also gained access to some of the world's most precious ancient sites. While the public witnessed ISIS's destruction in many of these sites, the group would loot smaller relics. There

---

[3] United Nations 1267 Monitoring Team Report. "The Islamic State in Iraq and the Levant and the Al-Nusrah Front for the People of the Levant: Report and Recommendations." November 14, 2014. Page 24.

remains ambiguity regarding how much ISIS benefited through the sale of cultural heritage, but there have been a range of efforts to document the wealth ISIS accumulated by virtue of its access. For example, in February 2015, FATF explained that ISIS absconded with valuable relics from ancient sites such as al-Nabuk in Syria. Indeed, according to multiple 2014 news reports, the Islamic State may have earned up to $36 million worth in antiquities from its access to the al-Nabuk site.[4]

ISIS's senior leadership interest in benefitting from antiquities was confirmed in the summer of 2015 when US Special Forces carried out a raid against a high-level member of ISIS's finance committee. Abu Sayyaf, the individual killed in the raid, was the head of ISIS's finance committee and in his possession at the time of his death were an Assyrian bible and ancient coins. The fact that such a high-level member of ISIS had these items in his possession is a direct example of the value senior-level members of ISIS placed on the exploitation of cultural heritage.[5]

Following the raid of the Abu Sayyaf compound, the United States government exploited documents found in his possession. The contents of these documents were later presented to the public at a public forum in September 2015. The documents made it clear that ISIS was engaged in a very organized effort to loot antiquities. The documents further illustrated that ISIS had a bureaucracy with a section within it that led ISIS's efforts to profit through the sale of oil, gas, and antiquities.[6] Within this division there was a diwan for natural resources under which the antiquities section was housed. It is also clear from the exploited documents that Abu Sayyaf cared deeply about how the group would benefit in the future from its loot. In correspondence to his subordinates, Abu Sayyaf directed his men

---

[4] FATF. "Financing of the Terrorist Organisation Islamic State in Iraq and the Levant (ISIL)." February 2015.

[5] Kerry, J. "Remarks at Threats to Cultural Heritage in Iraq and Syria Event," *U.S. Department of State*, September 22, 2014, https://2009-2017.state.gov/secretary/remarks/2014/09/231992.htm.

[6] A diwan is the Arabic term for division, or central finance department.

to hire people who are experienced in digging up ancient relics and that these relics would be moved by people who were knowledgeable about the value of ancient artifacts. In addition to the ancient sites, such as al-Nabuk, the group gained access to museums, perhaps most notably the Museum in Mosul, from which they were also able to profit from.

Just as ISIS benefited from controlling territory and gaining access to cultural heritage, the group's conquest of territory also allowed it to gain direct access to banks. For an example, you must look no further than Mosul – the site of ISIS's takeover of the Museum in Mosul. In 2015, ISIS would also take over the Iraqi Central Bank in Mosul, Iraq. When the Islamic State took over this bank, which they effectively fleeced, the group reportedly took 500 to 750 million US dollars from the Central Bank in Mosul. This is an astonishing figure, and while it is a one-time cash infusion and not a source of steady revenue, it is often cited as the reason why the group is seen as the richest terrorist group in history.

At the height of ISIS's power, there were reports that the group was making some, but not a lot of money, from the property it looted. As the Syrian and Iraqi armies fled, ISIS acquired abandoned vehicles and weapons. Ten years ago, an individual could scour the Dark Net and purchase from ISIS profiteers, Syrian and Iraqi government weapons and ammunition. Further, ISIS also took control of livestock and crops – pretty much anything innocent Syrians or Iraqis had in their collective possession. When foreign fighters travelled to ISIS's fledgling pseudo-state, they would bring all their worldly possessions with them and hand them over to ISIS. Finally, the group engaged in human trafficking as exemplified by the group's selling of enslaved minorities like Yazidi women.

ISIS's diversification of its finances was one of the primary reasons the group was such an effective fighting force. Without significant financing, the group would not have been able to pay its fighters, retain territory, and project a threat outside of Syria and Iraq by carrying out attacks in Paris, London, and Brussels (among many other locales). While it has been more than ten years since ISIS was dislodged from its territorial caliphate, the group remains a persistent threat to international peace and stability – as witnessed by its 2024 attack in Russia and the group's foothold in West Africa. Nonetheless, ISIS is a shell of its former self, and that is because of the comprehensive way the United States the global community would band together to counter the group's finances.

COUNTERING ISIS'S FINANCING

To counter ISIS, the United States created a strategy that had nine separate lines of effort, of which line of effort five was to counter the group's finances. These lines of effort remain in place as of 2024, even though ISIS has been evicted from Syria and Iraq. Unlike tackling the rise of the extreme radical right, the United States was able to harness a broad range of tools to degrade ISIS's financial capabilities. Some of these tools, such as the use of targeted financial sanctions, were being deployed against ISIS prior to the establishment of its caliphate. For example, in 2011, the US Department of State designated the future leader of ISIS (Abu Bakr al-Baghdadi) as a terrorist. Further, in 2004, the US Department designated ISIS's predecessor group, al-Qa'ida in Iraq (AQI) as a Foreign Terrorist Organization (FTO).The use of terrorist designations will be examined in more detail in Chapter 6, but for the purposes of this chapter, the US Department of State and Treasury would significantly ramp up the use of targeted financial measures, like terrorist designations, against scores of ISIS leaders, operatives, and financial facilitators. On August 29, 2017, the Department of the Treasury's Office of Foreign Assets Control (OFAC) would sanction Salim al-Mansur as a Specially Designated Global Terrorist (SDGT) pursuant to E.O. 13224 due to his role as a key financial cog in ISIS's moneymaking machine. The Department of the Treasury detailed al-Mansur's role as being responsible for fundraising for the group since 2009 and specifically for laundering and transferring funds associated with ISIS's extraction of oil from Iraq and Syria throughout 2015 and 2016. In announcing the designation of al-Mansur, the OFAC director, John E. Smith, would highlight how the sanction of Mansur would benefit the international effort to counter ISIS's finances. Smith would explain, "Treasury continues to work in close collaboration with the Government of Iraq to dismantle ISIS financial networks both inside and outside ISIS-controlled territory ... and underscores the United States' resolve to work with international partners to further restrict ISIS's ability to abuse the U.S. and Iraqi financial systems."[7] At ISIS's height, the US government, and international partners, would sanction dozens of ISIS and ISIS-linked individuals. The treatment of ISIS as a terrorist actor would allow the US government broad remit to use all its tools to go after ISIS's sources of profit. If a group is labeled a terrorist, it provides departments, like the Defense Department, greater leverage to effectively advocate for the use of military strikes to counter the terrorist group's financing.

Arguably, the most effective approach to tackling ISIS's wealth was the use of kinetic operations to degrade the group. This is also a method of fighting terrorism finance that is not frequently applied to groups. For instance, the extreme radical right has not been targeted by the tools of warfare because the groups within the pantheon of the radical right are often unsanctioned, as noted in Chapter 3, by the United States. Additionally, these far-right groups haven't posed the same level of threat to global order as ISIS. Nor have violent far-right actors taken control over the oil production of countries like ISIS did in Syria and Iraq.

When the United States started targeting for military strikes the ISIS oil-production and smuggling capacity, the trajectory of the conflict in Iraq and Syria would change. Beginning in 2015, under the name of Operation Inherent Resolve, the US government and its allies would begin its assault on ISIS's financial operations. In its inaugural press release in November 2015, US Central Command

---

[7] U.S. Department of the Treasury. "Treasury Collaborates with Iraqi Government to Sanction ISIS Finance Emir." *U.S. Department of the Treasury Press Releases.* https://home.treasury.gov/news/press-release/sm0149.

would explain, "among the targeted fronts are … financing mechanisms such as oil collection … in Ramadi, degrading oil revenue through oil strikes … in the past month alone key oil supply points [were struck]."[8] Between 2015 and 2019, the final year of ISIS's control of significant territory in Syria and Iraq, US Central Command would issue dozens of press releases documenting strikes against ISIS oil-producing, and trafficking, capacity. Typical of such a release is the July 2017 Inherent Resolve press release, "coalition forces struck ISIS targets … near Abu Kamal, a strike destroyed two ISIS oil tanks and an oil refinery building … near Dayr Az Zawr, six strikes destroyed 16 ISIS oil stills, 10 oil barrels, six oil trucks and two wellheads."[9] The author was inside the US government working to counter ISIS financing, and there was great apprehension about targeting Syria's oil infrastructure and the trucks involved in smuggling ISIS oil. First, several individuals involved in the smuggling of oil were civilians. Second, crippling a major profit center of a country, like Syria's oil industry, would require an expensive rebuilding later. The United States has a long history of paying for what it has broken on the battlefield, and an already expensive endeavor was a deep concern to policymakers. Spending more money to rebuild Syria in the aftermath of ISIS's ultimate eviction was a step too far for some policymakers. Ultimately, a decision to move ahead was made and the campaign to go after ISIS's assets would be known as Tidal Wave II – a name associated with the Allies' effort during World War II to counter Nazi Germany's access to Romania's oil production.[10] The US government would also mitigate the loss of

---

[8] Belser, J. "Operation Inherent Resolve Airstrikes Proving Effective in Iraq, Syria," *U.S. Central Command*, 2025. www.centcom.mil/MEDIA/NEWS-ARTICLES/News-Article-View/Article/885255/operation-inherent-resolve-airstrikes-proving-effective-in-iraq-syria/.

[9] U.S. Department of Defense. "U.S., Coalition Continue Strikes to Defeat ISIS in Syria, Iraq," *U.S. Department of Defense News*. www.defense.gov/News/News-Stories/Article/Article/1246136/us-coalition-continue-strikes-to-defeat-isis-in-syria-iraq/.

[10] Gordon, M. R. "U.S. Strikes Syria Oil Fields Used by ISIS," *The New York Times*, November 17, 2015. www.nytimes.com/2015/11/17/world/middleeast/us-strikes-syria-oil.html.

innocent civilian lives by often dropping leaflets prior to bombing truck drivers moving ISIS's illicit oil.[11] The US government made a decision that ISIS's financial nodes had to be knocked out and that the benefits of degrading ISIS's capabilities outweighed the negatives of a rebuild and the possible of loss of life associated with the smuggling networks engaged in moving ISIS's oil.

Destruction of ISIS's moneymaking capabilities did not come from the air alone. The US would deploy special forces on multiple occasions as part of an effort to remove important ISIS financial figures from the battlefield. As previously mentioned, US Special Forces were instrumental in killing Abu Sayyaf, a key ISIS leader with significant financial management responsibilities. Nor would US forces only kill ISIS facilitators in Syria and Iraq. In 2023, in northern Somalia, US Special Forces carried out a raid that resulted in the death of Bilal al-Sudani, a figure, according to Secretary of Defense Lloyd Austin, who was responsible for, "fostering the growing presence in Africa."[12] Al-Sudani was, according to George Washington University's Program on Extremism, able to facilitate the travel of foreign recruits and financed foreign fighter activity in [Somalia].[13] Bilal's removal from Somalia is illustrative of the fact that the lessons learned in Syria and Iraq continue to be applied against ISIS despite the collapse of the caliphate.

Sanctions and military strikes were only part of the US strategy to cripple ISIS's finances. The US government would arrest and prosecute several armchair ISIS supporters, some of whom operated from the comfort of their homes in the United States. As discussed in Chapter 6, one of the chief benefits of an FTO designation is that it provides the US Department of Justice the ability to prosecute individuals for providing material support to designated terrorist groups.

---

[11] Ibid.
[12] Macaulay, C. "Bilal al-Sudani: U.S. Forces Kill Islamic State Somalia Leader in Cave Complex," *BBC News*, January 27, 2023. www.bbc.com/news/world-africa-64423598.
[13] Bacon, T., & Doctor, A. C. "The Death of Bilal al-Sudani and Its Impact on Islamic State Operations," *George Washington University*, March 2, 2023. https://extremism.gwu.edu/death-of-bilal-al-sudani.

The case of a young woman named Zoobia Shahnaz is particularly instructive in understanding the value of the FTO regime to the countering of terrorist financiers. In 2017, Zoobia Shahnaz carried out a scheme involving credit card fraud where the proceeds of the fraud were used to acquire cryptocurrency, specifically over $60,000 in Bitcoin. Shahnaz also acquired a $22,500 loan which she also obtained through fraud. Next, she took the money she gained via the fake loan and credit cards and bought Bitcoin. Then she converted the Bitcoin back to cash to conceal the source of the funds. Essentially, Shahnaz used the crypto exchange to wash the money. She then transferred the currency to the Islamic State terrorist group. She started transferring the funds in a structured manner via a series of wire transfers. Ultimately, her activities, to include a review of her internet search history and her travel to Pakistan with a long layover in Turkey, were her undoing – more on role of financial intelligence in countering her terrorist financing in Chapter 5.

In December 2017, Shahnaz would be indicted by a federal jury in the Eastern District of New York (EDNY). The United States government would levy five initial charges against her, to include: bank fraud, conspiracy to commit money laundering, money laundering to conceal the proceeds of unlawful activity, money laundering to avoid transaction reporting requirements,[14] and most importantly, money laundering to support a designated FTO. Later, Shahnaz would later face an additional charge in February 2018 – that of providing material support to an FTO pursuant to 2339B(a)(1)(2) of the Immigration and Nationality Act. The material support tool to counter terrorist financing is among the most important in the Justice Department's arsenal and would lead to the undoing of scores of ISIS supporters, to include Shahnaz. In less than a year, on November 26, 2018, Shahnaz would plead guilty to providing material to ISIS, a designated FTO. Shahnaz would admit that she defrauded multiple financial institutions and

---

[14] This charge relates to the structuring, placing smaller than $10K worth of funds into the financial system to avoid suspicious transaction reports the bank would be required to file pursuant to US law that Shahnaz engaged in.

the laundering of the stolen proceeds out of the country with the intent to support ISIS. In 2020, Shahnaz would be sentenced to thirteen years of imprisonment by US District Judge Joanna Seybert. The FBI Assistant Director-in-Charge, William Sweeney, would highlight the power of terrorist financing prosecutions and how important of an instrument it is in the US government's toolkit. Sweeney explained,

> financing terrorist organizations shouldn't be viewed as any less dangerous of a crime than actually carrying out an act of terror itself. Make no mistake about it, Shahnaz funneled a significant amount of money into the hands of those who intended to use it in furtherance of ISIS objectives, and she set out to travel overseas with similar goals in mind.[15]

Shahnaz, an American citizen, is representative of the way the US government tried to counter ISIS financing by pursuing a law enforcement investigation that would result in a prosecution. The prosecution of Shahnaz, and others like her, would cut off funds from the United States to ISIS. This method is neatly tied to the use of terrorist designations. If ISIS wasn't a designated FTO, it is possible that Shahnaz's activities would not have merited investigation, much less more than a decade in a prison cell.

Prosecuting terrorists for financing designated terrorist groups has been in the US government's playbook since 1997. Less frequently deployed to counter illicit actors is the use of private sector engagement and the use of the US Government's Rewards for Justice program to stamp out terrorist financing. This odd combination of tools was deployed as part of a multiagency effort to counter ISIS's profiteering from the sale of ancient antiquities. Of course, as noted earlier, the US Special Forces eliminated Abu Sayyaf, one of the key individuals behind ISIS's exploitation of cultural heritage.

---

[15] U.S. Attorney's Office, Eastern District of New York. "Long Island Woman Sentenced to 13 Years' Imprisonment for Providing Material Support to ISIS," *U.S. Department of Justice*, March 13, 2020. www.justice.gov/usao-edny/pr/long-island-woman-sentenced-13-years-imprisonment-providing-material-support-isis.

Abu Sayyaf, however, was just one cog in ISIS's moneymaking empire. In an effort to counter ISIS's theft of antiquities, the US government engaged with the private sector, specifically working with museums and auction houses to alert the world of ISIS's plundering of Syria and Iraq's cultural heritage. This type of engagement was predicated on trying to dry up demand for Syria and Iraq's cultural heritage. The Department of State would try to curb demand for ISIS's sale of antiquities by deploying senior policymakers to engage with the art community. For example, Secretary of State John Kerry spoke at the Metropolitan Museum of Art in New York City in September 2014. In his speech, Secretary Kerry highlighted the ISIS threat to cultural heritage in Iraq and Syria. Kerry noted, "ISIS forces the people of Syria and Iraq to pay for their cultural heritage in blood. We are determined instead to help Iraqis and Syrians protect and preserve their heritage in peace."[16] The meaning behind Kerry's words was this, "if you buy these artifacts from Syria and Iraq for your art collections, you will have blood on your hands." It was a powerful message. Yet, the US government would do more than deliver speeches in an effort to counter this source of ISIS financing. The US Department of State's Cultural Heritage Center would work with International Council of Museums (ICOM) to create an Emergency Red List of Syrian Cultural Objects at Risk in 2013 and would do the same for Iraqi objects in 2015.[17] These lists were designed to highlight for the art market the types of items likely to be found in illegal ISIS excavations in Iraq and Syria. The dissemination of these lists was often coupled with law enforcement and other types of engagements as part of an effort to curb demand for illicit Syrian and Iraqi art.[18]

---

[16] Kerry, J. "Remarks at Threats to Cultural Heritage in Iraq and Syria Event," *U.S. Department of State*, September 22, 2014. https://2009-2017.state.gov/secretary/remarks/2014/09/231992.htm.

[17] U.S. Government Accountability Office. Report to Congressional Requesters: August 2016, *U.S. Government Accountability Office*. www.gao.gov/assets/gao-16-673.pdf.

[18] U.S. Government Accountability Office. "Report to Congressional Requesters: August 2016." *U.S. Government Accountability Office*. www.gao.gov/assets/gao-16-673.pdf.

Tackling the demand for illicit antiquities wasn't the only strategy deployed by the United States. Indeed, the US government literally put bounties on the heads of those responsible for financing ISIS's terror. In 2015, as part of an effort to curb the supply-side of ISIS's exploitation of antiquities, the US Department of State's Diplomatic Security Bureau issued a Reward for Justice (RFJ)[19] targeting ISIS's finance network. The RFJ, which remains in place as of December 2024, offers up to $10 million for "information leading to the disruption of the financial mechanisms of the terrorist group ISIS."[20] The RFJ page noting the offer depicts pictures of Syrian and Iraqi cultural heritage and explains that

> illicit oil operations and trafficking in looted archaeological objects from Syria and Iraq also have been key sources of revenue that generate hard currency ... ISIS's damage to and looting of cultural and historical sites in Syria and Iraq have destroyed irreplaceable evidence of ancient life and society. Ancient and historical coins, jewelry, carved gemstones, sculptures, plaques, and cuneiform tablets are among the types of cultural objects that ISIS has trafficked.[21]

The intersection of ISIS exploitation of antiquities and lawfare became apparent when the US government became aware of the crafts company Hobby Lobby selling Iraqi cultural heritage that was

---

[19] The author was the State Department's Counterterrorism Bureau representative to the RFJ committee, and the author was the author of the idea to use an RFJ to target ISIS's financing via the sale of cultural heritage. The idea met resistance from senior policymakers, including Ambassador Tina Kaidanow, who was the head of the Counterterrorism Bureau. Kaidanow and Undersecretary Kennedy were concerned about the costs associated with paying out a reward to a tipster. They were also skeptical of ISIS's profiteering via the sale of antiquities. Secretary Kerry, however, to his credit, supported the proposal, and ultimately it was broadened to include requests for information regarding ISIS's smuggling network engaged in the movement of natural resources like oil.

[20] U.S. Department of State. "Rewards for Justice: ISIS Financial Network," *U.S. Department of State*. https://rewardsforjustice.net/rewards/isis-financial-network/.

[21] Ibid.

unearthed and moved to the United Arab Emirates and then sold on its website. Hobby Lobby engaged in this activity during the height of ISIS's control of territory, and ultimately the US government became aware of the situation when an alert customs officer seized Iraqi artifacts destined for Hobby Lobby. In order to avoid criminal prosecution, Hobby Lobby agreed to pay a fine of $3 million and return more than 5,000 objects to Iraq.[22]

The Hobby Lobby case depicts well the fact that ISIS's financial activities touched all corners of the globe. As a consequence of ISIS's global operations, a multilateral approach would be adopted to counter ISIS's financing. The US government would play an instrumental role within a Global Coalition to Defeat ISIS. In fact, the United States, along with Italy and Saudi Arabia, would serve as one of three cochairs of a counter-ISIS finance subgroup within the global coalition to defeat ISIS.

On September 10, 2014, the United States government announced the creation of the Global Coalition to Defeat ISIS. The coalition, which still exists as of December 2024, outlined five pillars to counter ISIS. The third pillar was to counter ISIS's financing and funding. Within the coalition, the Counter ISIS Finance Group (CIFG), which remains active, has thirty-seven member states working together to, among other things, implement United Nations resolutions and to counter all forms of ISIS financing.[23] While the initial focus of the CIFG was battling against ISIS access to wealth derived in Syria and Iraq, the CIFG today takes a global approach to countering ISIS's access to finance. For instance, during a late January 2024 meeting, the CIFG met for the 19th time and touted ISIS's success at raising funds via crowdfunding via unwitting donors and the group's

---

[22] Connor, T., & Arkin, D. "Hobby Lobby Has Bought Tons of Antiquities. Where Do They Come From?" *NBC News*, July 8, 2017. www.nbcnews.com/news/us-news/spotlight-hobby-lobby-s-biblical-collection-after-smuggle-case-n780286.

[23] The Global Coalition. "Restricting Daesh's Access to Finance and Funding – The Global Coalition against Daesh," *The Global Coalition*, May 16, 2017. https://theglobalcoalition.org/en/mission/tackling-daeshs-financing-and-funding/.

ability to make inroads in West Africa.[24] Further, the CIFG would highlight several developments regarding ISIS financing and underscored the need to "increase timely information-sharing with relevant agencies, international partners, and financial institutions."[25] Given ISIS's global footprint, it is unsurprising that the CIFG underscored the importance of intelligence in countering ISIS's financing. The CIFG also explained the importance of taking a multilateral approach to fighting ISIS's wealth creation capability. The CIFG underscored this by noting, "all countries effectively implement the FATF recommendations."[26]

The coalition to defeat ISIS, the CIFG, and the United States have all emphasized the importance of a multilateral approach to combating ISIS. As will be discussed in Chapter 8, multilateralism is a critical component of fighting terrorist financing. Multilateral efforts, in the case of ISIS, have intersected frequently. In February 2016, for instance, the FATF convened a joint meeting with the CIFG. Among the many points emphasized at the February meeting was the "central role of the UN in combatting ISIL financing … and UNSCRS 2199 and 2253, which reaffirmed that trade in oil and other resources with ISIL is prohibited and directs new efforts by the ISIL and Al-Qaida Sanctions Committee to address the threat of ISIL in particular."[27] The FATF also published a one-off 2015 report outlining the methods of ISIS wealth accrual, but it has routinely emphasized the importance of countering ISIS via the deployment of multilateral sanctions. Indeed, for more than a decade the UN's ISIL and Al-Qaida Sanctions Committee (aka UN 1267 Committee) has

---

[24] U.S. Department of the Treasury. "Counter ISIS Finance Group Leaders Issue Joint Statement," *U.S. Department of the Treasury*, February 27, 2024. https://home.treasury.gov/news/press-releases/jy2131#:~:text=Global%20Coalition%20members%20will%20continue,ISIS%20and%20other%20terrorist%20groups.

[25] Ibid.

[26] Ibid.

[27] FATF-CIFG Communiqué. Financial Action Task Force. www.fatf-gafi.org/en/publications/Fatfgeneral/Fatf-cifg-communique-feb-2016.html#:~:text=The%20CIFG%2C%20co%2Dchaired%20by,degrade%20and%20ultimately%20defeat%20ISIL.

listed ISIS financiers and leaders as terrorists. In fact, the UN 1267 first listed ISIS's predecessor organization as a terrorist entity as far back as 2004.[28]

The focus on ISIS financing stands in stark contrast to the US attention, and global focus for that matter, on violent far-right terrorists. There may be good reason for this given the history of ISIS, its ability to conquer territory, and its ability to project a menace globally by virtue of the number of affiliate groups that continue to operate in places like West Africa. The approach to countering ISIS's financing nonetheless offers an interesting template for emerging threats, such as those from the radical right, as discussed in Chapter 3.

Countering the financing of violent terrorist and extremist groups requires intelligence, a required capability to deploy forms of economic warfare, such as sanctions and multilateralism cooperation. The remainder of this book will examine these counterterrorism financing methods, all of which are underpinned by intelligence, which will be the subject of Chapter 5.

---

[28] United Nations. "Al-Qaida in Iraq," *United Nations Security Council*. https://main.un.org/securitycouncil/en/sanctions/1267/aq_sanctions_list/summaries/entity/al-qaida-in-iraq.

5 Intelligence and the Countering of Terrorist Financing

The use of intelligence is foundational to countering terrorist access to finance. Intelligence collected by governments through human intelligence, signals intelligence, imagery intelligence, and other national technical means has been deployed against transnational terrorist groups. Additionally, open-source intelligence (OSINT) has been particularly helpful in recent times in understanding how terrorists leverage social media platforms like Twitter (now known as X), Facebook, YouTube, among others, to push sympathizers to support their nefarious activities. Finally, especially in a post 9/11 world, the use of financial intelligence (FININT) has been instrumental in curbing terrorists' access to funds. This chapter will explore how sensitive government collection, OSINT, and FININT, where the private sector plays a particularly pivotal role, have been deployed against terrorists.

HUMAN INTELLIGENCE (HUMINT)

Human intelligence, or HUMINT, is an intelligence discipline associated with the collection of information from human sources. HUMINT is critical to understanding capabilities, intentions, financing, and other aspects of illicit actors like terrorist groups. Often, it is the insider within a terrorist group or close friends and family members who may possess the most important intelligence that can help unravel an organization's capacity to do harm. HUMINT collection activities carried out by a range of US government actors, such as the Federal Bureau of Investigation, the Defense Intelligence Agency, the Central Intelligence Agency, and others, have been vital in countering terrorist facilitators and supporters. Many agencies increased their attention to terrorist financing intelligence collection post 9/11 – to include the use of human assets to understand the contours of terrorist financing.

The Department of Defense, for instance, as explained by Dennis Lormel in the Combating Terrorism Center's March 2008 issue, was passively involved in countering terrorist financing prior to 2004. According to Lormel, while DoD did not have any initiatives focusing on terrorist finance, DoD's intelligence components did provide intelligence to a range of government agencies who were heavily involved in the countering of terrorist financing. For example, Lormel notes that when the United States invaded Iraq, FBI agents were embedded within military intelligence to "collect information on al-Qa'ida."[1] It was also during this time that US Central Command stood up the Threat Financing Exploitation Unit (TFEU) to collect intelligence in Iraq during the insurgency. In testimony provided by US Department of the Treasury's Acting Assistant Secretary, Daniel Glaser emphasized that the TFEU "is designed to consolidate and share financial intelligence on terrorist and insurgency financial networks in Iraq."[2] In 2004, with US warfighters on the ground, collecting information via human sources by the DoD would prove valuable to multiple agencies, like the Treasury Department and the FBI. For Treasury, it would use this information to develop, like the State Department as explained in Chapter 6, terrorist designations packages. For the FBI, human intelligence provided by other agencies, like DoD, would provide indications and warning of potential plots against US interests at home or abroad.

In July 2005 testimony before the House Armed Services Subcommittee on Oversight and Investigations provided by Caleb Temple, Senior Intelligence Officer at the Defense Intelligence Agency

---

[1] Lormel, D. M., "Combating Terrorist Financing at the Agency and Interagency Levels," *Combating Terrorism Center at West Point*, March 2008, Volume 1, Issue 4. https://ctc.westpoint.edu/combating-terrorist-financing-at-the-agency-and-interagency-levels/

[2] U.S. Department of the Treasury, "Testimony of Acting A/S Glaser on Financing for the Iraqi Insurgency," *U.S. Department of the Treasury*, July 28, 2005. https://home.treasury.gov/news/press-releases/js2658.

(DIA) explained the importance of HUMINT to tackling terrorist financing. Temple explained the different types of DIA intelligence targets by way of broad example when he described the intelligence collection environment in Iraq during the height of the US invasion. He explained, "the intelligence instruments required for identifying and collecting on sophisticated international banking transactions are far different than the instruments required to identify and collect on a courier on a bike delivering a bag full of cash to the insurgency."[3] Temple, correctly, goes on to explain that collecting intelligence on both types of targets, HUMINT from the courier on the bike, or the financial intelligence in the form of the banking data was of equal import.

The Department of Defense and the DIA are not the only agencies collecting HUMINT to counter terrorist financing. Indeed, the lead agency in the US government for collecting HUMINT is the Central Intelligence Agency (CIA). In the aftermath of al-Qa'ida's attack on 9/11, a full spectrum review of the US posture against al-Qa'ida, to include the collection of terrorist financing information, was conducted by the 9/11 Commission – an independent body that assessed where the points of failure existed within the government that resulted in a successful terrorist attack – one that would be a watershed moment in US history. In the 9/11 Commission's analysis, it was noted that the CIA assessed that "Bin Laden's cash flow was steady and secure."[4] The state of the CIA's HUMINT collection related to al-Qa'ida financing, however, was, according to the commission, "speculative and sourced to general opinion in the Saudi business community."[5] The importance of human intelligence, and

---

[3] Temple, C., "Financing of Insurgency Operations in Iraq," *House Armed Services Subcommittee on Terrorism, Unconventional Threats, and Capabilities and House Financial Services Subcommittee on Oversight and Investigations*, July 28, 2005. Page 2. https://financialservices.house.gov/media/pdf/072805ct.pdf

[4] Roth, J., Greenburg, D., & Wille, S., "Monograph on Terrorist Financing," *National Commission on Terrorist Attacks Upon the United States*, Staff Report to the Commission. Page 30. https://govinfo.library.unt.edu/911/staff_statements/911_TerrFin_Monograph.pdf.

[5] Ibid, page 34.

terrorist financing to the mission of countering Bin Laden, however, was also clear from the Commission's findings. The key CIA subgroup responsible for countering al-Qa'ida was ALEC station, but its original name was CTC-TFL, Counter Terrorism Center – Terrorist Financial Links.[6] The Commission, chastised this structure, explaining that it underscored that the CIA only saw Bin Laden as a financier, not as a leader capable of directing an attack against the US homeland. In assessing the CIA's HUMINT collection posture, the Commission highlighted that the CIA's financial understanding was also tied to a single source – a walk-in who provided intelligence to the CIA's station in US Embassy Eritrea. Ultimately, the 9/11 Commission pointed to the CIA's HUMINT collection against al-Qa'ida as being "unsuccessful" despite having the legal authorities to disrupt cash couriers and hawaladars who were moving money on behalf of the terrorist group. The story of this HUMINT failure would drive US intelligence collection in the years in the aftermath of 9/11. Nonetheless, even having good human sources would not be enough to thwart a major terrorist attack or result in smoking gun intelligence that could unravel organizations fostering terrorist access to finance.

In the same report documenting the intelligence collection failures surrounding 9/11, the 9/11 Commission highlighted that the Federal Bureau of Investigation (FBI) "cultivated a good human source who provided useful information on BIF (Benevolence International Foundation), though never any smoking guns."[7] The BIF was an al-Qa'ida-linked charity based in the United States. In the lead-up to 9/11, al-Qa'ida secured most of its financing from access to charities that were either fronts (created by al-Qa'ida) or by inserting individuals within unaware and legitimate charities to siphon off money to benefit the terrorist group. In the lead-up to 9/11, the FBI was carrying out investigations against multiple AQ charities, but like the CIA,

---

[6] Ibid, page 35.
[7] Ibid, page 96.

the FBI failed in leveraging its HUMINT sources to stop the deadly attack. The 9/11 Commission explained that the FBI "operated a web of informants, conducted electronic surveillance, and engaged in other investigative activities."[8] This would not be enough, the FBI, as the 9/11 Commission described in detail, would not at a national level to ever have a systematic understanding of al-Q'ida financing within the United States. To their credit, however, FBI agents in various field offices would often collect useful intelligence, but they'd hit a wall once the money they were tracking went overseas, or was seemingly sent to an Islamic charity, raising the possibility that the money could be legitimate. Successfully exploiting HUMINT was not the only challenge in countering al-Qa'ida's terrorist financing' like the CIA, the 9/11 Commission called into question the FBI's "failure to create high-quality analytic products on al-Qa'ida financing."[9] Like the CIA, the FBI structure was lacking, with the 9/11 Commission noting that FBI did not have a unit focused on terrorist financing.

In the aftermath of 9/11, the FBI would not only double down on using intelligence but also would do so with great success to disrupt terrorist financiers. As discussed in Chapter 4, the disruption of Zoobia Shahnaz's financing of ISIS was a law enforcement success. During an interview with retired FBI Special Agent Ron Hendren, who directly worked the Shahnaz case, it was evident that a post 9/11 posture was responsible for the success in Shahnaz's prosecution. Hendren noted that "intelligence initiated" the Shahnaz case.[10] Indeed, it was a post 9/11 creation, according to Hendren, that was instrumental to the use of intelligence. The public record backs up Hendren's views. In testimony before Congress in September 2003, John Pistole, Assistant Director of the FBI's Counterterrorism Division, would explain that the FBI formed the

---

[8] Ibid, page 30.
[9] Ibid, page 32.
[10] Author interview with FBI Special Agent Hendren, December 13, 2024.

Terrorist Financing Operations Section (TFOS) to "exploit financial information in efforts to identify previously unknown terrorist cells."[11] FBI Special Agents in the field, working with TFOS, at FBI Headquarters, would use tried and true law enforcement tactics to go after terrorist facilitators and would-be supporters – resulting in their prosecution.

The FBI, like other components of the US Intelligence Community, is coy in how it uses intelligence. The FBI website says very little beyond that it uses techniques, such as interviews, wiretaps, and analysis to fulfill intelligence needs.[12] Among the most important tools the FBI can deploy against terrorist financiers is the use of undercover agents. In the 1970s and 1980s an FBI Special Agent by the name of Joe Pistone was instrumental in carrying out undercover work to develop human sources that were critical to dismantling the Bonanno crime family – a New York mafia syndicate.[13]

Just as the successful use of undercover operations (UCO) proves important in tackling organized crime, UCO was a critical intelligence-gathering tool deployed against Jabhat al-Nusrah (al-Qa'ida affiliate in Syria) and ISIS operatives in the mid 2010s – at the height of ISIS's takeover of territory in Syria and Iraq. More recently, the FBI continues to use HUMINT effectively to counter ISIS supporters. In describing a 2024 election day plot by ISIS supporter, Nasir Tawhedi, the Department of Justice documented how HUMINT was effectively used to foil the plot. The Department of Justice's October 2024 complaint documents how the FBI used a "Confidential Human Source (CHS)" to get close to Tawhedi. The

---

[11] Pistole, J. S., "Testimony before the House Committee on Financial Services Subcommittee on Oversight and Investigations," *Federal Bureau of Investigation*, September 24, 2003. https://archives.fbi.gov/archives/news/testimony/the-terrorist-financing-operations-section

[12] Federal Bureau of Investigation. "How We Investigate: Intelligence," *Federal Bureau of Investigation*. www.fbi.gov/how-we-investigate/intelligence

[13] Federal Bureau of Investigation. "Joe Pistone: Undercover Agent," *Federal Bureau of Investigation*. www.fbi.gov/history/famous-cases/joe-pistone-undercover-agent

CHS, who the FBI details as being a "highly reliable source for the FBI for nearly nine years,"[14] was used to learn more about Tawhedi's intentions. After an initial meeting with Tawhedi, the CHS would meet again later with Tawhedi and his coconspirator. At the meeting with Tawhedi and his coconspirator, the CHS was joined by a second FBI CHS as well as an "undercover FBI Employee (UCE)."[15] At the meeting, Tawhedi expressed an interest in buying multiple firearms and later the HUMINT information collected by FBI's sources would, along with other information, result in Tawhedi's undoing and ultimately him being charged, among other things, for providing material support to ISIS, a designated FTO pursuant to US law. In addition to plotting an attack against an Oklahoma City polling site, the FBI investigation of Tawhedi identified that he had previously contributed to a charity that was a front for ISIS and that he "completed two cryptocurrency transactions resulting in a transfer of approximately at least $540 to a Syria-based organization that engaged in an online fundraising campaign benefitting ISIS members and their supporters."[16]

The FBI's ability to thwart Tawhedi's attack and financing of ISIS was successful because of the use of HUMINT, but it would not be the only factor in his undoing. Other sources of intelligence, as you'll find later in this chapter, would provide useful information regarding Tawhedi's intentions.

SIGNALS INTELLIGENCE (SIGINT) AND IMAGERY INTELLIGENCE (IMINT)

Governments like the United States that have top-tier intelligence capabilities can fuse multiple types of intelligence to counter terrorists and their financiers. Among the most technically sophisticated

---

[14] United States District Court, Western District of Oklahoma. Criminal Complaint. October 8, 2025. Page 21.
[15] Ibid, page 25.
[16] Ibid, page 16.

methods of intelligence collection is the use of Signals Intelligence (SIGINT) and Imagery Intelligence (IMINT). The United States has a large constellation of spy satellites and other types of collection platforms, such as unmanned aerial vehicles that can provide useful intelligence that can be leveraged against a wide array of bad actors – to include terrorists. SIGINT involves the collecting of information from electronic targets, such as telephones, emails, and computers. Within the SIGINT discipline, it is communications intelligence (COMINT) that is relevant to the disruption of terrorist activities. Conversations, or emails, between individuals plotting an exchange of funds to advance a terrorist attack are an example of the type of SIGINT a government would want access to. Similarly, IMINT used with geospatial intelligence (GEOINT) can make it easier for governments to track individuals – in the case of counterterrorism financing activity, it would be used to track couriers who may be moving money or information on behalf of a terrorist organization. In fact, GEOINT would be critical in tracking the activities of one of Usama Bin Laden's couriers – a courier who would lead the United States right to Bin Laden's doorstep. The National Security Agency (NSA) is the key, but not the only, entity in the United States that collects SIGINT. The National Geospatial-Intelligence Agency (NGA) is most closely associated with the collection of GEOINT and IMINT. Like HUMINT, there are limited use case studies that are declassified that document how these national technical means have been used against terrorist financiers.[17] Nonetheless, there are a few concrete examples that can be examined.

During an interview with retired FBI Special Agent Ron Hendren, he explained that in the case of Zoobia Shahnaz, "TFOS's

---

[17] The author is a former member of the US Intelligence Community and was in a managerial policy role in countering terrorism financing. In those capacities he witnessed firsthand how the US counterterrorism activities, including the countering of terrorist financing, benefitted from an all-source (all types of collection) intelligence collection approach.

targeting unit looking at SIGINT from suspected financiers identified partial data that we downgraded[18] and passed on to our private sector partners, one of whom returned the initial positive hit."[19] Hendren describes the intersection of SIGINT with private sector held open-source information that allowed the FBI to identify (the positive hit) Shahnaz as an ISIS supporter. Hendren would further explain, "she was 100% unknown to the US Intelligence Community and off any radar and likely would have remained so."[20] The SIGINT allowed the FBI to begin digging into Shahnaz's financial trail – one that, as noted in Chapter 4, led to ISIS.

At the height of ISIS's strength when it controlled significant swaths of territory, it stands to reason that a combination of SIGINT, IMINT, GEOINT, and HUMINT would be vitally important for the success of Operation Tidal Wave II's targeting of ISIS assets. Without clear imagery and the use of mapping tools, the United States would not be able to successfully target ISIS's siphoning off oil and natural gas assets. Having clear IMINT, which would be declassified, provided the United States an ability to acquire – before and after- evidence of ISIS's looting of cultural heritage sites. In a report by the US Government Accountability Office, a June 2012 image of a cultural heritage site in Durra Europos, Syria, is shown in pristine condition. Later, another image from 2014, when ISIS controlled access to Durra Europos, demonstrates destruction. The report explains that the site, according to a Deputy Assistant Secretary at the US Department of State, is "an example of ISIS … looting of archeological sites as both a means of erasing cultural heritage of Iraq and Syria and raising

---

[18] Downgrading of information is a common approach used by US government agencies to share information more easily. It is likely in this instance the FBI took classified information and downgraded it to the Sensitive but Unclassified level so it could be shared with the private sector. Routinely, the US government will either downgrade or declassify information in order to tell an audience more about problematic behavior of individual, organization, or country that may be in violation of laws or international norms.

[19] Author interview with FBI Special Agent Hendren, December 13, 2024.

[20] Ibid.

money."[21] In this case, while satellite imagery does not stop ISIS's financing, it provides policymakers and the broader global community a story of ISIS's terrorist financing. That glimpse of destruction can shape policies designed to counter ISIS's access to money.

As discussed in Chapter 4, during Operation Tidal Wave II, coalition aircraft would drop leaflets over tanker trucks warning that they would soon be bombed and that the drivers should exit their vehicles. In this instance, a combination of intelligence approaches, including IMINT, would be vitally important for targeting transit nodes responsible for facilitating the movement of oil on behalf of ISIS.

Forewarning of impending doom would not be the only use of IMINT. Throughout the ongoing conflict against ISIS, the US government would strike ISIS facilitators by using multiple sources of intelligence. In remote parts of the world, using UAVs, which have their own imagery capabilities, to track and strike at ISIS leaders and operatives would be commonplace. Terrorist financiers would also face the brunt of US military efforts. Just because these individuals were not directing attacks did not mean they would be shielded from intelligence collection that would be used to conduct airstrikes.

One such ISIS terrorist financier who was in the crosshairs of coalition forces was Fawaz Muhammad Jubayr al-Rawi, a US Specially Designated Global Terrorist sanctioned by the US Department of the Treasury for moving millions of dollars on behalf of ISIS through the Hanifa Currency Exchange, which al-Rawi owned. In a June 23, 2017 press release, the Combined Joint Task Force operating under the aegis of Operation Inherent Resolve carried out an airstrike that resulted in al-Rawi's death. Removing an individual like al-Rawi from the battlefield requires precision, to include the use of overhead

---

[21] U.S. Government Accountability Office. "Report to Congressional Requesters: August 2016." *U.S. Government Accountability Office*. Pages 7–8. www.gao.gov/assets/gao-16-673.pdf.

assets like UAVs or imagery satellites to be successful. Al-Rawi would be one of many ISIS terrorist financiers who would face a fiery death. In the same press release, announced the killing of other ISIS facilitators and colleagues of al-Rawi, including Samir Idris, a "key ISIS financial facilitator for external terror attacks and international money launderer ... and Abdurakhmon Uzbeki ... an external terror attack facilitator."[22] The use of technical collection methods, just as with HUMINT collection, is a key component of degrading the operations of terrorist financiers.

OPEN-SOURCE INTELLIGENCE AND SOCIAL MEDIA INTELLIGENCE

Collecting sensitive and classified information on terrorists is critically important in the fight against terrorist financing. Just as important is the exploitation of OSINT and social media intelligence (SOCMINT) to counter terrorist access to capital. OSINT is the practice of gathering, analyzing, and disseminating information from publicly available sources to address specific intelligence requirements.[23] Such open sources may run the gamut from reporting from credible newspapers, such as the *New York Times*, television reports, message boards, to the panoply of social media websites. A subdiscipline of OSINT is SOCMINT, which is often defined as the techniques, technologies, and tools that allow for the collection of analysis of information from social media platforms.[24] The range of publicly available information is significant, and it often takes

---

[22] CJTF-OIR Public Affairs. "Coalition Forces Kill ISIS Financial Facilitator," *Combined Joint Task Force – Operation Inherent Resolve*, March 26, 2018. www.inherentresolve.mil/NEWSROOM/News-Releases/Article/1227052/coalition-forces-kill-isis-financial-facilitator/.

[23] Borges, Esteban. "What Is Open Source Intelligence (OSINT)?," *Recorded Future*, June 24, 2024. Accessed on December 28, 2024. www.recordedfuture.com/blog/open-source-intelligence-definition.

[24] Maltego Team. "OSINT Cybercrime Investigations Investigator Know-How: Everything about Social Media Intelligence (SOCMINT) and Investigations," *Maltego*, June 18, 2024. Accessed December 28, 2024. www.maltego.com/blog/everything-about-social-media-intelligence-socmint-and-investigations/.

significant data processing and analytical skills to exploit the volume of content available efficiently and effectively. The utility of OSINT was recognized long ago when the 2005 WMD Commission issued a report to President Bush on the intelligence shortfalls of the US Intelligence Community. The report hit the right notes when it explained, "open source information provides a base for understanding classified materials ... perhaps the most important example today relates to terrorism, where open source information can fill gaps and create links that allow analysts to better understand fragmented intelligence ... and open source materials can protect sources and methods."[25] This last point on protecting sources and methods is especially important because publicly known outcomes, such as a terrorist's designation or a terrorist's death via airstrikes, may in some cases be only possible if the underlying sources of information that allowed for that action to be taken are protected. In other words, freely available data may obscure the precise capabilities of technological assets like satellites, or HUMINT sources, like assets who infiltrate terrorist groups. OSINT coupled with sensitive intelligence not only paints a fuller picture but it also allows sensitive assets to be deployed effectively again at a later date.

The WMD Commission's report would prove prescient, especially in the context of terrorism financing. OSINT tools would, *inter alia*, be used to designate terrorists and provide the basis for prosecutions of terrorist financiers. In the case of Tawhedi, OSINT and SOCMINT would be key elements of the US government's case. Tawhedi would make his cryptocurrency contributions by first being directed from the group's Telegram (a social media application) feed to the cryptocurrency donation address.[26] The Telegram feed was

---

[25] The Commission on the Intelligence Capabilities of the United States Regarding Weapons of Mass Destruction, Report to the President of the United States. March 31, 2005. Pages 378–379. www.govinfo.gov/content/pkg/GPO-WMD/pdf/GPO-WMD.pdf.

[26] United States District Court, Western District of Oklahoma. Criminal Complaint. October 8, 2025. Page 16.

known to be pro-ISIS and the US government would go on to subpoena Apple to gain access to Tawhedi's iPhone, whereupon the FBI then gained access to private messages sent between Tawhedi and a known ISIS terrorist financier by the name of Abu Malik. In those conversations Tawhedi discussed how he would finance, to include the sale of his house, the purchase of arms to carry out the attack.[27] For Tawhedi, openly available tools, like his iPhone and the Telegram Application, would prove important for his plotting and financing of the attack. Yet, just as those tools were important for facilitating Tawhedi's operation, those same tools would accelerate his undoing. Tawhedi and his accomplice (a minor) would also use Google searches and Facebook to further their attack planning and financing of the attack. Specifically, the tandem would try to sell items, including Tawhedi's house, over Facebook Marketplace.[28] The duo would also communicate over Facebook messenger – all of which provided the FBI important SOCMINT, which would be used against Tawhedi and his accomplice in court. The FBI would also issue a search warrant to Google and gain access to Tawhedi's search history and his Google Drive – all of which allowed the US government to document Tawhedi's interest in ISIS, terrorist attack planning, and financing.[29] The FBI's use of SOCMINT to build a case against Tawhedi would be instrumental in disrupting a major attack. It was also reminiscent of how would-be ISIS foreign fighters and facilitators tried to support ISIS ten years prior to Tawhedi's activities. Just as then, the exploitation of SOCMINT use would prove instrumental in countering the financing of a terror plot in the United States.

In the case of Tawhedi, OSINT and SOCMINT would be used for a law enforcement prosecution. The use case of SOCMINT would also be important for another tool in the US government's counterterrorism financing arsenal – the designation of terrorists. In

---

[27] Ibid, pages 16–17.
[28] Ibid, pages 21–22.
[29] Ibid, pages 9–15.

August 2014, the US Department of the Treasury designated as terrorists pursuant to US law two Jabhat al-Nusrah and one ISIS facilitators for financial activities. The Treasury Department's press release explained "through fundraising appeals on social media and the use of financial networks Shafi al-Ajmi, Hajjaj al-Ajmi, and al-Anizi have been funding the terrorists fighting in Syria and Iraq."[30] As is customary[31] for the US government, it avoided language specifying which social media company was being leveraged by designated terrorists. The United Nations was less bashful, however, when the same individuals would be listed as terrorists pursuant to the United Nations 1267 Committee. The UN's listing of Hajjaj al-Ajmi just a week after the Treasury Department's designation specified, "he is responsible for at least one Twitter fundraising campaign."[32] In the case of both the US and UN terrorist designations, SOCMINT would be an important basis for the blackballing of Jabhat al-Nusrah and ISIS financiers.

OSINT and SOCMINT, like HUMINT, SIGINT, IMINT, and law enforcement investigative practices, help create a compelling financial picture that help counter terrorist financing.

FINANCIAL INTELLIGENCE

The range of intelligence tools that can be deployed by governments and the private sector also includes specialized methods to counter illicit finance, including terrorist financing. One of the most important laws in the United States to counter illicit financing was passed

---

[30] U.S. Department of the Treasury. "Treasury designates three key supporters of terrorists in Syria and Iraq," August 6, 2014, *U.S. Department of the Treasury.* home.treasury.gov/news/press-releases/jl2605.

[31] The United States government is cautious because of optics surrounding censorship and forcing companies to remove content from their platforms. This is, in part, why ISIS was especially effective in recruiting and fundraising online during the height of power between 2011 and 2017.

[32] United Nations Security Council. "Hajjaj bin Fahd al-Ajmi," *United Nations.* https://main.un.org/securitycouncil/en/sanctions/1267/aq_sanctions_list/summaries/individual/hajjaj-bin-fahd-al-ajmi.

in the 1970s, long before the United States and the international community, for that matter, began a concerted effort to counter terrorist financing. The United States Congress passed the Bank Secrecy Act (BSA) in 1970 as an effort to counter organized crime's money-making efforts by laundering the proceeds of crime through formal financial institutions like banks. The BSA tried to remedy this by creating reporting requirements for banks. Key aspects of the BSA's requirements included the filing of reports and keeping detailed records. As the Internal Revenue Service explains, "the documents filed by businesses under the BSA requirements are heavily used by law enforcement agencies, both domestic and international to identify, detect, and deter money laundering whether it is in furtherance of a criminal enterprise, terrorism, tax evasion or other unlawful activity."[33] Among the key types of reports filed is the currency transaction report (CTR). Banks, and other relevant businesses, must file a CTR for each transaction in currency of more than $10,000. These reports are vital forms of intelligence to law enforcement because the banks must verify and record the name and address of the individual carrying out the transaction. Additionally, the account number, social security or taxpayer identification number, among other details are also submitted. These details can augment law enforcement investigations and provide a money trail. Terrorist financiers and criminals will try to place ill-gotten proceeds of crime into financial institutions without detection. The first step in the money-laundering process is placement – that's when the criminal or terrorist financier will try to insert cash into a bank. Money in a bank takes on an appearance of legitimacy that can facilitate terrorist operations. The private sector, especially banks, thus plays an important intelligence collection role by providing important financial details that can shed light on the financing of a terror plot or criminal act.

---

[33] Internal Revenue Service. "Bank Secrecy Act," *U.S. Department of the Treasury*. www.irs.gov/businesses/small-businesses-self-employed/bank-secrecy-act#:~:text=Congress%20passed%20the%20Bank%20Secrecy,%2C%20tax%2C%20and%20regulatory%20matters.

Savvy criminals and terrorist financier are very aware of the $10,000 reporting threshold. As a consequence, structured transactions are a method deployed to get around the CTR reporting requirement. Structuring, also called smurfing, occurs when a person, or multiple people acting in a coordinated way, tries to conduct one or more transactions in currency under $10,000 with the purpose of evading CTR requirements. When a US bank believes structuring is occurring, pursuant to the BSA, it must file a suspicious activity report (SAR). In other parts of the world, as will be discussed in Chapter 8, SARs are referred to as suspicious transaction reports (STRs). SARs, or STRs for that matter, are not only filed upon the suspicion that structuring may be occurring. As the Federal Depository Insurance Corporation (FDIC) points out, "SARs are used to report all types of suspicious activity affecting depository institutions, including but not limited to cash transaction structuring, money laundering, check fraud and kiting, computer intrusion, wire transfer fraud, mortgage and consumer loan fraud, embezzlement...and terrorist financing."[34] In the United States, SARs and CTRs are sent to the United States government's Financial Intelligence Unit (FIU), which is based in the United States Department of the Treasury. The US FIU is called the Financial Crimes Enforcement Network (FinCEN) and it is the responsible legal authority in the United States for evaluating, analyzing, and disseminating SARs and CTRs that are not only coming from banks but also from DNFBPs, such as casinos, realtors, accountants, and other professions that may facilitate the transfer of funds or other types of assets that have value. The value of SARs and CTRs and other types of financial records are of high value to law enforcement and intelligence agencies that track illicit financial crime. However, these types of financial information come with significant challenges. First, the volume of reporting in the United States, for example, of SARs and CTRs is incredibly high. During

---

[34] Federal Deposit Insurance Corporation. "Connecting the Dots: The Importance of Timely and Effective Suspicious Activity Reports." www.fdic.gov/bank-examinations/connecting-dotsthe-importance-timely-and-effective-suspicious-activity.

fiscal year 2023, FinCEN reported that it received 20.8 million CTRs and 4.6 million SARs.[35] Second, as FinCEN evaluates the sensitive data, such as personally identifiable information, that comes in via banks and DNFBPs, it must take measures to protect the information to ensure it is not misused. Third, another challenge is that SARs and CTRs can result in accounts of innocent individuals being incorrectly frozen because their identity may be conflated with that of a designated terrorist who may, for instance, have a similar name. This issue, known as false positives, results in additional processing by personnel at banks and in the US government at places like OFAC and FinCEN to sift through. Nonetheless, the data contained in SARs and CTRs can provide valuable intelligence to intelligence agencies and law enforcement in countering terrorist financing. They can, in short, be the critical piece of information that allows law enforcement to "connect the dots." In highlighting a concrete example of this, FinCEN describes in a use case how the FBI utilized a SAR to counter terrorist financing in the Middle East. FinCEN noted, "the FBI initiated a material support of terrorism investigation based on a SAR filed by a bank detailing a series of overseas financial transactions totaling millions of dollars." FinCEN would further explain that the reporting bank was concerned about the unorthodox matter in which the transactions had been executed and that the recipients of the funds were suspected terrorists.[36] SARs and CTRs are among some of the best examples of the types of FININT that provide agencies, like the FBI, critical lead information that, when fused with other types of intelligence collection, can result in the demise of terrorist financiers and money launderers.

---

[35] Hardy, Peter D. & Danch, Siana. "FinCEN Releases Year-in-Review for FY 2023: SARs, CTRs, and Information Sharing," *Ballard Spahr LLP*, June 10, 2024. www.moneylaunderingnews.com/2024/06/fincen-releases-year-in-review-for-fy-2023-sars-ctrs-and-information-sharing/#:~:text=Collectively%2C%20they%20filed%20during%20FY,received%20in%20a%20trade%20or.

[36] Financial Crimes Enforcement Network, "Suspicious activity report initiates material support investigation," *U.S. Department of the Treasury*. www.fincen.gov/resources/law-enforcement/case-examples/suspicious-activity-report-initiates-material-support.

FININT is broad and includes SARs, CTRs, and other various types of records that provide valuable details into the inner workings of illicit actors, to include a group's funding, membership, planned activities, goals, and many other aspects of a group's actions, financial or otherwise. FININT is instrumental in the "follow the money" responsibilities of government agencies charged with countering terrorist financing. Among the key purveyors and consumers of FININT are FIUs. FinCEN is an example of an FIU. There are different types of FIUs based throughout the world, but one thing unites them – the use of FININT to combat terrorist financing and money laundering. FinCEN is an example of an administrative FIU, and it is part of the US Department of the Treasury. Administrative FIUs will typically be part of an agency, usually a Finance Ministry (such as the US Department of the Treasury) not affiliated with law enforcement or judicial authorities. In other cases, an administrative FIU can be a separate agency, regardless of its placement with the government, an administrative FIU's primary advantage is that financial institutions, such as banks, are likely to be more willing to share sensitive banking information with a non-law enforcement agency that will take measures to limit dissemination. This stands in contrast to the second type of FIU, law enforcement FIUs, which are directly connected to an agency with arrest powers. One advantage this type of FIU has over administrative FIUs is that it can limit the delay between applying law enforcement measures, such as arresting a terrorist financier, and the leveraging of key FININT reports, such as SARs. The third type of FIU is judicial FIUs that are contained within a judicial body. With this type of FIU, SARs are often provided directly to prosecutors, which can often trigger a financial crimes investigation. The key advantage of this type of FIU is that FININT is passed from the financial sector directly to a judicial agency that is often seen in many countries as being more immunized from politics and corruption. One key disadvantage of the judicial FIU is that they often will have a difficult time exchanging information with nonjudicial FIUs. Information sharing, especially given the global context of many terrorist groups, is critically important. As such, judicial FIUs have an inherent drawback relative to other types of FIUs that can share sensitive information, as will be discussed later in this chapter, more nimbly. The fourth type of FIUs is hybrid, which takes on two characteristics of the previously mentioned FIU types, such as administrative and law enforcement. Norway, for example, deploys a hybrid law enforcement and judicial FIU.

No matter the type of FIU, the core work remains the same – that is, receiving reports from a range of private sector entities, such as banks and casinos, that have responsibility for detecting financial irregularities. These entities will create reports in the forms of SARs and CTRs and then send them directly to the FIU. Next, the FIU will analyze and then, if appropriate, share the FININT with relevant stakeholders, such as prosecutors, law enforcement agencies, or other FIUs. This cycle of collection (of reports), analysis, and dissemination is fundamental to the successful exploitation of FININT to the disruption of terrorist financing.

The sharing of FININT does not only take place domestically. Because of the nature of financial transactions, which are global, coupled with the transnational aspects of many terrorist groups, such as ISIS, FIUs across the globe must cooperate and share intelligence. Intelligence sharing can be done bilaterally from FIU to FIU, or it can be done via a multilateral body. The Egmont Group is a multilateral body that is composed of more than 170 FIUs that has two core focus areas: FININT sharing and international cooperation, and implementation of international standards (such as those promulgated by the FATF and UN).[37]

To implement intelligence exchange and information sharing, the Egmont Group is organized along regional and thematic lines. Regionally, Egmont has groups working together to share intelligence

---

[37] Egmont Group of Financial Intelligence Units. "About the Egmont Group," https://egmontgroup.org/about/.

in the following areas: Americas, Asia and Pacific, East and Southern Africa, Eurasia, two areas of Europe labeled Europe I and Europe II, Middle East and Northern Africa, and West and Central Africa. This alignment by region is important because in countering terrorist finance, many of the groups' FIUs need to counter cross-border activities. As one example, groups like ISIS's West Africa Province will move between countries like Niger, Cameroon, and Nigeria. Having working groups that tackle terrorist group financing by region allows the Egmont's FIU membership to share intelligence on the financial modalities that groups are using that multiple countries in the same region are targeting. As important are the working groups Egmont has created along thematic lines. Egmont has four thematic working groups that focus on information exchange, membership, support and compliance, policy and procedures, and technical assistance and training. It is the first working group on information exchange that is most pertinent to the use of FININT. As the Egmont group explains, the information exchange working group conducts its work along three key work-lines. First, the working group works to support the exchange of intelligence at bilateral and multilateral levels. Second, it facilitates joint approaches to share knowledge regarding trends developing in the areas of money laundering and terrorist financing. Third, it works to help FIUs to develop their IT capabilities and better leverage technology to facilitate intelligence exchanges.[38] The Egmont Group is a crucial multilateral organization to counter terrorist financing and its objectives are consistent with the importance that the FATF has placed on using FININT effectively to counter terrorist financing.

While Chapter 8 will explore the importance of FATF and its recommendations that have been designed to tackle terrorist financing in more detail, it is important to emphasize that among the group's recommendations, multiple focus on the importance of

---

[38] Egmont Group of Financial Intelligence Units, "IEWG – Information Exchange Working Group." https://egmontgroup.org/working-groups/iewg/.

FININT and FIUs. FATF was created in 1989 with an initial focus on fighting against money laundering carried out by organized criminal groups (OCGs). Six years following FATF's founding, the Egmont Group was created with only fourteen FIUs coming together as founding members. Post 9/11, FATF, just as with the Egmont Group, moved its attention to battling terrorist financing. Early on, FATF recognized the importance of using intelligence to connect the dots between individuals and organizations who raised and moved funds to successfully carry out their terrorist attacks.

The FATF updated its various recommendations to countries on how to best counter terrorist financing and money laundering in 2012, and then amended those recommendations again in 2013.[39] Various FATF recommendations speak to the importance of intelligence, and sharing of intelligence, as a basis for countering terrorist financing. However, Recommendations 1, 2, and 29 are of particular note. First, Recommendation 1 calls on countries to take a risk-based approach to countering money laundering and terrorist financing. In this respect, countries carry out these risk assessments by using all forms of intelligence, especially FININT, to assess the threats by terrorist financiers and vulnerabilities to their financial systems that can be exploited by nefarious actors. In February 2024, the US Department of the Treasury, as part of its responsibilities pursuant to FATF Recommendation 1, published its 2024 National Terrorist Financing Risk Assessment (NTFRA). Among the top terrorist financing threats the Treasury Department identified were from domestic (far-right) violent extremists, ISIS, al-Qa'ida, Hizballah, and Hamas. Among the key vulnerabilities identified to the US government's financial health that could be exploited were, according to the 2024 Treasury Department report, "registered money services businesses," the use of cash for transactions, US banks' facilitation of transaction

---

[39] FATF, "International standards on combating money laundering and the financing of terrorism & proliferation, 2012–2025." *FATF.* www.fatf-gafi.org/en/publications/Fatfrecommendations/Fatf-recommendations.html.

with foreign-based correspondent banks, and the continued use of virtual assets, such as cryptocurrency, by terrorist groups.[40] Throughout Treasury's NTFRA, various intelligence assessments from multiple agencies, such as the FBI, ODNI, and others, are sourced as a basis for identifying threats and vulnerabilities.

In addition to FATF Recommendation 1, FATF Recommendation 2 underscores the importance of sharing information internally at the national level on financial issues conducted effectively to "ensure that policymakers, the financial intelligence unit, and law enforcement authorities" can combat terrorist financing.[41] This recommendation encourages FININT to be shared widely within governments so they can more effectively pursue funders of terror. In many ways, this FATF recommendation underscores the US government's 9/11 report, which underscored the lack of sufficient intelligence sharing between multiple agencies.

Finally, FATF Recommendation 29 calls on governments to establish FIUs so that they may serve as the focal point for the receipt and analysis of FININT. FATF also encourages other government agencies to work with their FIU so that they can pursue their mission effectively.[42]

FATF's recommendations 1, 2, and 29 serve as a call for governments to examine threats and vulnerabilities through the lens of assessments that are underpinned by intelligence. FATF has cast a shining light on the importance of FIUs in the fight against terrorist financing.

---

[40] U.S. Department of the Treasury, "2024 National terrorist financing risk assessment, February 2024." *U.S. Department of the Treasury*. https://home.treasury.gov/system/files/136/2024-National-Terrorist-Financing-Risk-Assessment.pdf.

[41] FATF, "International standards on combating money laundering and the financing of terrorism & proliferation, 2012–2025." *FATF*. www.fatf-gafi.org/en/publications/Fatfrecommendations/Fatf-recommendations.html.

[42] FATF, International standards on combating money laundering and the financing of terrorism & proliferation, 2012–2025, *FATF*. www.fatf-gafi.org/en/publications/Fatfrecommendations/Fatf-recommendations.html.

The use of intelligence by governments to counter terrorists does not come without controversy. The United States created the Terrorist Financing Tracking Program (TFTP) in the aftermath of 9/11. TFTP would become a critical intelligence tool in curbing illicit transactions conducted by terrorists. One key component of the TFTP program is managed by the US Department of the Treasury as part of an effort to identify, track, and pursue terrorist financial networks through transactions carried out through the Society for Worldwide Interbank Financial Telecommunication (SWIFT). The SWIFT system is instrumental in the movement of international money via secure communications that allow financial institutions to message each other quickly to facilitate the settling of payments between individuals and/or organizations.[43] The SWIFT messaging system provides banks key details regarding transactions that may be crucial on a case by case for government regulators, like the Treasury Department, charged with tackling terrorist financing. The Treasury Department issues subpoenas to SWIFT to gain access to "information on suspected international terrorists or their networks."[44] The Treasury Department issued these subpoenas between 2001 and 2009 directly to the Belgium-based company, SWIFT. In 2009, SWIFT ceased storing financial information on its servers and the data previously held by SWIFT has been held by the European Union (EU), a block of twenty-seven countries. As a result, the United States and the EU culminated an agreement in 2010 to process and exchange information as part of the TFTP. Since the US–EU agreement, according to the US Department of the Treasury, the TFTP has been instrumental in foiling several attacks or was instrumental to the investigative effort following a terrorist attack. The Treasury

---

[43] Shobhit, Seth. "How the SWIFT system works," *Investopedia*, September 14, 2023. www.investopedia.com/articles/personal-finance/050515/how-swift-system-works.asp.

[44] U.S. Department of the Treasury, "Terrorist finance tracking program (TFTP)," *U.S. Department of the Treasury*. Accessed on January 12, 2025. https://home.treasury.gov/policy-issues/terrorism-and-illicit-finance/terrorist-finance-tracking-program-tftp.

Department notes that FININT[45] was used in the aftermath of an ISIS-inspired 2020 attack in Vienna, Austria, that resulted in four deaths.[46] Additionally, the Treasury Department noted that the TFTP played an important role in the aftermath of the August 2017 terror attack in Turku, Finland; the 2017 La Rambla attack in Barcelona; the 2016 ISIS attacks in Brussels; the January and November 2015 ISIS attacks in Paris; and the 2013 Boston Marathon attack carried out by the Tsarnaev Brothers. The Treasury Department also noted that TFTP generated more than 160,000 shared leads with EU member states between August 1, 2010, and December 2022.[47]

Despite TFTP's apparent successes in following the money of terrorist financers, it has not come without criticism. The use of all forms of intelligence, including FININT, must be used responsibly to ensure that human rights, civil liberty protections, and privacy rights are not ignored. In Europe, there have been concerns that the EU has "effectively deputized the US Treasury to perform counterterrorism searches on European data."[48] This outsourcing has been a bone of contention for the decades the TFTP has existed. Mindful of these concerns, the US and the EU have conducted multiple studies to ensure effective data protection is in place. The EU's November 2022 review of the TFTP program encouraged the Treasury Department to "improve its mechanisms to review the necessity of retaining extracted data to ensure that this data is only retained as long as

---

[45] U.S. Department of the Treasury, "Terrorist finance tracking program: Questions and answers, U.S. Department of the Treasury." Accessed on January 12, 2025. https://home.treasury.gov/system/files/246/Terrorist-Finance-Tracking-Program-Questions-and-Answers.pdf.

[46] Bell, Bethany & Kirby, Paul. "Vienna Murders: Four Guilty of Helping Jihadist in Terror Attack," *BBC News*, February 1, 2023. www.bbc.com/news/world-europe-64482080.

[47] U.S. Department of the Treasury. "Terrorist finance tracking program: Questions and answers, U.S. Department of the Treasury." Accessed January 12, 2025. https://home.treasury.gov/system/files/246/Terrorist-Finance-Tracking-Program-Questions-and-Answers.pdf.

[48] Adam, Klein. "Statement by Chairman Adam Klein on the Terrorist Finance Tracking Program," *U.S. Privacy and Civil Liberties Oversight Board*, November 19, 2020, https://documents.pclob.gov/prod/DynamicImages/Generic/e426b076-928d-4a79-ac0c-9ed9efe9e4cf/TFTP%20Chairman%20Statement%2011_19_20.pdf.

necessary for the specific investigation or prosecution for which they are used for."[49] This improvement, among other modest proposals from the EU, would create more public confidence in the TFTP's implementation. The TFTP program is an example of bilateral CTF cooperation that underpins the relevancy of sharing FININT. In a world of global commerce and finance, tapping, quite literally, into SWIFT has been crucial to the follow-the-money policies that can thwart a terrorist attack.

As this chapter detailed, several types of intelligence are important to countering terrorist access to finance. Without an information edge, governments and multilateral bodies are at a disadvantage in the battle to curb illicit financing. Without intelligence, not only would it be difficult to follow the red trail of blood money, but it would be increasingly challenging to develop policies, such as the designations of terrorists – the topic of Chapter 6.

---

[49] European Commission. *Report from the Commission to the European Parliament and the Council on the joint review of the implementation of the Agreement between the European Union and the United States of America on the processing and transfer of financial messaging data from the European Union to the United States for the purposes of the Terrorist Finance Tracking Program*. November 11, 2022. European Commission. Accessed January 12, 2025. https://eur-lex.europa.eu/legal-content/EN/TXT/PDF/?uri=CELEX:52022DC0585.

6 Terrorist Designations – An Inside Look at the United States Department of State's Process to Sanction Terrorists

In the United States, the US Departments of State and Treasury are the two competent legal authorities responsible for designating individuals and groups as terrorists under US law. Other US government agencies, US foreign allies and adversaries, as well as the general public, understand the role the US Department of the Treasury plays in designating terrorists. What is less well understood, and the primary focus of this chapter, is the integral role the US Department of State plays in designating terrorists under its legal authorities. In fact, the Department of State has more legally available tools to designate terrorists than the US Department of the Treasury. Generally, the State Department can designate countries, groups, and individuals. The State Department is the lead authority in the US Government for designating countries as State Sponsors of Terrorism. Countries determined by the Secretary of State to have repeatedly provided support for acts of international terrorism are designated pursuant to three laws:

- section 6(j) of the Export Administration Act;
- section 40 of the Arms Export Control Act; and
- section 620A of the Foreign Assistance Act.

The Department of State also designates countries as "Not Fully Cooperating" with US counterterrorism efforts. These SST and NFCC tools of statecraft, both broad in scope, are used sparingly relative to the Department's more focused designations of terrorists as Foreign Terrorist Organizations (FTOs) under section 219 of the Immigration and Nationality Act and designations of individuals and groups as "Specially Designated Global Terrorists" (SDGTs) under

Executive Order (EO) 13224. The Department of State shares designation responsibility under EO 13224 with the US Department of the Treasury. The Department of State is also responsible for designating entities for the Terrorist Exclusion List (TEL) pursuant to Section 411 of the USA PATRIOT ACT of 2001 and shares EO 12947 authorities with the US Department of the Treasury. EO 12947 allows for the designations of groups and individuals who pose a threat to the Middle East Process. In practice, terrorist designations using either the TEL or EO 12947 authority are rare because they have been eclipsed by the broader and more effective powers associated with FTO and EO 13224 designations.

Why does the Department of State designate terrorists? After all, the amount of effort involved in sanctioning a terrorist is significant. Hundreds of hours are spent researching, drafting, editing, legally reviewing, and approving the underlying documents that culminate in a terrorist designation. Although the sanctioning of terrorists has been a tool available to the Departments of State and Treasury since 1995 with the issuance of EO 12947; and the authority to designate FTOs has been available to the Department of State since 1997, the increased usage of terrorist sanctions stems from the tragedy of September 11, 2001. Simply put, al-Qa'ida abused the US formal financial system in the lead-up to 9/11. The Staff Monograph on the Financing of 9/11 documented this fact in its investigative report when it determined that approximately 60 percent of the estimated $400,00 to $500,000 USD spent for the conduct of al-Qa'ida's plot moved through the US formal financial channels.[1] Al-Qa'ida used, among other mechanisms, checks, bank accounts, and ATM transactions to facilitate its 9/11 operations. Because of this abuse, President George W. Bush said shortly after 9/11, "we will direct every resource at our command to win the war against the terrorists, every means

---

[1] Roth, John, Greenburg, Douglas, & Wille, Serena B. "Monograph on Terrorist Financing: Staff Report to the Commission." Washington, DC: *National Commission on Terrorist Attacks upon the United States*, 2004. Page 13. Internet resource.

of diplomacy, every tool of intelligence, every instrument of law enforcement, every financial influence. We will starve the terrorists of funding."[2] It was against this backdrop that terrorist designations became entrenched as a part of the US government's counterterrorism architecture when President Bush acted on his words and promise of countering terrorism finance more aggressively when he signed EO 13224 twelve days after 9/11. Nearly thirty individuals, including Usama bin Laden, and entities were designated by the President in the annex of EO 13224.[3] Another result of his decision was the significant expansion of both Treasury and State Department powers in countering terrorism.

From 2008 to 2018, the author led a small office within the Counterterrorism Bureau at the Department of State that was responsible for writing the underlying documents that culminated in an individual or terrorist group's designation. What follows below in this chapter is a firsthand account of the process related to the Secretary of State's designations of individuals and entities pursuant to EO 13224, as well as the designations of groups as FTOs. This chapter will first address the legal criteria to which the Department of State must adhere in order to designate a terrorist, as well as a short discussion of the formal consequences of FTO and EO 13224 terrorist designations. Often lost in the discussion of sanctions as a counterterrorism tool is the importance of removing designated terrorists from the United States government's blacklist. This chapter will also discuss the benefits and importance of delisting terrorists. Finally, throughout the following narrative I will intersperse firsthand observations of policy discussions that centered on some of

---

[2] Office of the Press Secretary. "President Freezes Terrorists' Assets," *George W. Bush Whitehouse Archives*, September 24, 2001. https://georgewbush-whitehouse.archives.gov/news/releases/2001/09/text/20010924-4.html. Accessed February 25, 2018.

[3] "Blocking Property and Prohibiting Transactions with Persons Who Commit, Threaten to Commit, or Support Terrorism; 66, Fed. Reg. 186." September 23, 2001. www.gpo.gov/fdsys/pkg/FR-2001-09-25/pdf/01-24205.pdf. Accessed February 25, 2018.

the more controversial designations, such as why it took the United States government so long to designate the Nigeria-based Boko Haram group or the Pakistan-based Tehrik-e-Taliban movement.

LEGAL STANDARDS ASSOCIATED WITH DEPARTMENT OF STATE TERRORIST DESIGNATIONS

The legal authority for the Secretary of State's designations of FTO is derived from section 219 of the Immigration and Nationality Act (INA). There are three legal criteria that must be satisfied to designate an FTO.

- *The group must be a foreign organization.* In practice this means the organization cannot be primarily based in the United States. It should come as no surprise that the State Department, as the United States government's foreign ministry, is not inwardly focused on domestic groups. This means groups like the Animal Liberation Front, Environmental Liberation Front, various sovereign citizen movements, Ku Klux Klan, and the Weather Underground cannot be designated by the Department of State as terrorists. In practice, in evaluating whether a group is foreign based, various factors come into play. For instance, who are the leaders of the terrorist group under evaluation and are they foreign citizens? Does the group have training camps and are those camps based overseas? Does the group primarily carry out its attacks overseas? Does the group raise funds outside of the United States? For example, when the United States designated al-Qa'ida as an FTO in 1999, it was clear that the group's top leaders, Usama bin Laden and Ayman al-Zawahiri, were foreign citizens. It was also understood that the group's primary base of operations was in Afghanistan, where al-Qa'ida trained its operatives in camps such as the al-Farouq training camp near Kandahar, Afghanistan. As a general rule, this is the simplest legal criterion to satisfy. However, if there is any possibility of an organization having a significant US domestic presence, caution in proceeding with the designations process will prevail.
- *The group must engage in terrorist activity, or retain the capability and intent to engage in terrorist activity.* In practice, the Department of State has never designated a group as an FTO based solely on an entity's capability and intent to carry out an attack. Every group initially placed on the FTO list has carried out an act of terrorism. Examples of terrorist

attacks can range from suicide bombings, small arms attacks, and various forms of improvised explosive detonations to carrying out a chemical attack like the Japan-based Aum Shinrikyo group's attack against the Japanese subway system in 1995. Although the INA does not distinguish between attacks against combatants and noncombatants, in practice the Department of State has focused its efforts on organizational attacks carried out against noncombatants.

- *The group's terrorist activity or terrorism must threaten the security of US nationals or national defense, foreign relations, or economic interests of the United States.* This tends to be the most difficult prong of the three criteria to satisfy because many violent organizations do not directly target US interests. However, the INA's broad definition of US national security interests has allowed the Department of State to designate a broad array of terrorist groups – many of which the general US public may not see as a threat. Although it is intuitive that a group like ISIS is a threat to US interests given the fact it has beheaded US citizens, it is harder for the average American to understand how a group like the Spain-based Basque Fatherland and Liberty (ETA) threatens the security of the United States. In the case of ETA, the group historically satisfied the criteria because, especially at its height, the activities of the group had a destabilizing effect on Spain – a NATO member like the United States. Often the narrative for designating groups like ETA will center on how its activities are a direct threat to close US allies, or US trade and business interests more generally.

The 1977 International Emergency Economic Powers Act (IEEPA) provides the underlying legal authority that allows the State and Treasury Departments to designate groups and individuals as "SDGTs" under EO 13224. Pursuant to section 1(b) of EO 13224, the Secretary of State can designate individuals or entities that have committed, or pose a significant risk of committing, acts of terrorism that threaten the security of US nationals or the national security, foreign policy, or economy of the United States. The Treasury Department can designate individuals or entities owned or controlled by an already designated entity or individuals, or entities who assist in, sponsor, or provide financial, material, or technological support to an already designated entity. So, what are the practical outcomes in the US model where there are shared legal authorities between the State and Treasury Departments? The different legal criteria for each department drive the kinds of designations each pursue. In practice, while this is an oversimplification, it means the Department of State tends to focus on the leaders and operatives that constitute terrorist groups. For example, on October 4, 2011, the Department of State designated Ibrahim Awwad Ibahim Ali al-Badri, better known as Abu Bakr al-Baghdadi and the leader of the so-called Islamic State, pursuant to EO 13224.[4] An example of an operational figure that culminated in a March 24, 2011, State Department EO 13224 designation is that of al-Qa'ida in the Arabian Peninsula's (AQAP) bomb maker, Ibrahim al-Asiri.[5] In contrast, the Treasury Department tends to focus its legal authorities on individuals who move money and materiel on behalf of terrorist groups.

PROVIDING LEVERAGE – THE CONSEQUENCES ASSOCIATED WITH STATE DEPARTMENT TERRORIST DESIGNATIONS

State Department designations provide leverage to other US government agencies and the private sector to pursue their missions and various legal responsibilities. The formally stated consequences of an FTO designation are:

1. All funds under the control of a US institution are blocked.
2. Aliens are inadmissible to, and may be deported from, the United States.
3. It is illegal for persons subject to the jurisdiction of the United States to knowingly provide material support to the designated FTO. Those who provide material support are subject to civil and criminal penalties, to include prison time.

---

[4] U.S. Department of State. "Terrorist Designation of Ibrahim Awwad Ibrahim Ali al-Badri," *Bureau of Counterterrorism and Countering Violent Extremism*, October 4, 2011. www.state.gov/j/ct/rls/other/des/266629.htm. Accessed February 25, 2018.
[5] Ibid.

Assets blocked in US jurisdiction curb terrorist operations, as well as more mundane expenses such as purchasing safe houses, food, clothing, and acquisition of other materiel. The FTO designation also provides the legal basis for the compliance sections of financial institutions, as discussed in Chapter 9, to take action against questionable financial activity. But what is generally unknown to the nonexpert is that there is an intersection between FTO designations and the prosecutions of terrorist supporters or prospective terrorist supporters. FTO designations provide prosecutorial leverage to the Department of Justice and open the aperture for more expansive FBI investigations. For instance, in 2016 there was a significant spike in successful material prosecutions under §2339(b) of the INA.

This spike correlates to the phenomena of would-be US foreign terrorist fighters who have tried to join groups like ISIS or Jabhat al-Nurah in Iraq and Syria. For example, in November 2016, Mohammad Hamzah Khan of Bolingbrook, Illinois, was sentenced to forty months in federal prison and twenty years of supervised release for attempting to provide support to ISIS by attempting to join that group in Syria.[6] If groups like ISIS were not designated, it would be much more difficult for the US government to pursue material support-related prosecutions. It is for this reason that it is imperative to add groups to the FTO list, especially if there is a hint of support for that group in the United States. Finally, the designations of FTOs provide leverage to the Department of Homeland Security by giving a basis to reject known members of terrorist groups by rejecting visa applications and ensuring those individuals cannot enter the United States.

As a general matter, the consequences of an EO 13224 designation are comparable to that of an FTO designation. One key

---

[6] Department of Justice. "Illinois Man Sentenced to 40 Months in Federal Prison Attempting to Provide Material Support to ISIL," *Justice News*, Office of Public Affairs, November 18, 2016. www.justice.gov/opa/pr/illinois-man-sentenced-40-months-federal-prison-attempting-provide-material-support-isil. Accessed February 26, 2017.

difference though, and less of a legal consequence per se, is that a State Department designation of groups under EO 13224 is of critical importance to the US Department of the Treasury. Under EO 13224, the State Department has primary designation authority, while the Treasury Department has derivative, or secondary, authority. In essence, the Treasury Department must build upon an existing State Department group-related designation. For instance, if Treasury has identified a facilitator associated with an undesignated terrorist group, it would be difficult for Treasury to pursue that designation. However, if the facilitator is associated with a State Department EO 13224 designated group, such as Jabhat al-Nusrah, the Treasury Department could pursue the designation of that individual by linking the facilitator's activities to the State Department designated entity – in this case, Jabhat al-Nusrah. Thus, one result of a State Department primary EO 13224 designation is the leverage it provides the Treasury Department in pursuing the designations of terrorist financiers.

There are other nonlegal consequences associated with State Department designations. First, designations, in theory, are supposed to have a deterrent effect on donors who may be interested in giving to a cause. If a donor learns that the proceeds of their donations could result in a criminal prosecution, they may be deterred from giving to the designated entity. Second, in the past the US government has requested, via a *demarche*, that foreign governments remove terrorist content linked to US and UN designated terrorist groups. In the author's direct experience, in some cases foreign governments have taken concrete action, but others, such as Scandinavian countries, have been particularly reticent in removing content associated with terrorist groups. The US experience of working with Silicon Valley has been decidedly mixed, but in two very specific cases over the ten years the author worked on terrorist designation issues, he witnessed firsthand immediate results.

First, Denis Cuspert, aka Deso Dog, was a German rapper who toured the United States with the American rap artist known as DMX. Cuspert eventually joined ISIS and was one of its most nihilist members. The day after the State Department designated Cuspert pursuant to EO 13224, Apple removed all of Cuspert's music from its catalogue. Second, shortly after the Department of State's amendments to Lashkar-e Tayyiba's (LeT) FTO and EO 13224 designations to include the alias Al-Muhammadia Students (AMS) that were announced on December 28, 2016,[7] the author directly engaged with Facebook in an effort to remove the student group's Facebook pages. Initially, Facebook took quick action, but shortly after the removal of AMS's content, more pages[8] by the group cropped up and remained accessible to the general public.

Unfortunately, removing terrorist content, especially charities and student groups linked to terrorist groups, will remain difficult given the lack of terrorism experts in Silicon Valley. In 2017 and 2018, Western European governments, in particular France and the United Kingdom, have pushed Silicon Valley and the United States to do more in removing terrorist-related content. The difficulty in acceding to these requests lies in the First Amendment. What Western Europe and other countries like Russia and China, who consistently push to remove terrorism-related content, have not been savvy enough in doing, though, is pointing to terrorism content linked to designated terrorist groups. It should be hard for the United States and Silicon Valley to turn down requests to remove content associated with designated terrorists because those determinations have been vetted, as you will soon understand, through multiple layers of evaluation by terrorism experts and national security lawyers. As terrorist groups rely increasingly on those inspired to carry out violent attacks while not necessarily being members of these groups, it will become more important to remove terrorism content before it can be interpreted and acted upon by impressionable minds.

---

[7] U.S. Department of State. "Amendment to the Terrorist Designations of Lashkar e-Tayyiba," *Bureau of Counterterrorism and Countering Violent Extremism*, December 28, 2016. www.state.gov/j/ct/rls/other/des/266629.htm. Accessed February 25, 2018.

[8] "Al-Muhammadia Students." *Facebook*. www.facebook.com/AMSOfficial1/. Accessed February 27, 2017.

THE PROCESS OF DESIGNATING A TERRORIST

What follows is a description of the State Department's multistep process of designating terrorists under its two primary authorities. Throughout the process, an FTO and EO 13224 designation generally follow the same process path. In a few areas the process diverges, and where this occurs, I will be explicit in noting where those differences exist. Additionally, as a general rule, the Treasury Department follows the same process for its terrorist designations pursuant to EO 13224. The tradecraft noted later is little understood, but it is paramount in understanding how the United States government decides who is a terrorist. But, before diving into the nuts and bolts of the designations process, it is important to understand that, with very few exceptions, the process is consensus driven. Thus, while the State Department's Counterterrorism Bureau and Treasury's OFAC lead the process; they generally will not push forward with a terrorist designation unless the entire US national security apparatus supports the initiative. The terrorist designations process also takes many months, and in some cases, years, to unfold. One reason for this is that the US government wants to ensure its designations are appropriately applied and that an innocent person is not having their assets inappropriately blocked or frozen.

IDENTIFYING A TARGET FOR DESIGNATION

The first step in the designations process begins with the identification of the individual or group for possible sanction. At the Department of State, whether it is an FTO or EO 13224 designation, the Office of Counterterrorism Finance and Designations (CT/CTFD) within the Counterterrorism Bureau (CT) is the lead office at the Department of State on designation matters. Generally, there are three ways designation targets are identified. CT/CTFD personnel identify the vast majority of all State Department FTO and EO 13224 designation targets. How are these targets identified? The sanctions investigator likely had an "AHA Moment" while going through the daily morning intelligence and unclassified information they read. Often it is the raw intelligence reporting about a terrorist's misdeeds that begins the designations process. In some other cases, an investigator may be already working on a terrorist designation and during that research, they have identified a key figure in a terrorist group that is worth pursuing for designation. For instance, when looking into ISIS-West Africa's FTO designation, the analyst likely learned about the group's leader, Abu Musab al-Barnawi. It is not coincidental that both ISIS-West Africa and al-Barnawi were sanctioned on the same day – February 27, 2018.

In other cases, a designation target is identified by other government agencies. In these instances, the agency will request that CT/CTFD consider pursuing a designation. In the author's direct experience, the Departments of Justice and Treasury generally make the majority of the externally driven requests because their interest correlates to the benefits that emanate from State Department designations. For example, if a sanctions investigator was researching a terrorist facilitator, let's say one associated with Pakistan-based Jamaat al Dawa al Quran (JDQ), who was traveling to Saudi Arabia to raise funds for JDQ, but that over course of the research the investigator also found that JDQ was not designated as a terrorist group; that becomes a challenge. In this situation, the Treasury Department likely could not pursue the designation of the JDQ facilitator until after the Department of State designated JDQ pursuant to EO 13224. Treasury, as mentioned earlier, has derivative authorities and must essentially piggyback on an active terrorist designation. In this scenario, Treasury may request that CT/CTFD designate JDQ. In the case of the Department of Justice (DOJ), often at the behest of the Federal Bureau of Investigation (FBI), it will ask the CT/CTFD to pursue an FTO designation because there may be open investigations on individuals who are providing material support to an undesignated terrorist group. Pursuing material support charges against the FBI subject under investigation would be easier if the Department of State designated the group. As a consequence, it is not uncommon for DOJ or the FBI to identify a group for designation.

Other governments will often ask the State Department to designate terrorists. The specific reasons foreign governments make these requests vary significantly, but all cases are driven by overarching geostrategic interests. For instance, over the ten years of my directorship, the Chinese government requested on numerous occasions that the State Department add the East Turkestan Islamic Movement (ETIM) to the FTO list. In each instance, the State Department, correctly, rebuffed the Chinese. China's propensity to label all Uighurs as terrorists was problematic and ETIM is, according to the Chinese, a Uighur organization. The feeling in the US government was that the Chinese would use the FTO designation as a pretext to crack down harder on its Uighur population. Given the gross injustices and human rights abuses carried out by China against its Uighur citizens, an FTO designation was unpalatable to the CT Bureau. US regional experts and analysts also believed that ETIM was no longer, or never was, a functioning terrorist group. US experts felt ETIM was largely a concept pushed forward by the Chinese in an effort to broadly label Uighurs as terrorists. The United States pushed back on the Chinese narrative, noting that we saw a problematic group, but it was called the Turkestan Islamic Party, and for the most part it had relocated most of its operations to Syria to fight alongside Jabhat al Nusrah and that the group was composed of Arabs, not just Uighurs. This, however, was not a conversation the Chinese were interested in having. Instead, the narrative would shift back to ETIM. We learned through these engagements that one very important part of the reason the Chinese were interested in doing this was because they viewed the World Uighur Congress as part of the Uighur movement and as a possible alias for ETIM. The interest in drawing a line connecting ETIM to the WUC was flamed by China's angst over the activities of Rebiya Kadeer, a US resident and Chinese national. Kadeer, a Chinese national of Uighur ethnicity, advocated for Xinjiang independence, the home of many of China's Uighurs, was imprisoned in China, and once released came to the United States, where her advocacy has continued unabated. The Chinese government looks at a possible ETIM FTO designation as a novel way to possibly counter Kadeer's perceived anti-China stance. In essence, the Chinese care deeply about the US domestic designation of ETIM because it sees the FTO tool as leverage against the pro-Uighur narrative.

There are more benign reasons for a foreign government's request for the United States government to designate an individual or a group. Unsurprisingly, the United States works closely with the United Kingdom (UK) on terrorist designation matters. The UK also understands that in order for the United States to support designations at the United Nations ISIL and al-Qa'ida (aka 1267) Committee, it must first have a domestic designation in place. In 2016, the UK requested that the United States Department of State designate Alexanda Kotey and El Shafee Sheikh,[9] two members of the notorious ISIS Beatles cell that was responsible for horrific beheadings of US and foreign-based aid workers and journalists. The State Department worked to designate both Kotey, in January 2017,[10] and El Sheikh, in May 2017, as SDGTs pursuant to EO 13224. Not long after the US designations, the UK nominated both individuals for listing at the UN 1267 Committee and in July 2017, the UN listed both as international terrorists.[11]

The UK motivation, unlike the Chinese, was based on a sincere belief that Kotey and El Sheikh perpetrated heinous acts of terrorism against innocent civilians. Unlike the Chinese example, there was little dispute in the facts surrounding Sheikh's and Kotey's terrorist activities and, as such, the author directed his team to start work on the UK-identified terrorist designation targets. In the author's more than ten years as the Director of CT/CTFD, other governments, to

---

[9] U.S. Department of State. "State Department Terrorist Designation of Alexanda Amon Kotey," *Bureau of Counterterrorism and Countering Violent Extremism*, January 10, 2017. www.state.gov/j/ct/rls/other/des/266771.htm. Accessed March 2, 2018.

[10] Ibid.

[11] United Nations. "Security Council ISIL (Da'esh) and Al-Qaida Sanctions Committee Adds Two Names to its Sanctions List," *Security Council*, July 20, 2017. www.un.org/press/en/2017/sc12919.doc.htm. Accessed March 2, 2018.

include but not limited to Israel, Russia, France, Algeria, Kazakhstan, and Germany, have proposed individuals and groups for terrorist designation under the Secretary of State's authorities. In every case, the Department of State tried to find sufficient grounds for designation, but in some cases, the State Department was not able to cross the legal threshold. Telling another government, "no" is always difficult, but unless the identified target can get through the remainder of the designations process, as will be discussed later, "no" is the only answer. The designations process is guided by a deliberative policy and legal process that is designed to remain consistent with overarching US national security objectives. In some cases, a foreign government's request for a designation will be inconsistent with either the legal and due diligence standards built into the designations process, or the request may be outside the scope of US national security objectives.

THE EQUITY CHECK

Terrorist designations are an area where foreign policy, legal, and intelligence issues intersect. This intersection is most evident at the equity check stage of the designations process. The equity check is an executive summary document, comprised of all-source information, of the proposed designation target. In the proposed equity check of an individual, key information such as the person's date of birth, place of birth, passport or national identification number, as well as various aliases is highlighted. In addition, the terrorist activities of the individual, or group, as the case may be, are documented in a concise manner. The equity check is then sent electronically to various agencies and departments that may have equity in the proposed terrorist designation. If the equity check is of an organization, the executive summary discusses the attacks conducted by the organization and where the group is based and the composition of its membership. Every sentence in the equity check, including aliases and date of birth, is footnoted and traced back to the original source of the information. Theoretically, if it was determined that individual X, a

State Department proposed designation target, was born on March 28, 1979, and the source of that information was from the Pakistan-based newspaper, *Dawn*, a footnote would cite *Dawn*. Likewise, if individual X's place of birth was ascertained by a human intelligence source, the entity that collected the information from the source would be cited in a footnote. The purpose of documenting the origin of information in the equity check is to provide the national security community fidelity regarding the nature of the intelligence that could be used in the development of the terrorist designation.

The equity check is designed to ensure that the proposed designation of an individual or a group does not impair diplomatic, defense, law enforcement, or intelligence objectives. Typically, agencies are given two weeks to consider whether the proposed public designation of an individual or group would impair their operations. The designations of terrorists, whether carried out by State or Treasury Department, are always made public. Terrorist designations cannot be made in secret because the benefits of such a determination require action on the part of nongovernment entities, like banks. The possibility of financial transactions being blocked as a result of a terrorist designation requires the cooperation of financial institutions, which cannot occur unless the designation is ultimately made public. It is because of the public nature of terrorist designation that often leads to the terrorist designations process stalling. Why is this the case?

When equity is declared on a nominated terrorist designation target, the United States government agency that is concerned about the nomination will place a hold on the proposed State Department designation. These holds may stay in place permanently or they can be lifted. In the author's direct experience, holds have lasted weeks, days, months, years, and in some cases opposition to a designation continues indefinitely. In my experience, intelligence agencies are most likely to place a hold on a State Department proposed EO 13224 designation, and their concerns typically involve the nominations of individuals and not of groups. In past cases, a CT/CTFD sanctions investigator may have had an "AHA moment" and then developed an equity check. If the information the sanctions investigator read was all highly classified, and if that intelligence came from one specific agency only, there is a high probability the IC agency will place a hold on the proposal. Whether the single source comes from NSA technical means; a highly placed CIA human source with unique access; or an FBI informant with key information; all of these agencies will be concerned about their sources being compromised by the publication of a State Department designation. These agencies want to ensure the continued placement of their source and do not want to jeopardize their access to foreign intelligence. In these cases, it is prudent to pause the designation process. The State Department is not interested in jeopardizing continued access to key information that could result in a change of the possible target's pattern of life – especially regarding individuals who may be involved in planning terrorist operations.

The Department of Defense (DoD) will also, on very rare occasions, place a hold on a State Department designation proposal. Taking a policy action like a terrorist designation at the wrong time could negatively impact DoD kinetic strikes. If DoD has identified an individual subject to the use of authorized use of military force and has approval from the White House to carry out a military strike, it would be imprudent for the State Department to designate the individual. A designation, especially if it relies on a single strain of intelligence reporting, may lead the designation target to change their pattern of life. If that occurred, the designation could possibly jeopardize a military operation.

Although the intelligence community, law enforcement, and defense agencies have all placed holds on State Department CT/CTFD designation proposals; ironically, it is intra-State Department bureau disputes that are most likely to delay FTO designations. Geographic bureaus or Presidential special envoys responsible for geographic regions are the most likely to object to a CT Bureau FTO proposal. As CT/CTFD's Director, my office was engaged in multiyear or multimonth heated debates relating to the prospective FTO designations of the Haqqani Network, Tehrik-e Taliban Pakistan (TTP), and Boko Haram (BH). These intradepartmental debates centering on the TTP's and BH's FTO designations highlight some of the foreign policy concerns related to a terrorist designation proposal. Often, these concerns were driven by perceived, often incorrect, possible negative diplomatic repercussions associated with an FTO listing.

On May 1, 2010, TTP operative Faisal Shahzad attempted to ignite up a car bomb in Times Square, New York City. Shahzad failed and ultimately pled guilty to multiple charges. One charge absent was that of Shahzad's intent to provide material support to the TTP – which was undesignated at the time of Shahzad's attempted attack. The Times Square attack precipitated an intense State Department debate regarding whether the TTP should be designated as an FTO. In opposition to the designation was the Presidential Special Representative to Afghanistan and Pakistan (SRAP), Ambassador Richard Holbrooke, a foreign policy titan. Also against the designation was the US Ambassador to Pakistan, Anne Patterson, no lightweight herself with decades of foreign policy experience. However, neither was an expert on terrorism or counterterrorism. In favor of the TTP FTO designation, and my boss at the time of the discussion, was Ambassador Daniel Benjamin. In the years I worked in the Clinton State Department, the idea of split-view action memos, stating different opinions was anathema. The debate that raged around the TTP FTO designation was the one exception to the no-split memo rule. In this instance, the 7th Floor messaged to Ambassadors Benjamin and Holbrooke that it (the State Department leadership sat on the 7th Floor) would accept a split memo. At this juncture the CT Bureau, US Embassy Islamabad, and SRAP formulated arguments to convince Secretary Clinton to adopt their position.

The CT/CTFD arguments, endorsed by Ambassador Benjamin, were fairly straightforward. The TTP tried to attack the US homeland. It was a direct assault on the United States, and while the TTP effort failed, it illuminated the dangers posed by the group. It was not, contrary to the Ambassadors Holbrooke's and Patterson's opinion, a

Pakistan-based organization that solely focused on its local grievances. Instead, the TTP, in the CT Bureau's view, was a foreign-based group that already carried out terrorist activity that threatened US interests directly, and as such easily met the criteria for FTO designation. We also explained that Pakistan, itself, had designated the TTP under its own domestic legal authorities in 2008, and it would be peculiar for the United States to not designate a group that Pakistan already designated. The CT Bureau also explained that by not designating the TTP, it would not provide leverage to the Department of Justice to prosecute possible TTP material supporters. We noted the fact that Shahzad, himself, could not be prosecuted for material support to the TTP because the TTP was undesignated at the time of his attack. Why would the United States, we argued, not use all of its counterterrorism tools against a group that tried to blow up Times Square? We also explained that if you did not designate the group under US law, there was nothing preventing it from using the formal financial system to move funds between Pakistan and the United States. We noted while it was unlikely that the group availed itself of the formal financial system, it was nonetheless important to understand that sanctions are inherently a preventative tool and we should make every effort to block the TTP's theoretical access to the US system of finance. Finally, we explained that the credibility of the US terrorist designations list was at stake. If you did not add groups like the TTP to the list, how could US or international audiences take the United States FTO list seriously?

Holbrooke and Patterson explained that they had met in July 2010 with Pakistan President Asif Ali Zardani and General Ashfaq Parvez Kayani on the possibility of the TTP's FTO designation by the United States. Both men objected, noting that it would elevate the TTP's status and aid in the group's recruitment efforts. Holbrook and Patterson took back the message to Washington and Secretary Clinton that Pakistan opposed the US FTO designation and for this reason, and others, it should not be pursued. Holbrooke and Patterson both believed that the designation would somehow dilute Secretary Clinton's foreign policy power by shifting influence to the

Departments of Justice and Treasury. They argued that it made no sense to dilute the Secretary's foreign policy influence when, in their view, there was no practical benefit to the designation. Ambassador Patterson specifically argued that the TTP terrorist designation would make it harder to reconcile with the group at some future point.

Ambassador Patterson was always under the impression that terrorism designations made it impossible to negotiate with FTOs, which is not the case. In fact, as of March 2018, members of the Revolutionary Armed Forces of Colombia, a US designated FTO, are running for political office. The US, especially US envoy to the peace talks, Bernard Aronson,[12] played a role in the rapprochement between the FARC and the Colombian government despite the FTO listing. More to the point regionally, at the time of the debate, the US had been trying and willing to negotiate with the Afghan Taliban, despite the fact it is designated as a terrorist entity pursuant to EO 13224. These points were also lost on Holbrooke, who also opposed the TTP designation because he believed it would have a snowball effect whereupon the designation would lead to pressure on the State Department to designate other groups, like the Afghan Taliban, as FTOs (which incidentally still has not occurred as of March 2025). In 2012, this was the same argument that Holbrooke's successors at SRAP trotted out when it opposed the FTO designation of the Pakistan government supported Haqqani Network. Finally, with some merit to the argument, Holbrook argued that the TTP was an umbrella organization with no central cohesiveness. The CT Bureau countered that the group did have a clear leadership and we noted that the lawyers at State, Justice, and Treasury Departments all agreed that the group was united enough to designate.

In the end, Secretary Clinton signed the CT Bureau's recommendation line in the split action memo to designate the group and

---

[12] Otis, John. "The American Diplomat Who Helped Bring an End to Columbia's War," *NPR Parallels (Audio)*, September 24, 2016. www.npr.org/sections/parallels/2016/09/24/495185560/the-american-diplomat-who-helped-bring-an-end-to-colombias-war. Accessed March 4, 2018.

disapproved Ambassador Holbrooke's and Patterson's recommendation. The Secretary of State realized that groups that try to attack the United States homeland directly should not be allowed to do so with impunity. Shortly after Secretary Clinton's signature dried, the TTP was designated on September 1, 2010, as an FTO. It, however, took many months to reach a resolution on this issue and the TTP's action was held up in the equity check process for months. In the end, Holbrooke and Patterson were incorrect in their view that the TTP designation would not have any practical effect. Approximately one year later after the designation, three individuals were successfully charged for trying to provide material support to a designated FTO. In the September 2011 hearing in front of US District court judge John D. Bates, three defendants, Irfan Ul Haq, Qasim Ali, and Zahid Yousaf, pled guilty for trying to provide support to the TTP.[13]

Like the TTP debate, the CT Bureau and the Africa Bureau disagreed on whether BH should be designated under US law as an FTO. When the author joined the CT Bureau in 2008, one of my first meetings was with the Africa Bureau when I approached them with the possibility of designating BH as an FTO. I was laughed out of the room when the Africa Bureau staffer, who I will not name in order to preserve his anonymity, said that the group was nothing but guys on motorbikes. In other words, the Africa Bureau did not see BH as a serious threat. I countered their points by noting the atmosphere in which BH operated was one that could allow it to grow in strength, but this argument about projecting the future threat the group posed fell on deaf ears. Like all equity checks, though, the CT Bureau would check in regularly with the Africa Bureau to see if they had a change of heart. In the case of BH, the CT Bureau would check in every few months for nearly four years before CT was finally able to convince the Secretary of State to label BH an FTO.

---

[13] U.S. Immigration and Customs Enforcement. "3 Plead Guilty to Conspiracy to Provide Support to the Pakistani Taliban," *ICE Newsroom*, September 11, 2011. www.ice.gov/news/releases/3-plead-guilty-conspiracy-provide-material-support-pakistani-taliban. Accessed March 4, 2018.

Why did it take so long, and who was behind the delay? One reason for the delay was that the Africa Bureau did not feel the BH's activities merited designation. This perception changed to an extent, however, when BH carried out a successful suicide bombing attack on a United Nations facility in Abuja, Nigeria, on August 26, 2011.[14] Despite this attack that left at least twenty-one people dead, it took the Department of State more than two years to designate the group as an FTO. The chief impediment to the designation was the Africa Bureau's Assistant Secretary Johnnie Carson. Carson fought at every turn to push back on the designation, even though a coalition of senior government officials were in support of the BH's designation. On February 23, 2012, Admiral William H. McRaven, the Commander Officer of Joint Special Operations Command, sent a letter to Secretary Clinton noting his support for the designation. In that letter, Admiral McRaven highlighted the need to designate the group given its violent actions, most notably the group's attack on the UN compound. Admiral McRaven also explained the benefits the designation would provide to the Treasury and Justice Departments. McRaven was not alone; also around the same time, Lisa Monaco, who was then head of the Department of Justice's National Security Division, sent a letter to the State Department's Coordinator of Counterterrorism, Daniel Benjamin, noting the need to put the group on the FTO list.[15]

Why did Assistant Secretary Carson stridently resist the designation? While there has been speculation and news articles[16] written about the topic, these stories only scratch the thin veneer.

---

[14] Murray, Senan & Adam Nossiter. "Suicide Bomber Attacks U.N. Bomber in Nigeria," *The New York Times*, August 26, 2011. www.nytimes.com/2011/08/27/world/africa/27nigeria.html. Accessed March 12, 2018.

[15] Hosenball, Mark & John Shiffman. "U.S. Justice Dept Urges Terror Label for Nigerian Militants," *Chicago Tribune*, May 17, 2012. http://articles.chicagotribune.com/2012-05-17/news/sns-rt-us-usa-security-bokoharambre84h01i-20120517_1_haqqani-network-militant-group-terrorist-group. Accessed March 12, 2018.

[16] Kessler, Glenn. "'Boko Haram' Inside the State Department Debate over the 'Terrorist' Label," *The Washington Post*, May 19, 2014. www.washingtonpost.com/news/fact-checker/wp/2014/05/19/boko-haram-inside-the-state-department-debate-over-the-terrorist-label/?utm_term=.156ab90832c7. Accessed March 12, 2018.

Like many Foreign Service officers, especially those at senior levels, there is great angst in doing anything as a matter of policy that may unnecessarily upset a delicate bilateral relationship. In Carson's view, the designation would upset the Nigerian government. In fact, the Nigerian government was opposed to the designation. Carson cited the fact that in May 2012, Owaye Azazi, the Nigerian national security advisor, opposed the designation because it would give BH "prestige." The government of Nigeria also was worried that the FTO designation would adversely affect trade and tourism into Nigeria. Ironically, Carson also opposed the FTO designation because he felt it would look like the US government was condoning Nigeria's heavy-handed tactics, such as extrajudicial killings of BH members. Instead, Carson believed that the US should work with the Nigerian government to address the underlying issues that BH exploited and led to the alienation of northern Nigeria's population. Carson's views heavily mimicked those of a group of prominent academics who wrote to Secretary Clinton in May 2012. The twenty-one academics, led by Paul Lubeck from the University of California in Santa Cruz, believed that, inter alia, the FTO designation would internationalize BH's status and, interestingly, "would prevent independent scholarly inquiry about Boko Haram and increase suspicion in the future about researchers with no governmental ties. Public policy benefits from dialogue with public scholars, and an FTO designation would effectively criminalize broad categories of research." Thankfully, this far-fetched reasoning did not win the day, and ultimately, shortly after Johnnie Carson departed the Department of State, the group was designated as an FTO. But the damage was already done. The long delay led to Congressional interest and to the introduction of bills that would, if passed, compel the Department of State to designate the group as an FTO. Ultimately, this leverage Congress provided was of use to the Counterterrorism Bureau as it tried to push the designation forward in an effort to lift the Africa Bureau's hold on the FTO designation.

On November 13, 2013, BH was formally designated as an FTO. The Department of State explained that BH was a group with links to al-Qa'ida in the Islamic Maghreb that has carried out numerous indiscriminate attacks against women and children.[17] From the time the author had his first meeting with the Africa Bureau to the time the designation transpired, five years had passed, and hundreds had been killed in the meantime. Would have the FTO designation of the group prevented these deaths? In all likelihood, no. The delay, however, had other political consequences.

New Jersey Governor Chris Christie, in his July 2016 speech at the Republican National Convention, blamed Secretary Clinton for ignoring the problem of BH. In his speech, Christie, while incorrectly conflated terrorist watch listing with terrorism designations the broader point was clear – Secretary Clinton ignored a problem in the eyes of the Republicans. Christie said,

> In Nigeria, Hillary Clinton amazingly fought for two years to keep an al-Qa'ida affiliate off of the terrorism watch list. Now, what happens because of this reckless action by the candidate who is the self-proclaimed champion of women all around the world? These al-Qa'ida terrorists abducted hundreds of innocent young women two years ago. These girls are still missing today. And what was the solution from the Obama-Clinton team? A hashtag campaign.[18]

While Governor Christie inaccurately conflates watch listing with terrorist designations, the perception that Secretary of Clinton was weak on terrorism was problematic and could have been avoided with a timely sanction of BH as an FTO.

---

[17] U.S. Department of State. "Terrorist Designations of Boko Haram and Ansaru," *Bureau of Counterterrorism and Countering Violent Extremism*, November 13, 2013. www.state.gov/j/ct/rls/other/des/266565.htm. Accessed March 24, 2018.

[18] Reilly, Katie. "Read Chris Christie's Convention Speech Attacking Hillary Clinton," *TIME*, July 22, 2016. http://time.com/4419974/chris-christie-republican-convention-speech/. Accessed March 29, 2018.

The damage could have been worse though for the Obama Administration. In his speech, Governor Christie was referencing the 2014 BH kidnapping of 276 girls from the northeast Nigerian town of Chibok and the accompanying hashtag Twitter campaign #BringBackOurGirls.[19] Yet, that kidnapping occurred after Secretary John Kerry designated BH as an FTO in 2013. If BH were undesignated at the time of the Chibok kidnapping, the political and public outcry would have been more damaging. Instead, the damage was limited to a political speech and a Trevor Noah comedy skit on Comedy Central.[20] More than five years after the group's FTO designation, none of the group's assets have been blocked or frozen, nor has there been any material support prosecutions in the United States because of the BH designation. Does this mean, though, that the delayed designation was appropriate? Not necessarily, because ultimately an FTO designation is about blocking a group's access to the formal financial system. Moreover, the Africa Bureau's hold on the BH designation had political consequences and damaged the credibility of the State Department's FTO list. A group that kills, maims, kidnaps, and rapes thousands of civilians for political objectives needs to be treated for what it is – in the case of BH, a terrorist group.

THE ADMINISTRATIVE RECORD

As a general matter, the terrorist designations process stalls during the equity check process. If, after a two-week period, no agencies express equities regarding the proposed target's designation, the next step in the designations process is the drafting of the administrative record. The administrative record is the essence of the individual's or group's designation as a terrorist entity. The administrative

---

[19] "Nigeria Chibok Abductions: What We Know." *BBC News*, May 8, 2017. www.bbc.com/news/world-africa-32299943. Accessed April 2, 2018.

[20] "Boko Haram RNC Viewing Party." *The Daily Show with Trevor Noah*, July 21, 2016. www.cc.com/video-clips/ewuqz6/the-daily-show-with-trevor-noah-boko-haram-rnc-viewing-party. Accessed April 2, 2018.

record is comprised of classified and unclassified information. For example, an administrative record may contain human intelligence (HUMINT), signals intelligence (SIGINT), foreign government intelligence information, and imagery intelligence (IMINT), as well as State Department diplomatic reporting, which may be either classified or unclassified. Unclassified sources are equally wide-ranging. Examples of unclassified sources of information may range from the reporting of US-based newspapers like the *New York Times* to foreign language printed news sources. Social media sources of information like YouTube, Facebook, and Twitter are also highly relevant information sources, where groups will frequently take credit for their attacks using social media platforms. Reliable classified and unclassified information is the foundation for a credible administrative record. How reliability is established will be examined in more detail in the next section, but first it is important to establish the three key components of a State Department administrative record; (1) the foreignness section; (2) terrorist activity; and (3) terrorist activity that threatens US national security.

FOREIGNNESS

In the case of an individual's EO 13224 designation, the administrative record is the "story" of that person's activities. First, this narrative highlights the bio-identifiers of the individual. For a designation to have maximum effectiveness, the full name, various aliases, birthdate, place of birth, nationality, passport number, and current location should, when possible, be documented in detail. For a Department of State designation, this information will confirm that the prospective designee is a foreign person because the Department of State does not designate US persons.

In the case of a group's FTO designation by the Department of State, relevant information collected and discussed in the administrative record may focus on identifying the leaders of the group and their nationality. In the context of the relevant law guiding FTO determinations, Congress left undefined the term "foreign organization" in section 219 of the INA. As a consequence, the Department of State has been guided by various factors when determining whether a particular terrorist group may be a foreign-based entity. These factors may include, but are not limited to:

1. The leaders of the group are located or live primarily outside of the United States;
2. The organizations nonviolent activities in the United States or overseas are directed or controlled by members who do not primarily reside in the United States;
3. The group's headquarters and training camps are located outside of the United States;
4. The group's violent activities in the United States or abroad are directed by members who do not primarily reside in the United States;
5. Funding or other material support of the organization, such as travel documents, operational logistical support, planning, or information-gathering activities, comes from outside of the United States from foreign nationals or from state sponsors of terrorism; and
6. Some of the group's terrorist activities take place outside of the United States.

An instructive way to consider whether a group may satisfy these criteria is by examining the composition of a specific group, such as al-Qa'ida (AQ). AQ was cofounded by Usama bin Laden (UBL), a Saudi national. UBL directed al-Qa'ida's operations from outside of the United States – whether from his Sudan safe haven in the 1990s or from his Afghanistan perch in the early 2000s. AQ's attack on 9/11 was perpetrated by citizens of Saudi Arabia, the UAE, Lebanon, and Egypt. AQ's financing, especially pre-9/11, as determined by the National Commission on Terrorist Attacks Upon the United States, derived primarily from Persian Gulf-based charities. Once an organization is determined to be foreign based, the next step in the process is to document terrorist activity of the group or individual.

TERRORIST ACTIVITY

The second substantive section of the administrative record documents the terrorist activity of the prospective designation target and how these activities meet the relevant statutory criteria.

The State Department designates individuals or groups under section 1(b) of EO 13224. Section 1(b) allows the Department to designate individuals who have committed, or pose a significant risk of committing, acts of terrorism. Section 3(d)(i) of EO 13224 defines terrorism as involvement in a violent act, or act dangerous to human life, property, or infrastructure and, per section 3(d)(ii), appears to intimidate or coerce a civilian population, influence a policy of government, or affect the conduct of a government by mass destruction, assassination, kidnapping, or hostage taking. This means that the State Department designates individuals or groups that have carried out terrorist attacks or have the capability and intent to commit acts of terrorism. EO 13224 limits the Department of State's ability to designate a diverse range of individuals operating within terrorist groups. In practice, section 1(b) limits Department of State designations to leaders directing attacks or the operatives conducting attacks. A good example of a State Department EO 13224 designation of an operative is that of Ibrahim al-Asiri, a member of al-Qa'ida in the Arabian Peninsula (AQAP). Designated on March 24, 2011, Asiri was described in a Department of State press release as "AQAP's primary bomb maker … who gained notoriety for the recruitment of his younger brother as a suicide bomber in a failed assassination attempt of Saudi Prince Muhammad bin Nayif."[21] Al-Asiri was a strong candidate for a Department of State designation because he played a key operational role within AQAP and constructed the bomb dedicated to premeditatedly kill a senior Saudi government official.

Like EO 13224, the Department of State can only designate a group as an FTO if it either engages in terrorist activity or retains the

---

[21] Department of State. "Department of State's Terrorist Designation of Ibrahim Hassan Tali Al-Asiri," *Bureau of Counterterrorism and Countering Violent Extremism*, March 24, 2011. www.state.gov/j/ct/rls/other/des/266641.htm. Accessed April 17, 2018.

capability and intent to engage in terrorism or terrorist activity.[22] Terrorist activity relevant to FTO designations is defined in section 212(a)(3)(B) of the INA and includes:

1. The hijacking or sabotage of any conveyance.
2. The seizing or detaining, and threatening to kill, injure, or continue to detain, another individual in order to compel a third person to do or abstain from doing any act as an explicit or implicit condition for the release of the individual seized or detained.
3. A violent act upon an internationally protected person or upon the liberty of such a person.
4. An assassination.
5. The use of any biological agent, chemical agent, or nuclear weapon or device, or (b) explosive, firearm, or other weapons or dangerous device, with intent to endanger directly or indirectly the safety of one or more individuals or to cause substantial damage to property.
6. A threat, attempt, or conspiracy to do any of the foregoing.

If there is ample reporting on a group, determining its involvement in terrorist activity is fairly straightforward. The Department of State's September 1, 2010, press release describing the FTO designation of TTP contains details relevant to establishing a group's engagement in terrorist activity. The State Department attributed the following acts of terrorism to the TTP:

- A 2009 suicide attack on a US base in Khowst, Afghanistan;
- A 2010 suicide bombing against the US Consulate in Peshawar, Pakistan; and
- Faisal Shahzad's failed explosives detonation in New York City's Times Square.

The factual case for developing evidence that the TTP was engaged in terrorist activity was significantly easier than, as demonstrated earlier, achieving consensus during the equity check stage of the designations process.

---

[22] Bender's Immigration and Nationality Act Pamphlet (2011 Ed.), INA, at Section 219(a)(1).

TERRORIST ACTIVITY THREATENS US INTERESTS

The final substantive section of the administrative record is whether the prospective State Department EO 13224 for FTO designation target is a threat to US national security interests. Of the three elements of the administrative record, this tends to be the most difficult to determine.

EO 13224 makes clear that the State Department can only designate an individual or group if their terrorism or the threat of their terrorism "threatens the security of U.S. nationals or the national security, foreign policy, or economy of the United States."[23] EO 13224 allows the Department of State to broadly interpret what or who may constitute a threat to the United States. An individual or group can be designated by the State Department even if they may not pose a threat to the US homeland. EO 13224, by noting threats to US foreign policy or economic interests, also provides the Department great latitude in establishing how an individual or group may meet the final designation criteria. The best way to demonstrate how an individual may meet the threat to US interests' criteria is by examining a specific example.

On September 1, 2010, the US Department of State designated TTP's leader Hakimullah Mehsud pursuant to EO 13224. According to the Department of State's press release announcing the designation at the time, "[the] TTP has carried numerous attacks against US interests under Mehsud and Rehman's leadership."[24] The State Department's press release also documents a few of the attacks carried out by Mehsud, but what further demonstrated Mehsud's threat to US interests was the rare timing of a Department of Justice charge by criminal complaint of Mehsud that was announced on September 1, 2010. According to the FBI press release, Mehsud was "charged with conspiracy to murder U.S. citizens abroad and conspiracy to

---

[23] Blocking Property and Prohibiting Transactions with Persons Who Commit, Threaten to Commit, or Support Terrorism; 66, Fed. Reg. 186. September 23, 2001. www.gpo.gov/fdsys/pkg/FR-2001-09-25/pdf/01-24205.pdf. Accessed February 25, 2018.

[24] Department of State. "Designations of Tehrik-e Taliban Pakistan and Two Senior Leaders," *Bureau of Counterterrorism and Countering Violent Extremism*, September 1, 2010. www.state.gov/j/ct/rls/other/des/266652.htm. Accessed April 22, 2018.

use a weapon of mass destruction (explosives) against U.S. citizens abroad."[25] Illustrating the threat Mehsud posed to US interests was therefore simple and straightforward.

Unlike Mehsud's EO 13224 designation, the November 2010 FTO designation of Jundallah, an Iranian-based terrorist group, provides an opportunity to demonstrate the creativity required to label a group as a threat to US interests. The Department of State's press release documenting Jundallah's terrorist activity notes an array of suicide bombings, ambushes, and targeted assassinations against civilians.[26] Jundallah is a group that has, however, primarily focused its attacks within the borders of Iran. For instance, in 2007 the group attacked Iran's Islamic Revolutionary Guard Corps soldiers, killing eleven.[27] How could an organization that primarily attacks an enemy of the United States also pose a threat to US interests? In the case of Jundallah, the State Department explained that the group's attacks, especially those against Iranian and Pakistani border patrol elements along a porous border, created instability and the freedom of movement of violent extremists, whether by Jundallah or other groups, such as al-Qa'ida. In the case of Jundallah, its terrorist activity was antithetical to US foreign policy interests because it allowed for the movement of terrorists, finance, and materiel to conflict zones, such as Afghanistan, where the United States had a vested interest. While demonstrating that terrorist activity is a threat to US interests is the most difficult legal prong to satisfy, the Jundallah example illustrates the ease in which it can be satisfied.

---

[25] Department of Justice. "Pakistani Taliban Leader Charged in Terrorism Conspiracy Resulting in Murder of Seven Americans in Afghanistan." *FBI*, September 1, 2010. https://archives.fbi.gov/archives/washingtondc/press-releases/2010/wfo090110.htm. Accessed April 22, 2018.

[26] Department of State. "Secretary of State's Terrorist Designation of Jundallah," *Bureau of Counterterrorism and Countering Violent Extremism*, November 3, 2010. www.state.gov/j/ct/rls/other/des/266649.htm. Accessed April 28, 2018.

[27] Sahimi, Muhammad. "Who supports Jundallah?" *PBS (KQED)*, October 22, 2009. www.pbs.org/wgbh/pages/frontline/tehranbureau/2009/10/jundallah.html. Accessed April 28, 2018.

The time it takes to research and write the administrative record varies, but in general can take either a few days or weeks to complete. If the United States has ample intelligence collection on a group or individual proposed for designation, the drafting of the administrative record may be expedited. If, however, the designation target is obscure, the administrative record drafting process may take weeks.

INTERAGENCY REVIEW AKA "THE CLEARANCE PROCESS"

Once the administrative record is drafted, whether it is an FTO or EO 13224 designation, attorneys from the Departments of Justice, State, and Treasury Departments must then conduct a legal review. This part of the designations process takes the longest period of time and in some cases has taken years to complete the interagency legal review process. There are many factors that prolong the clearance process. First, it is important to note that all of the Department of State's terrorist designations are subject to judicial review. In the case of EO 13224 designations, the first court of review is the applicable United States district court. If there is a legal challenge of an FTO designation, the first court of review is the United States Court of Appeals District of Columbia Circuit. Because State Department FTO and EO 13224 designations can be challenged and overturned in court, interagency lawyers scrutinize every sentence in the administrative record. The intensity of the review cannot be overstated – the legal review process is deliberative and robust. The administrative record, once completed, is the academic equivalent of a dissertation on a terrorist or terrorist organization. Nearly every sentence in the administrative record is cited and reviewed to ensure that the underlying exhibit is correctly noted. As discussed in the previous section, the administrative record is comprised of classified and unclassified information. While vetting this information, interagency lawyers are considering the sourcing behind the statements that undergird the basis for the individual's or group's designation. Administrative records are generally based on raw reporting, as opposed to finished analytical intelligence products, because the reviewing interagency attorneys believe that a judge can better understand the bona fides of each source statement. The best way to describe this bias toward raw reporting is by example. Human intelligence informs terrorist designation decision-making and human source intelligence is often reviewed carefully by interagency lawyers since it comes in various forms.

Human sources can have different kinds of proximity to information. A source may have collected information directly, or firsthand, or indirectly, second, third, or fourth hand. The closer the access or proximity to the information, the better for purposes of the administrative record, if the reliability and reporting record of the source has been established. Reliability and reporting history of the source is often noted clearly by US intelligence agencies. An ideal example of human source derived sentence in an administrative record could look like this, "According to information provided on September 12, 1977 from a reliable and vetted source with a five year reporting record who claims firsthand access to the information, Person X carried out and assassination that led to the death of Person Y, a U.S. citizen." In a finished intelligence product, the same sentence could look like this, "We assess with high confidence that Person X killed Person Y on September 12, 1977." In the first example, a reviewing judge would understand the basis for the assertion that Person X carried out an act of terrorism. In the case of the finished intelligence, however, the judge does not have access to the sourcing. As a consequence, it is more difficult for the judge to independently and credibly assess the basis for the analytical viewpoint that person X carried out an act of terrorism.

Technically derived information, whether from imagery or SIGINT, is preferred over other types of information because there is higher confidence in the source's reliability. Human sources tend to embellish, alter, or simply forget the precise nature of a conversation. A technical source is not as prone to these weaknesses. Open-source information, such as unclassified information derived from newspapers, X (formerly Twitter) feeds, television or radio interviews, and Facebook posts, is also used in the construction of administrative records. These kinds of sources tend to be scrutinized closely for reliability. Using sources of information from publications that have a clear slant, especially foreign-based newspapers or online publications based in government-controlled authoritarian states, will usually not be approved for use in an individual or group's designation unless the information is corroborated by other sources, such as SIGINT. Less controversial is the use of self-incriminating information from an individual's tweets. For instance, if a possible designation target takes credit for an attack via his X (Twitter) account, it will likely be incorporated into the administrative record. In most cases, however, there will be efforts to corroborate the fact that the individual or group actually carried out the attack they claimed to have conducted. Often, groups and individuals will claim attacks for which they had no role in an effort to increase fear in its target population. In other cases, a group may take credit for an attack in an effort to increase its prestige in jihadist circles so that it can raise more money or add recruits to the organization. For these reasons, corroboration of open-source information is vital.

Once the interagency lawyers agree that an individual's designation pursuant to EO 13224 is justified, they will "clear" the administrative record. FTO designations, however, have an extra step in the process following interagency legal approval. Since 1997, the formality of receiving a "Letter of Concurrence (LOC)" from senior members of the Treasury and Justice Department has been part of the FTO process. The LOC, however, is not a legal requirement and it often delays the finalization of the FTO designation. On average, FTO designations take at least a few months longer to complete than EO 13224 designations. Until 2018, a key reason for this delay correlated to the fact that Department of Justice sent its LOC from the Attorney General (today the Assistant Attorney General sends the letter). The Treasury Department delegates the LOC down to the Director of OFAC. In the author's more than ten years of heading up CT/CTFD, I never saw the LOCs as adding any value to the terrorist designations process.

THE SECRETARY OF STATE'S DETERMINATION

The final package for the Secretary of State's determination includes an action memorandum that explains, in a few paragraphs, the justification for the recommended individual or group designation. The action memo may have from three to ten other supplementary documents appended to it. The administrative record is the primary document appended, but other documents sent to the Secretary of State include: a Federal Register Notice (FRN); a document explaining the legal background for FTO and/or EO 13224 designations; and (only for FTO designations) a letter to Congress because FTO designations require seven days advance congressional notification pursuant to the INA. The decision package sent to the Secretary of State is meant to both inform and ensure that certain legal requirements of the terrorist designations process are adhered to. For instance, for an FTO designation to take effect, the FRN must be published. The action memorandum is meant to encapsulate in a few paragraphs the administrative record, a document that often is longer than ten pages in length. The most ironic part of the designations process is that the shortest process part is the Secretary of State's final determination and signing of the FRN and action memorandum. Secretary Clinton would usually sign off on designations in a week, while Secretary Kerry was known to sign in a matter of a few days. Secretary Tillerson would take weeks to sometimes a month to sign, but even during his short tenure he designated more than fifty terrorists and terrorist groups.

POST-SECRETARY OF STATE DECISION – THE UNITED NATIONS, CONGRESSIONAL, AND PUBLIC NOTIFICATION

Once the Secretary of State decides to designate an individual or group, the next step in the process is to publicly announce the sanction. It is also at this time when the United States holds internal deliberations on whether to nominate the individual or group the Secretary approved for domestic listing for simultaneous listing at the United Nations. Of the UN's various sanctions committees, the one that is most relevant to terrorism designations is the ISIS and al-Qa'ida (aka 1267) Sanctions Committee. The process for UN listings at the UN 1267 Committee involves a two-week prenotification cable that is sent to key US Embassies overseas. Political and economic foreign service officers then demarche host governments in an effort to generate support and interest in the US nomination of the individual's UN listing. The cable sent to embassies overseas will generally outline the individual's bio-identifiers and terrorist activities. If it is a group listing, the cable will generally outline the attacks conducted by the group as well as its links to either al-Qa'ida or ISIS. Following that, a formal statement of the case is presented at the UN 1267 Committee. That starts a ten-day no-objection period in which any member of the UN Security Council can stop or pause the proposed nomination before the UN adopts it. While the CT Bureau at State, especially earlier in the author's tenure, had a great appetite for nominating individuals and groups for listing at the UN. UN listings have an incredibly strong multiplier effect. In the case of a US designation, only one country, the United States, establishes an asset freeze against the designated entity. In the case of a UN listing, more than 190 countries are obligated to implement an asset freeze against the designated entity. Additionally, UN member states are also obligated to implement an arms embargo and travel ban against listed individuals. A UN listing, especially given the UN's inability to define terrorism, also carries significant symbolic weight.

For these practical and symbolic reasons, CT/CTFD was keen to pursue UN listings whenever possible. That all changed in the wake of the Syrian civil war and Russia's invasion of Crimea. Since 2014, the Russian Federation has become increasingly difficult to collaborate with the UN. In 2017, for example, the Russian Federation, Saudi Arabia (via Senegal as a proxy), and Egypt blocked the United States proposal to list ISIS-Libya, ISIS-Yemen, ISIS-Saudi Arabia, and ISIS-Khorasan at the UN 1267 Committee. A few years prior to that blocking of ISIS listings, the Russian Federation blocked the

US proposal to list ISIS-Caucasus Province (ISIS-CP) at the same UN committee. Why would these countries block US efforts to sanction ISIS's branches? For the Russian Federation, it was about the perception that it did not have a handle on terrorists in its backyard. That's why the Russian Federation blocked the ISIS-CP proposal. It blocked the 2017 proposals because the Russian Federation was worried about the slippery slope that would be created. The theory that sparked Russia's opposition was that if it supported the US 2017 proposal to sanction other ISIS branches at the UN, the United States might try again to nominate ISIS-CP for listing. Egypt's and Saudi Arabia's calculations were not unlike those of the Russian Federation. Both Egypt and Saudi Arabia were concerned about the optics that they did not have a tight lid on ISIS within their borders. Another irritant in UN listing efforts has been China's willingness to serve as a proxy for Pakistan at the UN Security Council. China has consistently blocked, at Pakistan's behest, US efforts to sanction Lashkar-e-Tayyiba (LeT) and Haqqani Network (HQN) linked individuals and entities. It is no secret that Pakistan has proactively provided funding and operational support to LeT and HQN via the auspices of its intelligence agency, the Inter-Services Intelligence (ISI). China, acting as Pakistan's proxy, has set back international efforts to counter LeT and HQN, and as a consequence, the United States and other countries are left with domestic designations as the primary sanctions tool to counter terrorist freedom of movement and access to materiel.

If the designation is only announced domestically, the United States Department of State will still notify key countries in advance of the US public announcement. The advance notification will outline the individual's or group's terrorist activity and request that countries take similar action pursuant to their own domestic legal authorities. In extremely sensitive cases where there is fear of a leak that could tip off the designated target of the impending sanction that could result in the possibility of asset flight, the US will not prenotify. This tends to be the case with Pakistan, given ISI's close relationship with HQN and LeT. For FTO designations, the Department of State must, pursuant to statute, prenotify Congress seven days in advance of the public announcement. Congressional notification takes the form of a classified executive summary document that outlines the activities of the group or individual being designated. The Department of State is not required to prenotify Congress of its EO 13224 designations.

The general public is notified of State Department FTO and EO 13224 designations in three ways. First, for every Department of State designation, a Federal Register Notice (FRN) is published. The FRN simply notes the group or individual designated, who signed off on the designation (usually the Secretary of State), and under what legal authority (FTO or EO 13224) the designation was made. Second, every Department of State designation is published on the US government Specially Designated National (SDN) list. The Department of the Treasury's Office of Foreign Assets Control (OFAC) maintains the SDN list. The Director of CT/CTFD sends a memo that contains the identifiers of the designated individual or entity to the Director of OFAC. In essence, the SDN list is how the United States conveys to financial and nonbank financial institutions the names of individuals and groups that should be blocked from the US financial system. Third, for every new or amended Department of State designation, a press release is distributed to the public. The press release outlines the activities of the individual or group designated by the Secretary of State. The press release will contain more specific details of the entity or individual's terrorist actions than either the SDN listing or the FRN publication. Public notifications are a vital element of the terrorist designations process. The US government cannot designate terrorists in secret. Announcing in an open manner the reasons for the Secretary's determination best maximizes the impact of a designation. Without that openness, banks would have more difficulty in blocking nefariously transferred assets. Without this transparency, the general public, US and overseas law enforcement, as well as border officials, would have less insight into the threat posed by designated individuals. Just as important, public announcements serve as the last piece of the due process for the individual. They have been notified of the US decision and, if they have standing to do so, can legally challenge their listing as discussed in the interagency review section.

DELISTING TERRORISTS

The process of delisting terrorists designated as FTOs or SDGTs pursuant to EO 13224 is nearly identical to that of listing a group or individual. The process will begin with the identification of a deceased individual or defunct group and then move to the equity check stage and culminate in the Secretary of State's determination that revocation[28] of the designation is appropriate. Removing terrorist groups from the FTO and EO 13224 is vital to the credibility of the United States' terrorist designations regime. A list that contains dormant groups itself is dormant and prone to ridicule. Despite clear legal criteria for revocation, removing FTOs from the list is extremely difficult and time-consuming. Before proceeding, it is important to understand the standard for revocation.

FTO listings are, per the INA as amended, reviewed every five years. Over the course of the research for an FTO's five-year review, it may become apparent that there is an absence of open source or classified reporting that is indicative that the organization under review is no longer extant. When this occurs, the delisting process begins. Revocation occurs according to the legal standard set forth in §219 (a)(6)(A) of the INA. There are three ways for an FTO to be delisted:

1. *The circumstances that were the basis for the designation have changed in such a manner to warrant revocation.* This simply means the FTO is either defunct or has modified its behavior in a manner that does not allow for the group to continue to meet the legal criteria for designation. Generally, this occurs when a group morphs from a terrorist group into a legitimate political organization. A possible future example of this is the

---

[28] The terms "revocation" and "delisting" are used interchangeably in this section.

FARC in Colombia. Another contemporaneous example is the Spanish-based ETA group that announced its dissolution on May 2, 2018.[29] The group went as far as even saying, "ETA recognizes the suffering caused as result of their struggle."[30] While short of an outright apology, ETA's rhetoric and disbandment are indicators that the group should soon be delisted. Groups delisted since the inception of the FTO list, with one exception, have been removed because of a change of circumstances, and in each of those cases the revocation occurred because the FTO was deemed defunct. A few examples of this type of FTO delisting include the Algeria-based Armed Islamic Group, the Libyan Islamic Fighting Group, Greece-based 17 November, and the Moroccan Islamic Combatant Group.

2. *The national security of the United States warrants a revocation.* A delisting in this manner would imply that it is in US national security interests to remove the FTO from the list. This type of delisting has never occurred before, and it is hard to foresee this happening in the future given the implications of such a maneuver. The implication of a national security-based delisting is that the United States sees the FTO as a group it can leverage to benefit foreign policy or defense interests.

3. *The Secretary of State has the discretion to revoke an FTO designation at any time he or she sees fit.* Only once, on September 28, 2012, has the Department removed an FTO from the list based on a discretionary determination. In this case, Secretary Clinton used her discretion to remove the MEK from the FTO list in order to resolve what was rapidly becoming a human-rights quagmire in Iraq. At the time of the MEK's delisting, nearly 3,000 MEK members were living in Camp Ashraf, Iraq. The Government of Iraq wanted the group out of Iraq, but no country would seriously entertain the notion of welcoming members of a US-designated FTO. At the same time, the United States was attempting to find a country to host the MEK, the Islamic Revolutionary Guard Corps (IRGC) was lobbing rockets into Camp Ashraf. The MEK's presence was an irritant to US–Iraq bilateral relations; the group's

---

[29] Minder, Raphael. "Basque Group ETA Disbands, After Terrorist Campaign Spanning Generations," *The New York Times*, May 2, 2018. www.nytimes.com/2018/05/02/world/europe/spain-eta-disbands-basque.html. Accessed May 10, 2018.
[30] Ibid.

membership was likely to be picked off by the IRGC, which would result in a human rights catastrophe; and the group was seen as a pariah until the FTO designation was removed. The Federal Register Notice (FRN)[31] and the State Department's press release[32] noting the MEK's delisting is telling. Neither the FRN nor the press release contains the phrase "change of circumstances." The State Department also goes out of its way to explain its "serious concerns about the MEK as an organization." This phrase, and the previous paragraph noting the MEK's direct involvement in the deaths of Americans, makes clear the group's designation was not revoked out of US national security interests. In the end, Secretary Clinton had little choice but to remove the MEK from the FTO list, and under her watch the Department did not countenance the MEK's past misdeeds.

Unlike the FTO regime, there is no legally mandated time-specific review process for groups and individuals designated pursuant to EO 13224 by the Department of State. However, while the author served as the CT/CTFD director between 2008 and 2018, the State Department delisted eighteen individuals and groups previously designated pursuant to EO 13224.[33] In the majority of the cases, the groups were deemed defunct or the individuals were determined to be deceased. In an effort to ensure our designations regime was dynamic, we invested limited resources to pursue the delistings of deceased individuals and defunct groups. In most of these cases, the determinations were fairly straightforward. For example, in 2013, it was widely reported that AQAP's second-ranking leader, Said Ali al-Shihri, was killed in a late 2012 counterterrorism operation.[34] Later in 2013, AQAP eulogized and confirmed

---

[31] "Department of State: Public Notice 8050; 77, Fed. Reg. 193." September 21, 2012. www.gpo.gov/fdsys/pkg/FR-2012-10-04/pdf/2012-24505.pdf. Accessed May 12, 2018.

[32] Department of State. "Delisting of the Mujahedin-e Khalq," *Bureau of Counterterrorism and Countering Violent Extremism*, September 28, 2012. www.state.gov/j/ct/rls/other/des/266607.htm. Accessed May 12, 2018.

[33] Department of State. "Individuals and Entities Designated by the State Department Under E.O. 13224." *Bureau of Counterterrorism and Countering Violent Extremism*. www.state.gov/j/ct/rls/other/des/143210.htm. Accessed May 12, 2018.

[34] Mazzetti, Mark. "No. 2 Leader of Al Qaeda in Yemen is Killed," *The New York Times*, January 24, 2013. www.nytimes.com/2013/01/25/world/middleeast/said-ali-al-shihri-qaeda-leader-in-yemen-is-dead.html. Accessed May 12, 2018.

al-Shihri's death.[35] In 2014, the State Department, after corroborating news reports, removed him from the list of designated terrorists. Reviewing all-source information to ensure that an individual like al-Shihri is truly deceased is the key attribute in the EO 13224 delisting process. Delistings of terrorists pursuant to EO 13224 are handled cautiously because terrorists have a penchant for obfuscation to elude counterterrorism efforts designed to bring them to justice. It is partly for this reason that the pace of delistings is significantly slower than the pace of adding individuals to the US terrorism designations lists.

RECAP AND CONCLUDING THOUGHTS

Why spend so many human resources and multiple months, in some cases years, to designate terrorists? The benefits of designations are often lost on the general public, scholars, and so-called terrorism experts. Most myopically believe that the only benefit of a designation is a freezing or blocking of an asset and, to be sure, that is a key attribute of a terrorist designation. In 2017, the Treasury Department published its yearly Terrorist Assets Report (TAR) and documented 2016 statistics of blocked funds relating to designated FTOs and SDGTs. At the end of the calendar year 2016, according to this report, nearly $35 million USD of terrorist assets were blocked.[36] That is demonstrative of the positive impact State and Treasury terrorist designations have in blocking terrorists from using the US formal financial system. As discussed in some detail earlier, one of the most important benefits, and often least understood, of an FTO's designation is the prosecutorial leverage it provides the Department of Justice. Since the inception of the FTO regime in 1997, hundreds of people have been prosecuted for 18 USC §2339B violations of providing material support to designated FTOs. In 2017, Mohamad Khweis, a

---

[35] Roggio, Bill. "AQAP Confirms Deputy Emir Killed in US Drone Strike," *FDD's Long War Journal*, July 17, 2013. www.longwarjournal.org/archives/2013/07/aqap_confirms_deputy.php. Accessed May 12, 2018.

[36] Department of Treasury. "Terrorist Assets Report: Calendar Year 2016," *Office of Foreign Assets Control*, 2016. Page 10. www.treasury.gov/resource-center/sanctions/Programs/Documents/tar2016.pdf.

former bus driver from Alexandria, Virginia, was sentenced to twenty years for fighting with ISIS.[37] While there are few concrete statistics of the immigration consequences of an FTO designation, there have been determinations made in which suspected or known terrorists interested in traveling to the United States have been denied a visa. These benefits that correlate to FTO and EO 13224 designations highlight the importance of the terrorist designations regime. Given how important these benefits are to preserving US national security, should it really take so long to sanction an individual or group as a terrorist? In the author's view, shaped by more than ten years as director of CT/CTFD, the answer is both yes and no. There are very few changes to the process I would recommend making. Taking away someone's assets or their liberty, if there is a material support prosecution, ought to require intense deliberations before a terrorist designation is adopted. *One* change that should be made is dispensing with the Letters of Concurrences (LOCs) provided by the Departments of Justice and Treasury to the Department of State at the end of the interagency FTO review process. The LOCs can delay the FTO process unnecessarily for months, and there is no legal requirement for an LOC to be provided. *Second*, the US government has no established mechanism to prioritize terrorist designations. There is no one authority at the National Security Council (NSC) to prioritize a State Department action over a Treasury action, and the result has been, more often than not, a self-prioritization of Treasury's actions. The NSC, whether during a Democratic or Republican administration, needs to do a better job at racking and stacking priorities. *Third*, there are too few lawyers at the State, Treasury, and Justice Departments reviewing FTO and EO 13224 designation packages. The lawyers

---

[37] Weiner, Rachel and Ellie Silverman. "He Joined the Islamic State, Then Fled. Now, He's Been Sentenced to prison for 20 Years," *The Washington Post*, October 27, 2017. www.washingtonpost.com/local/public-safety/he-joined-the-islamic-state-then-fled-now-he-will-go-to-prison-for-20-years/2017/10/27/9c8a34c2-b813-11e7-9e58-e6288544af98_story.html?noredirect=on&utm_term=.4230c93b9aa1. Accessed May 13, 2018.

who conduct the legal interagency review are oversaturated with terrorist designation packages, and the consequence of this is that often it will be ninety days before the package is picked up and reviewed by any lawyer. *Fourth*, the State Department's authorities to sanction terrorists under its FTO and EO 13224 are outdated. One of my great frustrations as Director of CT/CTFD was that we were severely limited in the kinds of targets we could pursue. Times have shifted since 1997 and 2001, when the FTO and EO 13224 authorities were provided to the Department of State. The State Department should be provided new and explicit authorities to sanction terrorists using social media platforms to propagate terrorist messaging. Today, it is exceedingly difficult for the Department of State to do this, and until Congress or the White House provides the Department of State greater legal or executive authority to pursue terrorist messengers, the US government and international community's ability to counter violent ideology will continue to be unnecessarily hampered. Finally, the State Department's CT/CTFD needs to be empowered to work directly with Silicon Valley and other content providers to remove designated terrorist group's and individual's screeds from their platforms.

On this last point, I will leave you with an image Figure 6.1, that of Hafez Saeed waving to you from the Milli Muslim League's Facebook page. Saeed is an SDGT pursuant to EO 13224, and the Facebook page below is that of the Milli Muslim League (MML), an organization the Department of State designated as an alias under LeT FTO and EO 13224 in April 2018. Yet, as you can see from the following image, MML's most recent post on the Facebook platform was from May 4, 2018, which was accessible at least two weeks after its initial posting. In the future, terrorist designations should play an even more important role in countering terrorist ideology. Taking down terrorist-related content based on terrorist designation determinations is reasonable; especially when you consider the above-noted level of deliberation that surrounds the terrorist designations process. Without social media platforms, terrorist rhetoric will have a more difficult

FIGURE 6.1 Milli Muslim League Facebook Page.

time finding a larger audience. Until that day occurs, the United States and international community will continue to be at a disadvantage when it tries to limit the violent actions, finances, recruitment, and propaganda of groups like ISIS, Jabhat-al Nusrah, and LeT. In late summer of 2018, Facebook finally took the MML's Facebook page down, but despite content removals like MML, the cat-and mouse game of social media content creation and removal between designated terrorists and social media companies will continue.

7 Countering State Sponsors of Terrorism

Terrorism, or acts of violence against civilian targets intended to achieve a political goal, is hardly a novel concept in the present age. The terrorist attack of 9/11 continues to reverberate in both the popular consciousness and American political scene over twenty years since it was gruesomely enacted and left a looming question for nations to answer: how best to counter an entity with no established borders who insists on attacking civilian targets? The United States initially opted to declare a "War on Terror," in response, but as countless scholars have pointed out in the aftermath, waging war on the concept of a human emotion is as vague an idea as it is as hopeless a notion. More delicate tools, like sanctions, would have to be employed.

The first step was to follow the adage: follow the money. Commercial planes do not typically intentionally fly into large buildings without a good deal of prior planning and, more pertinently, funding. The members of al'Qaida who hijacked the airliners had received a good deal of prior training in how to bypass the security checkpoints at the airport, in addition to the necessary flight lessons required to steer the planes in a direction other than a random patch of earth. Similarly, no matter how much their leader, Bin Laden, would boast about the sheer cost efficacy of the action relative to the amount of spending the United States was investing into their security, a small percentage of a very large number is still, on its face, a large number; spending one dollar for every thousand a government puts into defending its borders is still an extraordinary lump sum. In addition, one cannot forget the human element – terrorists are still human and bound by all human limitations, such as a requirement for shelter, food, and water, all of which require an active effort to fulfill on the part of the group. Al'Qaida's solution to the issues of these up-front costs was a common one – find a state sponsor. In the case of al-Qaida, its relationship with the Taliban, and prior to that Sudan, allowed the group to gain the sanctuary it needed to plot contemporary history's deadliest attack – resulting in the deaths of nearly 3,000 Americans.

Simply put, state sponsors of terrorism offer a neat answer to a variety of these problems; a small terrorist organization of 100 people might have difficulty housing and funding that many (as any small organization would), but an established government can provide the liquid capital or infrastructure necessary to house and feed a small number of people quite easily. The question remains, of course, what kind of government would want to fund terrorists to begin with? And, if this is a transactional relationship, what kind of services is the government expecting in this exchange?

The answer is as obvious as it is unfortunate and cynical. Nations such as the United States have established militaries with substantial global reach, a nuclear arsenal, and an overwhelming amount of conventional firepower. Many other western nations can claim one or more similar characteristics – France and Israel might lack the same global reach but possess their own nuclear arsenals and are not hesitant to retaliate in an overwhelming conventional fashion when they are threatened or attacked. Nevertheless, the ability to protect oneself, one's allies, and one's borders hardly precludes developing enmity with rivaling nations, nations who might rightfully recognize that a conventional war with a militarily superior foe is as stupid as it is fruitless. However, there are other avenues to violence than war.

Terrorist organizations offer states an opportunity to target opposing states with violent but deniable action. With no money officially changing hands and no members of their own militaries or state departments found on the books of these organizations, it is easy enough to claim ignorance over a terrorist organization or even denounce it entirely – to do otherwise would entirely defeat the point. Terrorists are the "dagger" in term "cloak and dagger;" they strike without warning, and it is unclear where they came from or who ordered the strike to begin with.

Nations have borders, interests, economies, obligations, and ideologies. Terrorist organizations are considerably more fluid. Owning a warehouse and a bunker in the middle of a desert is a substantially different notion than holding sovereign territory, which can be invaded and/or held. An attack from an established army is an act of war. An attack from an independent organization, housed at an unknown location, with no official ties to any known nation, is a substantially different affair. The War on Terror proved that waging conflict on an emotion is pointless, but even narrowing the scope further to a War on Terrorist Organizations opens a whole host of semantic and legal questions regarding what is or is not a terrorist organization and who is, or is not, funding them.

Nevertheless, confronting terrorist organizations is an affair of difficulty, not of possibility or impossibility. Just because it might be time-consuming or expensive for a state to confront and counter terrorist attacks does not mean that it should not be done. The United States and her allies did not collectively throw up their hands after 9/11 and resign themselves to a future filled with co-opted airliners, but instead took pains to identify and counter the possibility of it happening again. While physically uprooting their own military to take the fight to the terrorists did not ultimately prove effective (one cannot wage a conventional war against unconventional opponents), they did find substantially more success in instead targeting their foes financially; if a state is discovered to have supported terrorists financially, then they would be sanctioned by the largest economy in the world, with other nations urged to follow suit.

The first list of State Sponsors of Terrorism (SST) was released in 1979 by the State Department. During the early days of the SST list, it was a tool that was sparingly used, consisting of rogue nations like Iraq, Libya, Syria, and South Yemen (which dissolved in 1990). Fast forward nearly fifty years, and the SST list remains sparingly used. As of 2024, the list consists of Iran, Cuba, North Korea, and Syria. To be designated a State Sponsoring Terrorism, the Secretary of State must determine that the nation has repeatedly rendered assistance to the terrorist organization(s).[1] They will retain the designation until it is lifted by following statutory criteria; the President of the United States determines that the nation has either not provided any support for terrorists in the past six months and has "provided assurances they will not do so in the future," or there is a sudden and massive change in leadership and policies, no indication that the new leadership is sponsoring terrorists, and they have provided assurances they will not sponsor terrorists in the future.[2] Being placed under the list comes with a bevy of disadvantages, chiefly economic sanctions on the basis that the United States does not want any money (or arms exports) that would come from trade with them ending up within the possession of terrorists. These sanctions would also cause the United States to de facto vote against any International Monetary Fund loans to the target nation.

Less severe than the SST list is the Not Fully Cooperating Countries (NFCC) list, which designates the country as not being fully compliant with US efforts to counter terrorism. The sanctions against these nations are not as punishing as those levied against those on the SST list; however, it is still a fate ideally to be avoided. Present members of this list as of 2024 include North Korea, Syria, Iran, and Venezuela. Cuba was removed in May 2024, after being controversially added in early 2021 by the Trump administration.[3]

---

[1] Office of the Director of National Intelligence, "Counterterrorism guide: Terrorist groups," www.dni.gov/nctc/groups.html#:~:text=To%20designate%20a%20country%20as%20a%20State%20Sponsor,designation%20is%20rescinded%20in%20accordance%20with%20statutory%20criteria.

[2] U.S. Department of State, Bureau of Counterterrorism, *Country Reports on Terrorism*. 2021. www.state.gov/reports/country-reports-on-terrorism-2021/.

[3] This is not a typo, the Trump Administration's (Trump 1) decision to add Cuba to the SST list was technically adopted via the publication of a Federal Register Notice that was published during the early days of the Biden Administration.

The United States' NFCC list has come under fire by critics from both within and without for being used as a political cudgel for the US government, to be employed whenever being opposed by foreign entities to whom they were already negatively predisposed. Critics, including myself, have argued that "much of the international community that reject broad-based unilateral U.S. sanctions will not bend to a unilateral U.S. SST listing," citing that nations such as Russia and even the European Union are coming up with creative ways to maneuver around sanctions that they see little reason for existing.[4] This also produces an unfortunate secondary side effect of muddying the waters for when an NFCC or SST designation is valid, weakening the overall potency of the list, in essence reproducing a national scale, "The Boy Who Cried Wolf" phenomenon. As I've written alongside my coauthor Stephen Tankel, the NFCC list is also employed in a deliberately discriminatory fashion such that it degrades its overall credibility; Pakistan was known to support numerous terrorist organizations during the War in Afghanistan, however, the critical role it played supporting the United States meant that it avoided placement on the NFCC list.[5] "If the NFCC certification were applied more judiciously," we argued, "it could provide a mechanism to taking a more balanced approach to dealing with problematic partners."

In short, the current method of designating a party on a strict binary of "innocent" or "terrorist-sponsoring scumbags" makes the United States look inherently hypocritical as it ignores nations that would otherwise be in the "terrorist-supporter" category for the sake of its own interests, or places nations that would otherwise be considered "innocent" on the list for scoring easy political points for the sake of that presidential administration.

---

[4] Blazakis, Jason M. "Using a Terrorism List to Squeeze Cuba and Venezuela," *Lawfare*, May 31, 2020. www.lawfaremedia.org/article/using-terrorism-list-squeeze-cuba-and-venezuela.

[5] Blazakis, Jason M., & Tankel, Stephen. "The Growing Irrelevance of State's List of Countries Not Cooperating on Counterterrorism," *Just Security*, June 4, 2020. www.justsecurity.org/70529/the-growing-irrelevance-of-of-states-list-of-countries-not-cooperating-on-counterterrorism/.

No better example might be when the Trump Administration considered adding Venezuela to the NFCC list in 2018, which the author criticized.[6] While the Maduro presidency was indeed deeply destructive to its own citizens and was unarguably a narco state, the author argued that Russia and Saudi Arabia deserved the designation far more, and placing Venezuela on the list would be done for purely political reasons – a desperate attempt by an outside entity to force change on a corrupt regime. Unfortunately, as terrible as the Maduro presidency might have been for its own citizens, its myriad crimes did not include sponsoring terrorists and only raised the question for our allies of why this nation was being singled out when Russia had attempted to assassinate Sergei Skirpal in London less than a year before, in 2017. Like Russia, North Korea has used assassinations to threaten its enemies. Unlike Russia, however, North Korea's Kim Jong Un's decision to kill his half-brother at the Kuala Lumpur International Airport in Malaysia with VX nerve agent resulted in North Korea's relisting as an SST by the first Trump Administration in 2017.[7] The juxtaposition between Russia's absence from the SST list and North Korea's addition underscores the inconsistent application of the underlying laws that govern SST determinations.

This questionable discretion for the designation of problematic actors can also extend to the Foreign Terrorist Organization list, the core focus of Chapter 6. While it is undebatable that the organizations on the FTO list have earned their place, as Jamshidi points out in their paper "The World of Private Terrorism Legislation," sixty-six of the total eighty-six organizations added to the list since its formation in 1997 have been Arab or Muslim, resulting in a disproportionate number of suits filed and violence committed against Arab and

---

[6] Blazakis, Jason M. "Labeling Venezuela a Terror-Supporting State Doesn't Fit," *The Hill*, December 3, 2018. https://thehill.com/opinion/international/418984-labeling-venezuela-a-terror-supporting-state-doesnt-fit/.

[7] Shear, Michael D., & Sanger, David E. "Trump Returns North Korea to List of State Sponsors of Terrorism," *The New York Times*, November 20, 2017. www.nytimes.com/2017/11/20/us/politics/north-korea-trump-terror.html.

Muslim communities and a reinforcement of the notion that these peoples are predisposed toward terrorism.[8]

The seeming flippancy at which nations or organizations are added to these lists has not gone unnoticed abroad – following the withdrawal of the United States from the Joint Comprehensive Plan of Action, Iranian Foreign Minister Mohammed Javad Zarif decried the US's approach to terrorism designations as a game, complaining:

> In 1984, the United States removed Saddam Hussein from its terrorism list and put Iran on it's the (sic) terrorism list. Again, in the 1990s, Saddam was again on the terrorism list in 1998 the United States put (the) MEK on the terrorism list, in 2012 they took them off the terrorism list. This is a game. This game needs to stop.[9]

While being designated by the US as an FTO, SST, or NFCC is a fate to be avoided, the apparent looseness of criteria has reduced how seriously nations abroad treat these designations. Instead of refusing to partner with these nations because the US has claimed they are supporting terrorists, they now seek legal loopholes to work around in order to maintain existing trade partnerships, because the United States has been enforcing these punitive lists very selectively, and "has angered the current presidential administration (and is convenient to target)" does not force the same reaction from even allied nations if the lists were applied more judiciously. The original SST list was intended to be used as a means of export control and combating terrorism globally. Instead, it is increasingly being used as a tool to penalize nations regardless of their compliance.

---

[8] Jamshidi, Maryam. "The World of Private Terrorism Litigation," *Michigan Journal of Race & Law*, 2022: University of Florida Levin College of Law Research Paper No. 22-25, https://papers.ssrn.com/sol3/papers.cfm?abstract_id=4138659.

[9] Sanford, Melissa. "'This Is a Game': A History of the Foreign Terrorist Organization and State Sponsors of Terrorism Lists and Their Applications," *History in the Making* 13 (2020): Article 10. https://web.archive.org/web/20220619225117/https:/scholarworks.lib.csusb.edu/cgi/viewcontent.cgi?article=1140&context=history-in-the-making.

As a silver lining, it is possible for the United States to lift these designations in accordance with their stated guidelines, and one need not look even that far back in history to do so. The Colombian-based FARC was removed from the FTO list by Secretary of State Anthony Blinken in 2021, after languishing on the list since its initial release in 1997.[10] While one of its successors, FARC-EP, was simultaneously added to the list, the main group was acknowledged for having laid down their arms and attempted to peacefully integrate into the Colombian government. This helps reinforce the (hopefully true) notion that these lists are intended as a means of reducing terrorist activity globally rather than as a strictly punitive measure to be levied at the slightest sign of disagreement with the United States.

However, the removal of the FARC from the FTO list is a less politically loaded maneuver than the recission of a country's listing as an SST. SST additions and subtractions should occur more frequently if the list is to be seen as credible. Simply put, removing nations from the lists who provably have been working to avoid funding terrorists helps reinforce that they are intended as an incentive to produce better behavior, and not simply being wielded a punitive political tool.

However, the United States has one additional major element to their counterterrorism approach that strains their international credibility. While national sovereignty is typically a given for international law, the United States has seen fit to uniquely include a loophole to allow victims of terrorism to engage in lawsuits against state sponsors of terrorism who might have been responsible, directly or indirectly, for harming them or their family members. Canada has seen fit to follow suit in this legal peculiarity, but this has done little to stymie claims from nations such as Iran that these nations are breaching customary international law.

---

[10] Blazakis, Jason M. "U.S. Has Taken FARC Off Its Terrorist List, Giving Insight into Biden's Foreign Policy," *The Conversation*, January 26, 2022. https://theconversation.com/us-has-taken-farc-off-its-terrorist-list-giving-insight-into-bidens-foreign-policy-174667.

Canada and the United States possess a unique approach to their counterterrorism efforts by ignoring what is considered international customary law; both nations ignore state sovereignty to prosecute sponsors of terrorism. The United States amended their own Foreign Sovereignty Immunity Act (FSIA) in 1996 to include a terrorism exception through the Justice Against Sponsors of Terrorism Act (JASTA). The original iteration only targeted nations designated as SSTs by the government already, but it was subsequently amended in 2016 to include even nations not presently designated as SSTs, generating substantial global criticism.[11]

Canada's own Justice for Victims of Terrorism Act (JVTA) presently retains the restriction of only allowing citizens to pursue lawsuits against states that have been listed as sponsoring terror; however, even this more limited approach has attracted criticism. As of late 2024, only two nations have been placed on the list, Syria and Iran, both added in 2012 at the list's formation. Only the US and Canada possess the sovereignty exception to terrorism, both of which have experienced a great deal of pushback abroad due to its supposed violation of international customary law.

Iran would ultimately bring a case against Canada on June 2023 within the International Court of Justice both to dispute its own designation as a state sponsor of terrorism and to officially designate Canada's JVTA as a violation of international law. While Canada is the official target of Iran's case, it is likely that Iran is going after the United States by extension since it is the only other nation with this terrorism exception, and they are trying to force an official stance by the International Court of Justice on whether these terrorism exceptions are violations of customary international law.[12] These laws were intended to permit private citizens of these

---

[11] Dodge, William S. "Does JASTA Violate International Law?" *Just Security*, September 30, 2016. www.justsecurity.org/33325/jasta-violate-international-law-2/.

[12] M. Jamshidi, "Iran's ICJ case against Canada tests the terrorism exception to sovereign immunity," *Just Security*, July 24, 2023. www.justsecurity.org/87357/irans-icj-case-against-canada-tests-the-terrorism-exception-to-sovereign-immunity/.

nations to seek reparation for damages inflicted by terrorists funded by the nations who sponsored them; however, the occasional irreverence of the United States in their designations of these nations, as well as the 2016 amendment to JASTA, has made the opposition to these acts quite credible due to the sheer breadth of potential legal actions. Canada might be the official target in the legal dispute, but it is clear that they are tired of being targeted by the US and are seeking a "softer" opponent in Canada in the international stage.

Whether JASTA and the JVTA violate customary international law may not be as important as determining if they are bad policy or not. While it is true that no other nations possess this terrorist exemption, it is also true that it was not until the 2016 amendment to JASTA that the laws saw significant pushback and promises of reciprocation from opposing nations.[13] UC Davis law professor William Dodge explained that while JASTA may not be in clear violation of international law, it is also not good policy, as it alienates key allies while doing nothing to help victims from attacks such as 9/11. Dodge further explained that then President Obama, who in 2016 had attempted to veto the amendment to the law before being overridden, had also stated that the underlying law did not benefit the victims of 9/11.[14] In matters of both legality and efficacy, JASTA and JVTA are on shaky footing and point toward the overall unfavourability of using tools intended for counterterrorism as political bludgeons.

In both instances of the SST/NFCC lists and the JASTA/JVTA, we see tools created by nations intending to curtail sponsors of terrorism through economic and legal pressure being turned into political cudgels with which to bash at their foes ineffectually. The prior addition of nations such as Cuba or Venezuela drew criticism from

---

[13] Dodge, William S. "Does JASTA Violate International Law?" *Just Security*, September 30, 2016. www.justsecurity.org/33325/jasta-violate-international-law-2/.

[14] The White House, Office of the Press Secretary, "Veto Message from the President – S.2040," September 23, 2016. https://obamawhitehouse.archives.gov/the-press-office/2016/09/23/veto-message-president-s2040.

within and without, and while Canada has seen fit to follow the US's suit in allowing private citizens to initiate lawsuits against state sponsors of terrorism, the rest of the international community is not quite so keen. Iran correctly saw Canada's implementation of JVTA as a weakness through which the difficult-to-target United States might be attacked on the international stage; they saw Canada's siding with the United States in this instance as an irregularity to be attacked rather than a new status quo. In leveraging and unevenly applying legal tools against nation-states, the United States is not measurably countering terrorism.

Does it really matter whether or not countries have domestic legal tools to sanction entire countries as state sponsors of terrorism like the United States and Canada. As terrorism expert Daniel Byman has written extensively on the topic, countering state sponsors of terrorism is extremely difficult. Byman lays out several reasons for why this is the case in his book, Deadly Connections. Among the most important reasons, according to Byman:

1. States that use terrorism as a political tool are often resigned to the fact that there will be consequences for their sponsorship. A state's willingness to weather criticism makes countering a state's support more difficult.
2. A country that is willing to use proxies to carry out violent activity is an act of desperation, while the state being targeted is unlikely to face an existential threat by the terrorist act. Byman calls this an imbalance of stakes, which leads to a dwindled likelihood of stern action being directed toward the state sponsor.
3. Because state sponsors perceive that terrorism is generally the only avenue for affecting change and advancing policy interests, countering an internalized perception is almost impossible.
4. Some state sponsors of terrorism, such as Iran, are ideologically driven. States like Iran are difficult to coerce because they are not necessarily driven by issues, such as economic growth for instance, that tend to drive decision-making in most states.
5. Another limitation, according to Byman, is the too narrow scope in which states define sponsorship of terrorism. Byman believes that

countries only consider the active or operational context in which countries support terrorism, while ignoring the most important aspects of support a state can provide to a terrorist group. For instance, the passive support that is provided in the form of sanctuary is often overlooked, according to Byman.[15]

Byman's points are critically important and square with this author's direct experience of adding and taking countries off the US Department of State's State Sponsor of Terrorism List between 2008 and 2018. In that time period, North Korea was removed from the SST list in 2008 and then readded in 2017. North Korea, simply put, never modified their behavior because of unilateral decision-making by the United States. This underscores that unilateral sanctions, without the support of allies and more broadly the international community, often lack clear results. As such, multilateral approaches have become increasingly important, especially as a feature of countering terrorist financing.

---

[15] Byman, Daniel. *Deadly Connections: States That Sponsor Terrorism.* Cambridge University Press, 2005. Pages 259–273.

8 Multilateral Approaches to Countering Terrorist Access to Finance

A Look at the Roles Played by the Financial Action Task Force and the United Nations

In Chapter 5, we examined the importance the Financial Action Task Force (FATF) places on the use of intelligence to counter terrorist financers and money launderers. In this chapter, we will take a broader look at the various ways FATF counters terrorist financing. Founded in 1989, FATF is an intergovernmental body that consists of nearly forty countries and regional bodies. Upon its founding by the Group of Seven (G-7) countries, FATF initially focused its energies on countering criminal groups by going after their money laundering operations. To combat criminal financing, FATF created standards for countries to follow in their battle against illicit finance. These standards were first codified in 1990 when FATF published its first set of forty recommendations, which would serve as the starting point for countries to follow as they try to disrupt organized crime flows of finance. Following the events of 9/11, FATF would expand significantly its work to counter terrorist access to financing by adopting in October 2001 eight special recommendations. In the years that would follow, FATF would continue to tinker with the various recommendations guiding work to counter money laundering and terrorist financing.

In 2012, FATF would revise its recommendations again by integrating all of its money laundering and terrorist financing recommendations into one set of forty recommendations. At the same time, FATF would also include new provisions to incorporate proliferating financing related to the development of Weapons of Mass Destruction into its work line.

Nearly all of the forty FATF recommendations are important for countering terrorist access to finance. For instance, Recommendations 1 and 2 focus on broad AML/CFT policies that countries should adopt to improve their understanding of the risks they face from terrorist financiers and money launderers and the importance of interagency coordination. While Recommendations 3 and 4 focus on money laundering and the importance of confiscation of assets, terrorist financiers, like their criminal financiers' brethren still have on occasion the need to 'clean' the proceeds of their ill-gotten gains. Among the buckets of FATF Recommendations that may be most relevant to countering terrorist financing are Recommendations 5, 6, and 8. Recommendation 5 encourages countries to criminalize the financing of terrorism. In other words, countries that do not have the underlying legal modalities to prosecute those who finance terrorism would become subject to scrutiny, as will be discussed in more detail later in this chapter, by the FATF. Recommendation 6 focuses on the need for countries to designate terrorists in compliance with relevant UN Security Council Resolutions. In the case of countering terrorist financing, as will be discussed in the UN subsection of this chapter, UNSCRs 1267 and 1373 are most relevant to the countering of terrorist financing. As described earlier in this book, terrorist groups like al-Qa'ida have exploited nonprofit organizations (NPOs) to finance their misdeeds. As a consequence, Recommendation 8 calls on countries to protect NPOs from terrorist financing abuse.

In FATF recommendations 9–23, a range of preventative tactics are highlighted for countries to adopt as a means of encouraging the private sector to enlist in the battle against terrorist financing. For instance, Recommendations 10 and 11 encourage financial institutions to carry out customer due diligence and keep detailed records to ensure that they are not facilitating illicit criminal activity, such as terrorist financing. Further, Recommendations 20 and 21 highlight the need for financial institutions to file with regulatory authorities suspicious transactions that may be indicative of terrorist financing or money laundering. The role of the private sector is pivotal in recommendations 9–23, among the most important are those that focus on the responsibilities of designated nonfinancial businesses and professions (DNFBPs) in countering illicit finance. For example, Recommendation 22 explains that casinos, real estate agents, dealers of precious metals and gemstones, as well as lawyers, notaries, trust companies, and accountants have the same responsibility as financial institutions in understanding who their customers are and how they have derived their wealth. Recommendation 23 also encourages DNFBPs, like financial institutions, to file suspicious transaction reports. The role of the private sector in facilitating terrorist financing, as well as their role in combatting it, will be the focus of Chapter 9.

FATF Recommendations 26–35 examine the importance of empowering regulatory and other competent authorities, such as law enforcement and customs agencies, to battle against terrorist financing and money laundering. For example, Recommendation 32 highlights the importance of countries adopting provisions in law to detect physical cross-border[1] transportation of currency and bearer negotiable instruments. This recommendation also calls on countries to create declaration systems for those moving currency across borders. This recommendation is especially important at ports of entry, such as at airports, where cash couriers may be moving hard cash to facilitate terrorist operations. As such, customs and border patrol officials play a leading role in countering the movement of cash by terrorist groups.

Finally, FATF Recommendations 36–40 focus on the importance of international cooperation in countering terrorist financing and money laundering. In designing these recommendations, FATF shines the light on the importance of tackling terrorist financing through cooperation. Groups like al-Qa'ida and ISIS cross borders to raise finance and conduct operations, and as a consequence, bilateral and multilateral approaches to tackling terrorist financing are

---

[1] FATF, "International standards on combating money laundering and the financing of terrorism & proliferation," 2012–2025, *Financial Action Task Force*. www.fatf-gafi.org/en/publications/Fatfrecommendations/Fatf-recommendations.html.

critical. For example, Recommendation 36 points to several international instruments that countries should implement domestically, such as the United Nations Convention for the Suppression of the Financing of Terrorism. Like Recommendation 36, Recommendation 37 encourages cooperation between countries by highlighting the importance of mutual legal assistance. In this recommendation, FATF explains that countries should, "rapidly, constructively and effectively provide the widest possible range of mutual legal assistance in relation to ... terrorist financing investigations, prosecutions, and related proceedings." Recommendation 37 also zones in on the importance of sharing information that can be used in court to prosecute money launderers and terrorist financers. Recommendation 38 is closely linked to recommendation 37 because it emphasizes that mutual legal assistance agreements should also take into account the freezing and confiscation of assets identified by foreign countries. Hitting terrorist financiers and money launderers by taking their ill-gotten gains is among the most important ways governments can deter terrorist financing and money laundering.

FATF does not have an enforcement mechanism in the traditional sense. It does not have law enforcement officials on the prowl issuing fines or jail time for government officials who are not following the guidelines issued by FATF. However, governments, for the most part, try to comply with FATF Recommendations. The FATF also has a range of mechanisms in place to help countries meet their recommendations. For example, FATF has working groups that member countries' personnel can participate in during FATF meetings – generally convened three times a year. One working group is the Risk, Trends, and Methods Working Group (RTMG). RTMG analyzes money laundering and terrorism financing methods that are trending globally. RTMG is essential in developing long-form products, like reports and typologies that dive into the details of how terrorist groups are financing their misdeeds. RTMG played, for instance, a vital role in the development of FATF's 2015 report on ISIS's financing. That report, and others like it, help governments and private sector entities, like banks, understand the latest trends in terrorist financing. Another FATF group is the Policy Development Group (PDG). The PDG plays a critical role in examining the FATF Recommendations and makes updates to them as needed. In particular, the PDG provides governments with guidance on how to most effectively implement the recommendations so they can reach compliance with FATF standards. One way the PDG can do this is by issuing guidance or statements on developing technologies, like virtual assets, that can be abused by terrorists – the subject of Chapter 10. For example, the PDG issued updated guidance on risk-based approaches governments should take in working with virtual asset service providers. In 2021, the PDG guidance, among other things, provided instructions on how FATF Recommendations could be applied to stablecoins.[2] The PDG also provided guidance on the risks and tools available to countries to address the risk of terrorist financing for peer-to-peer transactions involving virtual assets. The PDG's work is especially important as cryptocurrency becomes more ubiquitous.

Another critical FATF working group is the Evaluations and Compliance Group (ECG). The ECG plays an important role in evaluating the peer review reports that are key to whether countries are implementing FATF recommendations to combat money laundering and terrorist financing. These reports are known as Mutual Evaluation Reports (MERs). MERs are written by counterterrorism financing and antimoney laundering experts from FATF, or FATF style regional bodies (FSRBs) member states. These experts are assessing whether countries are compliant with the forty recommendations. If a country is deemed to be noncompliant or partially compliant with twenty or more recommendations or has low compliance on some combination of fewer, but core FATF recommendations, such as Recommendation 6 on compliance with UN Resolutions on terrorism sanctions, it can

---

[2] A stablecoin is a type of cryptocurrency that is pegged to a reference asset, such as fiat currency. This way it retains a stable price and does not experience the sudden fluctuation in value as you may see with other forms of cryptocurrency, such as Bitcoin.

be sent to a special review process where the country may become the focal point of another FATF subgroup known as the International Cooperation Review Group (ICRG). MERs are core to understanding how countries' regulatory, enforcement, and private sector system is designed to counter terrorist financing. Countries that are noncompliant or partially compliant on relevant terrorist financing-related recommendations are at higher risk of being exploited by terrorist financers.

FATF's ICRG will push countries to what the public calls the 'grey' or 'black' lists if countries are not complying with a sufficient number of FATF recommendations. When a country receives poor ratings in its MER, the country does receive some time to resolve the issues cited before being slapped onto the 'grey' list. Generally, follow-on reports are drafted to assess the progress made since the original MER. If the follow-on reports show no or slow progress, the country is likely to be added to the grey list. Decisions to add countries to the grey or blacklist are made cautiously because the impact of such a decision will have possible negative effects on the economy, potentially leading internationally-based businesses to derisk (leave) from the financial, commercial, and economic sectors of that country. In other words, being on the grey list has consequences, and while the FATF does not have a police force to assure countries are abiding by recommendations, addition to the grey list acts as a strong enforcement mechanism. As of late January 2025, there are twenty-four countries on the FATF grey list. These countries are under increased monitoring by FATF, but they also are, according to FATF, "actively working with the FATF to address strategic deficiencies in their regimes to counter money laundering, terrorist financing, and proliferation financing."[3] Being on the grey list means that governments are typically deficient in their laws or how they operationalize their laws to counter terrorist financing. For the most part, countries on this list lack the capacity to address the underlying challenges identified in the MER. Examples of

---

[3] Financial Action Task Force (FATF). "Countries under FATF's Black and Grey Lists," *Financial Action Task Force*, January 25, 2025. www.fatf-gafi.org/en/countries/black-and-grey-lists.html.

countries on the grey list include Haiti, South Sudan, Nigeria, Mali, Mozambique, and many other countries in Africa. These countries do not have the infrastructure to combat terrorism, including terrorist financing, in a meaningful way. Some, like Haiti and South Sudan, are not functioning states and are unable to devote government resources to countering money laundering or terrorist financing when they are unable to provide even the most basic of government services.

While lack of capacity and insufficient laws are a recipe for a country's addition to the grey list, additions to the FATF blacklist are more likely based on a country's antipathy toward the international community of states and FATF's role as a global watchdog that highlights gaps in a country's architecture to fight against terrorist financing and money laundering. In FATF's parlance, there are three countries, as of late January 2025, that are high-risk jurisdictions that are subject to a call of action. The countries on FATF's blacklist are: North Korea, Iran, and Myanmar. By being added to the blacklist, FATF is calling on countries to take active countermeasures against these states. This stands in deep contrast to the grey list countries that are actively working within FATF constructs to resolve their terrorist financing deficiencies. FATF's October 2024 statement detailing why North Korea, Iran, and Myanmar are on the blacklist paints a picture of recalcitrance. The three countries on the blacklist are working actively against FATF recommendations – in the case of North Korea, for instance, is on the blacklist because of its active development of a WMD program, and thus violating UN resolutions, and thus FATF recommendations related to proliferation financing. The FATF call against North Korea is stark, noting that North Korea has continued to fail to address significant deficiencies in combatting the financing of terrorism.[4] The October 2024 FATF statement calls on countries to also block North Korea from

---

[4] Financial Action Task Force. "Call for Action: High-Risk and Other Monitored Jurisdictions," *Financial Action Task Force*, October 2024. www.fatf-gafi.org/en/publications/High-risk-and-other-monitored-jurisdictions/Call-for-action-october-2024.html.

using their financial system by terminating correspondent banking relationships with North Korean banks, closing subsidiaries of North Korean banks in their countries, and to limit business relationships and financial transactions with any North Korean citizen.[5] These are among the countermeasures FATF wants governments to impose on North Korea so its access to the international financial system is constrained.

That Iran is on the FATF blacklist should be no surprise given its long history of supporting designated terrorist groups like Hizballah. FATF's concern regarding Iran's ineffectiveness in countering terrorist financing is not new. In 2016, for example, FATF detailed the deficiencies it needed to remedy in order to be in good standing with its countering the financing of terrorism responsibilities. Time and again, FATF detailed inaction on the government of Iran's part. In October 2024, FATF again underscored significant issues in Iran's compliance with multiple recommendations, including the need to criminalize terrorist financing; identifying and freezing terrorist assets consistent with UN Security Council Resolutions; the need to ratify the UN Terrorist Financing Convention, among many other issues.[6] Iran, like North Korea, is a pariah state when it comes to countering terrorist financing and as a consequence, economic investment in Iran (and North Korea for that matter) is far less than it could be if the country made any effort in tackling terrorist financiers.

Countries that are added to FATF's list, unless they are actively working to support terrorist, WMD, or criminal financing that is out of tune with the global community, are not left without assistance. While FATF as an international body may seem exclusive with fewer than forty nation-states that comprise the group, it is, in fact, very inclusive. For example, FATF style regional bodies (FSRBs) dot the globe. FSRBs are part of the broader FATF global network. The Asia

---

[5] Ibid.
[6] Ibid.

Pacific Group on Money Laundering (APG), Caribbean Financial Action Task Force (CFATF), Eurasian Group (EAG), Eastern and Southern Africa Anti-Money Laundering Group (ESAAMLG), Action Group Against Money Laundering in Central Africa (GABAC), Financial Action Task Force of Latin America (GAFILAT), Inter Governmental Action Group against Money Laundering in West Africa (GIABA), Middle East and North Africa Financial Action Task Force (MENAFATF), and the Committee of Experts on the Evaluation of Anti-Money Laundering Measures (MONEYVAL) play critical roles as FSRBs. Among these nine FSRBs, nearly every country in the world has representation. The FSRBs are instrumental in identifying experts to conduct MERs. Further, where there are deficiencies that are identified, FSRBs often will devote staff time, training, and funding to improve the capabilities of member states that are not compliant with FATF recommendations. Simply put, FATF and FSRBs, do not adopt a sink-or-swim approach, and for the most part every effort is made to depoliticize the activities of the FATF.[7] FSRBs are also critically important because countries in regions often share similar threats – to include the specific types of novel methods terrorist groups may engage in with respect to financing their activities. Countries regionally sharing typologies and terrorist financing tradecraft during FSRB meetings and in other engagements is important for developing strategies, laws, and tactics to counter the sources of terrorist financing. FSRBs provide such a platform.

The wealthy countries that populate the main FATF group also do their part to build the capacity of countries that are not achieving compliance with FATF recommendations. For example, the United States, which plays a key role within FATF, routinely announces

---

[7] There are some exceptions. For instance, FATF suspended Russia's membership in FATF in 2023 due to Russia's illegal invasion of Ukraine. In explaining FATF's decision, a February 2023 statement noted that the "Russian Federation's actions unacceptably run counter to the FATF core principles aiming to promote security, safety and the integrity of the global financial system." www.fatf-gafi.org/en/publications/Fatfgeneral/fatf-statement-russian-federation.html.

notice of funding opportunities (NOFO) to build the capacity of countries that are in need of technical assistance. On July 22, 2022, the United States Department of State's Counterterrorism Bureau published a notice seeking "applications to strengthen the Federal Republic of Nigeria's capacity to successfully implement its anti-money laundering and countering the financing of terrorism (AML/CFT) regime, with a particular focus on meeting international standards set by the FATF."[8] The State Department NOFO sought to fund the implementer to the tune of nearly $3 million. Nigeria was at the time of the NOFO's publication on FATF's grey list because of several deficiencies, among them less than stellar compliance with FATF Recommendation 6. The State Department's Counterterrorism Bureau is among the most important funders in building the capacity and its 2022 NOFO on Nigeria was awarded to the Global Center on Cooperative Security, a NPO.[9] Governments, not just the United States, often fund NPOs to work directly with governments to remedy FATF recommendation-related shortfalls. US interest in providing capacity-building assistance to help Nigeria get off of the grey list is logical given that several terrorist groups, such as Boko Haram and ISIS-West Africa, operate in the country and the surrounding region. If Nigeria remains incapable of implementing FATF standards to protect it from terrorist financing abuse, the country would be at a disadvantage in countering both Boko Haram and ISIS's province in West Africa.

The FATF, FSRBs, and its member states play key roles in countering terrorist financing. Inherently, FATF is designed to promote collaboration as part of an effort to counter the financing of terrorism. Indeed, several of its underlying recommendations tout the importance of global multilateral efforts to combat terrorist financers. FATF's emphasis on key UN initiatives is among the most

---

[8] U.S. Department of State. "AML/CFT Capacity Building in the Federal Republic of Nigeria." Winter 2022.

[9] Global Center on Cooperative Security. June 28, 2022. https://x.com/GlobalCtr/status/1541758566440255496.

important aspects of FATF's work. Simply put, because the financial system is global, it takes a global coalition to defeat terrorist financing.

THE UNITED NATIONS

The United Nations has more than a fifty-year history of trying to reach an agreement on defining the term terrorism. In the wake of extreme forms of terrorism perpetrated by groups like Black September, a group tightly connected to Yasir Arafat's Palestinian Liberation Organization (PLO). Black September triggered the countries of the west, such as the United States, to push for defining terrorism and to commit UN member states to counter a broad range of transnational actors who threatened nation-state stability. The United States was met with firm opposition from a block of countries that were former colonial subjects that pushed, sometimes violently, against what was viewed in their eyes as western-sanctioned oppression. One block of more than fifty countries in particular, through the auspices of the Organization of the Islamic Conference (OIC), was critical to stopping UN efforts to define terrorism. The OIC wanted to preserve violence as a recourse for Palestinians that were seen as being subject to colonial rule by the relatively newly minted Government of Israel. The OIC, simply put, did not want the Palestinian groups, such as the PLO, to bend to the will of Israel. The OIC wanted a Palestinian state and if the UN defined terrorism, it could then define the PLO as terrorists – decreasing the chances of eventual statehood for the Palestinian people.

While the Israel–Palestinian conflict continues and the UN still has not yet defined terrorism, the UN has nonetheless both substantive resolutions and structures aimed at fighting against terrorism. As part of the multilateral effort to combat terrorism, the UN has devoted significant energy to fighting against the financing of terrorism. In this portion of the chapter, we will examine the key resolutions and structures that guide the UN's work in countering terrorism financing.

THE UN 1267 SANCTIONS COMMITTEE

Since its inception in 1999, the UN Security Council's 1267 sanctions regime has been a vital component of the multilateral community's effort to combat terror finance, prohibit terrorist travel, and deny arms to listed individuals and entities. The 1267 Sanctions Regime is based on a Security Council Resolution (UNSCR) that was adopted unanimously by the Security Council on October 15, 1999.[10] When the regime was created now more than twenty-five years ago, the 1267 Committee began to symbolize the international community's shared commitment to combating al-Qa'ida and the Taliban. The 1267 Committee was, and remains to be, the primary way for governments to globalize their own domestic terrorist sanctions. Because of this, and the implications of a UN 1267 listing, the 1267 Committee is generally viewed as the most useful multilateral counterterrorism financing tool because it creates avenues for countries to work with one another as they try to fulfill their UN obligations to deter threats posed by listed persons or entities. The FATF, as discussed earlier in the chapter, sees it the same way, and as a consequence, it enshrines the UN terrorist financing sanction regime in its sixth recommendation.

The foundation for which the UN 1267 sanctions regime stands is a process for UN member states to propose individuals and organizations for listing as terrorists. The UN 1267 sanctions regime must be reviewed and renewed by the UN Security Council every eighteen months. Generally, upon completion of this eighteen-month review, a new Security Council resolution is adopted that amends aspects of the UN 1267 regime's work. As such, while Security Council Resolution numbers can be associated with the UN 1267 regime, experts in the field and diplomats will still refer to the work of this sanctions committee by its original name – the UN 1267 Sanctions Committee. For example, the Security Council rolled over

---

[10] United Nations. "Security Council Meeting Record S/PV.4051," October 15, 1999. https://docs.un.org/en/S/PV.4051.

the work of the UN 1267 Sanctions Committee by adopting Security Council Resolution 2734 on June 10, 2024. The basic mechanics of listing individuals and organizations did not change with the adoption of Security Council Resolution 2734, nor that of its predecessors. However, several of the successor resolutions to 1267 would introduce reforms and calls to action. For example, UNSCR 2734 emphasized that the "Committee's designation criteria, further recognizing ISIL, AQ, and associated individuals, groups, and entities' use of sexual and gender-based violence, including when associated to trafficking in persons ... is a tactic of terrorism an instrument to increase their finances."[11] UNSCR 2734 represented the first time the UN Security Council called on countries to explicitly consider countries to designate as terrorists individuals who sexualize their victims. The Security Council has made several technical, legal, and operational reforms since UNSCR 1267 was adopted in 1999. Many of these changes would be critical for allowing for continued sanctions against terrorists linked to al-Qa'ida, and later, ISIS.

Despite the UN 1267 sanctions regime being a critical feature in the global community's arsenal in tackling terrorist financing, it is important to note that the work of the UN has been criticized for a perceived lack of due process for listed persons. In the early days of the UN 1267 sanctions regime, those listed as terrorists had virtually no ability to challenge the basis of their listing. This lack of transparency and due process was frequently viewed by many countries and the human rights community as a problem. Due to these concerns, some of which were driven by legal challenges in Europe, European member states put in a great amount of work within the UN Security Council to address transparency-related criticisms. For example, in June 2008, the UN passed Security Council resolution 1822, which incorporated reforms such as requiring the release of public reasons for listings and mandating a review of all listings on

---

[11] United Nations. "Resolution 2734 (2024) Adopted by the Security Council at Its 9649th Meeting," June 10, 2024. https://docs.un.org/en/S/RES/2734(2024).

a triennial basis. In December 2009, the Security Council resolution 1904 created, among other things, the Office of the Ombudsperson to provide greater access to individuals seeking delisting from the UN 1267 regime. Canadian Judge Kimberly Prost was selected as the Ombudsperson in June 2010. Shortly thereafter, she began to carry out a number of reviews of listed individuals who petitioned for removal from the UN 1267 list. Over time, the Ombudsperson's reviews would, in the majority of the cases, result in individuals' or entities' removal from the 1267 list. For many concerned about human right and due process, these two resolutions were seen as critical improvements to the UN 1267 terrorism listing process.

For others, UNSCRs 1822 and 1904 would prove instrumental in ensuring the solvency of the UN 1267 Sanctions Regime. If not for these changes, the regime may have folded. The 1267 regime once faced a direct confrontation by the European Union ("EU") courts, and the basis for UNSC sanctions listings was put into question.

The EU's General Court (a subordinate court to the European Court of Justice) issued a ruling in September 2010 annulling for the second time an EU regulation imposing an asset freeze on Yassin Kadi[12] pursuant to the 1267 regime. The Court found that Kadi's due process rights were violated because the relevant European Commission regulation did not ensure him access to the evidence supporting his listing so that he could mount an effective challenge and have effective judicial protection. The Court did not challenge the principle that UN member states have a binding obligation under international law to comply with decisions of the Security Council, but nevertheless effectively said that EU institutions had to adhere foremost to rights, principles, and procedures "fundamental" to the European system. The General Court's decision in Kadi went to appeal at the European Court of Justice ("ECJ"). Ultimately the EU

---

[12] Yassin Kadi was a citizen of Saudi Arabia and sanctioned by the United States and the United Nations due to his alleged links to Usama bin Laden. Not only would the EU litigation serve as an impetus for Kadi's removal from the UN 1267 list but he would also be later removed from the US government's own terrorist designation list.

courts in 2008 annulled an earlier version of the EU regulation, and Kadi ended up winning in his court case in Europe

The result of Kadi court cases and the looming noncompliance of EU member states with their UNSC obligations created a fundamental threat to the authority of the Security Council. The United States was reticent to create avenues of reform to the work of the UN 1267 Sanctions Committee but in the end acceded to Resolutions 1822 and 1904 because the alternative, EU member states' noncompliance would thus present a basic threat to the US government's ability to continue to use the Security Council to promote US foreign policy goals. No other country nominates as many individuals and organizations for listing as terrorists as the United States, and in order to continue that work, the United States had to accept due process and human rights reforms.

Due process and human rights calibrations by UN 1267 Sanctions Committee were not the only modifications instituted during the history of the committee's work. In July 2011, the UN Security Council adopted Security Resolution 1988, which separated the Taliban and Qa'ida names by forming two separate committees. The 1988 Committee, which still exists as of January 2025, at the UN would focus on Taliban-related sanctions, while al-Qa'ida and associated individuals and entities would be governed by Security Council Resolution 1989 (also adopted in July 2011). Four years later, in 2015, the al-Qa'ida Sanctions committee would be renamed the ISIL and al-Qa'ida Sanctions Committee when the Security Council rolled over the work of the 1267 Sanctions Committee. UN 1267 and the ISIL and al-Qa'ida Sanctions Committee are terms that can be used interchangeably. The 2015 change was the most important, until the inclusion of gender and sexualized violence as a designation criterion in 2024, a modification made by the UN Security Council to the work of the UN 1267 Sanctions Committee. The UN change would be critical in highlighting the need for the global community to combat the rise of ISIS and its financing. In the years that would follow, the UN, chiefly led by proposals made by the United States, would add every meaningful ISIS province, with few exceptions. For example, as discussed in Chapter 6, ISIS's Caucasus Province was nominated for listing by the United States, but Russia, a permanent member of the UN Security Council, wielded its veto power to block the US proposal. Politics was at play with Russia's maneuver because Vladimir Putin did not want to accept the notion that ISIS was making inroads – to do so would risk Putin's strongman reputation as a terrorist-busting leader.

Politics is certainly more at play at the UN 1267 Sanctions Committee than it is at FATF, but for the most part the work of the committee is apolitical, at least until 2022 with the Russian illegal invasion of Ukraine. Since 2022, there has been only a trickle of new UN 1267-related terrorism listings. Nonetheless, the tool remains an important multilateral tool to FATF and the UN Security Council because hundreds of terrorists groups and individuals remain sanctioned. As such, implementation of the UN Sanctions Committee's decisions is critical in the fight against terrorist financing.

The UN Sanctions Committee list serves for many countries as the de facto list of banned terrorists nationally, and without it there would be little or no effort – or legal authority – to prohibit bad actors from engaging in terrorist activities within their borders. There are three very important legal implications associated with a UN terrorist designation. Once an individual or organization is listed at the UN 1267 sanctions regime, member states must do three things: implement an asset freeze; institute a travel ban; and subject individuals and organizations that are sanctioned to an arms embargo. These are the three formal consequences of a UN terrorist listing, but the regime is important in other ways. For example, listings help define the threat to global security. As discussed earlier in the chapter, the UN has never successfully defined terrorism, but in practice the UN does define who terrorists are by labeling them as such by the UN 1267 Sanctions Committee. The importance of this is difficult to overstate, but there are some limitations.

For example, the UN Sanctions Committee's listing criteria is narrowly focused. The work of the committee focuses only on ISIS and al-Qa'ida, or ISIS- and al-Qa'ida-linked, individuals and groups. The three key criteria for listing that member states include:

- Participating in the financing, planning, facilitating, and preparing of acts or activities in conjunction with a group or individual already on the list could result in a listing.
- Supplying, selling, or transferring arms and related material to ISIS- and al-Qa'ida-linked entities can serve as a basis for listing.
- Recruiting for or otherwise supporting acts or activities of ISIS, al-Qa'ida or any cell, affiliate, splinter group, or derivative thereof can result in a listing.

Based on these criteria, any member state of the UN, not just the fifteen countries that sit on the UN 1267 Sanctions Committee, can propose an ISIS- or al-Qa'ida-linked group or individual to be sanctioned. The author, a former head of a counterterrorism office in the US government, led US nominations for scores of individuals and groups linked to ISIS and al-Qa'ida. The process the US adopts for UN 1267 Sanctions Committee related proposals is well established. First, the United States only proposes a UN listing if it has already established domestic legal sufficiency, meaning that the Department of State or Treasury has already established a legal basis, often pursuant to Executive Order 13224, for the individual or group's listing as a terrorist. As discussed in Chapter 6, the United States would pre-notify allies and key countries, such as Security Council members, of its intent to designate and would seek support from countries for the listing. The culmination of any proposal at the UN, whether led by the United States or another country, is a narrative that appears on the UN's website. That narrative outlines the basis for the individual's or group's sanction and key bio-identifiers, such as the name, aliases used, date of birth, place of birth, address, passport details if known, among other key pieces of information. Without these details, the private sector, such as financial institutions, would not be able to implement the legally required asset freeze.

The UN 1267 Sanctions Committee terrorist listings create a global requirement to fight terrorist access to finance, and it is, arguably, the most important global tool used against al-Qa'ida and ISIS. Additionally, twice a year the UN 1267 Sanctions Committee's Monitoring Team (MT)[13] produces an in-depth report that examines the terrorist financing threat, among other issues. The MT's July 2024 highlighted Member State concerns regarding the rising use of cryptocurrency by terrorist groups. Specifically, it explained that "the expansion in ISIL's use of digital platforms is a growing concern for Member States ... One Member State noted that while the use of cash couriers and hawala are preferred for transferring funds into conflict areas, ISIL has purposely migrated to cryptocurrencies and online payment systems."[14] This trend, the use of cryptocurrency by terrorist actors, which is a focus of Chapter 10, highlighted by the MT, is an example of the value-added provided by the UN 1267 Sanctions Committee. The MT's work is shaped by exchanges its personnel have with member state's intelligence representatives, who are often on the forefront of countering terrorist access to finance. Understanding the current trends, such as increasing ISIL interest in cryptocurrency, can position countries to better fight against a new source of finance or new method of transferring funds. Additionally, the twice-per-year reports produced by the MT also highlight the implementation of the three consequences, such as the asset freeze, of a UN 1267 listing.

The UN 1267 Sanctions Committee and the underlying Security Resolution that gave it life provide an example of both an international legal requirement and a structure to combat terrorist

---

[13] The Monitoring Team consists of individual experts who work with representatives of UN member states to evaluate the threats posed to global security by groups listed as terrorists by the United Nations. Among their many responsibilities is drafting a twice yearly report that examines various aspects of the terrorist threat.

[14] United Nations. "Letter Dated 19 July 2024 from the Chair of the Security Council Committee Pursuant to Resolutions 1267 (1999), 1989 (2011), and 2253 (2015) Concerning Islamic State in Iraq and the Levant (Da'esh), Al-Qaida and Associated Individuals, Groups, Undertakings and Entities Addressed to the President of the Security Council," July 22, 2024. https://docs.un.org/en/S/2024/556

financing. UN Security Council Resolution 1373, in contrast, only provides a compelling international obligation for countries to act against terrorism financing. Unlike UNSCR 1267, UNSCR 1373 does not have among its outcomes a list of terrorists for countries to act against. Nonetheless, UNSCR 1373 is among the most important outcomes of fighting terrorism and its financing in a post 9/11 world.

UN SECURITY COUNCIL RESOLUTION 1373

UNSCR 1373 was adopted by the Security Council in the aftermath of al-Qa'ida's attack against the United States. On September 28, 2001, UNSCR 1373 was adopted with an eye toward preventing the financing of terrorism. In its operative paragraphs, the UN explained that states should "prevent and suppress the financing of terrorism ... criminalize the willful provision or collection of ... funds by their nationals ... that could be used ... to carry out attacks ... freeze without delay funds associated by terrorists."[15] One implication of UNSCR 1373's adoption is the push to freeze assets of terrorists operating in their countries, and to do that, the mechanism of terrorist designation would become critical. After 9/11, countries adopting a domestic terrorist designation regime would point to the obligations pursuant to UNSCR 1373 as the basis for doing so. The United States, as detailed in Chapter 6, would create Executive Order 13224 to fulfill its UNSCR 1373 obligations. Moreover, the FATF would consistently cite UNSCR 1373 as a critical component in the fight against terrorist financing, to include the use of domestic terrorist designations to achieve compliance with FATF Recommendation 6. In FATF's 2013 report on international best practices on targeted financial sanctions related to terrorism financing, FATF is explicit in explaining the importance of UNSCR 1373. The 2013 report notes, "Recommendation 6 requires countries to have procedures or mechanisms, to identify and initiate designations of persons and entities

---

[15] United Nations. "Resolution 1373 (2001) Adopted by the Security Council at Its 4385th Meeting," September 28, 2001. Page 2. www.unodc.org/pdf/crime/terrorism/res_1373_english.pdf.

pursuant to UNSCR 1373."[16] UNSCR 1373 would expand the world of terrorist designations beyond that called for by UNSCR 1267 – which only looks at ISIS and al-Qa'ida and associated individuals and organizations. While UNSCR 1373 does not result in a listing regime like UNSCR 1267, it provides an avenue for countries to designate a broader range of terrorist groups than those within the constellation of ISIS or al'Qa'ida's orbits. For instance, countries can justify domestic designations sanctioning Hamas and Lebanese Hizballah, two groups not sanctioned at the UN 1267 Sanctions Committee, by highlighting requirements within UNSCR 1373 and FATF Recommendation 6. Similarly, countries like the United States can leverage UNSCR 1373 and FATF Recommendation 6 to pressure countries to use their domestic designation regimes to sanction groups like Hamas.

UNITED NATIONS OFFICES DEDICATED TO FIGHTING TERRORIST FINANCING

The United Nations' work to counter terrorism financing has evolved significantly over the past several years. Created in 2005 at the UN General Assembly, the Counter-Terrorism Implementation Task Force (CTITF) for twelve years focused on executing the UN's Global Strategy to Counterterrorism. In 2017, the United Nations would create the UN Office of Counter-Terrorism (UNOCT), where responsibilities of CTITF and other[17] aspects of the UN's work to counterterrorism would be folded into the day-to-day work of the UNOCT. Within the UNOCT's sprawling organizational structure, its countering the financing of terrorism unit plays a key role in tackling terrorist access to finance. The UNOCT also has the responsibility

---

[16] Financial Action Task Force (FATF). "International Best Practices: Targeted Financial Sanctions Related to Terrorism and Terrorist Financing (Recommendation 6)," June 2013. Page 7. www.fatf-gafi.org/en/publications/Fatfrecommendations/Bpp-finsanctions-tf-r6.html#:~:text=FATF%20Recommendation%206%20requires%20countries,accordance%20with%20the%20relevant%20UNSCRs.

[17] United Nations Office of Counter-Terrorism. "New Avenues to Address Terrorist Financing," *UN Counter-Terrorism Centre (UNCCT)*, 2022. www.un.org/counterterrorism/cct/countering-the-financing-of-terrorism.

of coordinating a broad range of the UN's counterterrorism initiatives with the UN's Counter-Terrorism Committee (CTC), which was formed in the wake of 9/11, and upon its panel sit fifteen UN Security Council Member States. A support organization within the CTC is the UN's Counter-Terrorism Executive Directorate (CTED). The CTC and CTED do not maintain sanction lists like the UN's 1267 Sanctions Committee. However, the work of CTC, CTED, and the UNOCT are important bodies for implementing various aspects of the UN's broader strategy to counterterrorism, of which countering terrorism financing and the implementation of its sanctions regime are important aspects.

A recent initiative of the UNOCT has been its focus on impeding terrorist profiteering through kidnapping for ransom[18] (KFR) and other forms of terrorist financing by "organizing capacity building workshops for interested Member States on topics to enhance the capacity of national authorities to improve their work on suppressing the financing of terrorism." This work in capacity building, according to the UNOCT, is coordinated with other UN bodies, such as CTED and the UN's Office of Drugs and Crime (UNODC). An element of the capacity building that the UNOCT provides, along with UNODC, is the provision of software to assist FIUs with their tracking of terrorist financing. Specifically, the UNOCT and UNODC have provided software and web applications like goAML and goFintel to assist FIUs in the detection of terrorist financing and money laundering. In June 2024, the UNOCT announced the soft launch of goFintel as an emerging technology solution that would ingest new data sources, consolidate data, and enhance automated screening for FIUs.[19]

Providing technology directly to countries is not the only way that the UN contributes to the countering of terrorist financing.

---

[18] In 2019, the United Nations passed Resolution 2482, which expressed the UN's concern regarding how terrorists can benefit financially from kidnapping for ransom.

[19] United Nations Office of Counter-Terrorism. "Soft Launch of the GoFintel Software," June 25, 2024. www.un.org/counterterrorism/events/soft-launch-gofintel-software.

The UN's CTED conducts in-depth studies and reports that provide countries a template for understanding the financial dimensions of terrorism. The challenge of foreign terrorist fighters (FTFs) was among the most significant threats to global peace and stability between 2012 and 2016. This phenomenon coincided with the rise of ISIS in Syria and Iraq. In November 2024, CTED produced a comprehensive report looking at FTF-related financing between 2014 and 2024 and among the key findings was the rapid diversification of FTF-related footprints, including operations beyond the Middle East – to include the development of regional financial hubs in places like Turkey and Somalia.[20] In detailing the trends related to FTF financing, CTED attunes a country to the evolution of a threat in its backyard and, as a consequence, helps that country better push resources to counter the development.

Like CTED and the UNOCT, the UNODC plays a pivotal role in countering terrorism financing and money laundering. Within the UNODC there are two units that focus on countering terrorist access to funds. First, the UNODC's Global Program Against Money Laundering (GPML) initiative works directly with countries in countering both money laundering and the financing of terrorism. In addition to providing technology like goAML to countries directly, GPML deploys instructors to work with country law enforcement and regulators to develop skills to track illicit financing and confiscate the assets of criminal actors. GPML has also developed online course modules to improve the skills of financial crime fighters.[21] The dualistic approach of providing direct training and technology is also one taken by the UNODC's sister office, the Terrorism Prevention

---

[20] United Nations Security Council Counter-Terrorism Committee Executive Directorate (CTED). "Trends Tracker: Evolving Trends in the Financing of Foreign Terrorist Fighters' Activity: 2014–2024," November 2024, www.un.org/securitycouncil/ctc/sites/www.un.org.securitycouncil.ctc/files/cted_trends_tracker_evolving_trends_in_the_financing_of_foreign_terrorist_fighters_activity_2014_-_2024.pdf.

[21] United Nations Office on Drugs and Crime. "Training & Tools." www.unodc.org/unodc/en/money-laundering/global-programme-against-money-laundering/training-and-tools.html.

Branch (TPB). The TPB's approach differentiates itself from GPML in that its focus tends to be more on developing countries' underlying laws so that they conform with UN obligations. For instance, in December 2024, the TPB organized a workshop in Jordan to help Jordan become more efficient at implementing its responsibilities pursuant to UNSCR 1373.[22]

The UN's role in the area of countering the financing of terrorism focuses on the underlying resolutions and conventions that provide a basis for member-state action against terrorist financers. Once those obligations are on the books, however, the UN does not leave countries to their own devices. The UN provides significant resources via the dissemination of technology or direct training to countries that lack capacity but have political will to make change. Without question, the UN and FATF are the key multilateral bodies targeting terrorist financing, but they are not the only game in town.

OTHER MULTILATERAL BODIES THAT FOCUS ON TERRORIST FINANCING

In Asia, there are multiple organizations that tackle terrorism and its financing. The Association of Southeast Asian Nations (ASEAN) Regional Forum's Counterterrorism and Transnational Crime Committee (ARF/CTTC) was established in 1993 and today consists of more than twenty-five countries in the Pacific Rim, including the United States, which is bordered by the Pacific Ocean. The ARF/CTTC develops three-year plans to fight against terrorism and crime in the region, which often takes on unique properties in the region given the importance of the various waterways of the Pacific. For example, in 2005 the United States and Singapore worked jointly as cochairs to build resiliency in ARF/CTTC capacity to prevent terrorism in the Strait of Malacca – a water passageway known for piracy

---

[22] United Nations Office on Drugs and Crime. "UNODC Supports Jordan to Implement UN Security Council Sanctions," 2024. www.unodc.org/unodc/en/terrorism/latest-news/2024_unodc_-unodc-supports-jordan-to-implement-un-security-council-sanctions.html.

and kidnapping for ransom – forms of illicit financing. Additionally, the 2011 ARF/CTTC meeting in Malaysia agreed to add counter-terrorism financing and implementing UNSCR 1267 and 1373 obligations as one of its four key pillars of focus. More recently, in its 2024 workplan, the ARF/CTTC touted a workshop it conducted in Indonesia that explored the dimensions of terrorist financing and money laundering.[23] The ARF/CTTC in its workshops convenes experts to discuss trends specific to the ASEAN region in the area of terrorist financing and money laundering. Additionally, the group also gets involved in hands-on activities such as tabletop and field exercises, which are designed to improve implementation of international and regional agreements, which can include ASEAN member state compliance with UNSCRs 1267 and 1373.[24]

Also, in Asia, the Asia Pacific Economic Cooperation (APEC) group created in 2001 a subgroup to tackle counterterrorism. That group, the APEC Counter-Terrorism Task Force (APEC-CTTF), focuses on protecting the region's economy and commerce from forms of illicit financing, such as the financing of terrorism. A good example of APEC-CTTF's concern regarding the protection of its financial systems was the 2014 project focusing on securing finance systems from terrorist abuse of new payment systems (NPS).[25] The project sponsored and funded by the United States was a tabletop exercise to highlight gaps in government regulatory systems that would allow for possible financing of terrorism through NPS.[26]

---

[23] ASEAN Regional Forum. "Work Plan for Counter Terrorism and Transnational Crime 2024–2026," 2024. Page 13. https://aseanregionalforum.asean.org/wp-content/uploads/2024/07/6.-ARF-2024-2026-CTTC-Work-Plan_26-July_FINAL-CONSENSUS.pdf.

[24] Ibid, Page 7.

[25] Asia-Pacific Economic Cooperation (APEC). "*Secure Finance Workshop on Countering the Financing of Terrorism with New Payment Systems,*" 2014. https://aimp2.apec.org/sites/PDB/Lists/Proposals/DispForm.aspx?ID=1525.

[26] NPS includes a broad set of payment schemes that from use of cryptocurrency to pay for goods/services to other forms contactless payment via mobile devices. It can also include the use of gift cards.

In Latin America, like Asia, a specialized regional group tackles terrorism and its financing. The Inter-American Committee against Terrorism (CICTE) of the Organization of American States (OAS), which the United States is a member of, coordinates assistance and develops efforts for member countries to tackle challenges like terrorism financing. In 2011, for example, OAS CICTE provided technical assistance and funding to build the capacity of government officials in Paraguay's ministry of finance, FIU, foreign ministry, and customs officials so they can better counter the financing of terrorism and money laundering.

Turning to Europe, the Organization for Security and Cooperation in Europe (OSCE) has its "Action against Terrorism Unit" that works to improve the capacity of member states to counter terrorism financing. The OSCE recently highlighted its joint work with the UNODC's GPML to implement multiyear training programs for its member states that specifically counter illicit financing.[27] The OSCE's track record is long in countering terrorism financing. Like the OAS CICTE, it has also focused on building the capacity of FIUs in the region. In 2008, for example, the OSCE provided expert advice and training for a conference devoted to improving Kyrgyzstan's Financial Intelligence Unit. In 2012, an OSCE training course on anti-money laundering and countering the financing of terrorism was held for Kazakhstani nonfinancial businesses and professions. The workshop was organized by the OSCE center in Astana and brought together fifty-five representatives of nonfinancial businesses in an effort to educate participants about methods to prevent money laundering.

The Group of Seven (previously known as the Group of Eight), through the Roma/Lyon working group, has focused on countering terrorism and crime by working on joint projects. Within the context of the G7, the Roma group focuses on matters pertaining to

---

[27] Organization for Security and Co-operation in Europe (OSCE), "The role of the OSCE in countering the financing of terrorism," 2024. www.osce.org/secretariat/482445.

terrorism, while the Lyon group focuses on law enforcement and crime. Within the Roma group there are several subgroups, such as the Counterterrorism Practitioners sub-group (CPSG). At the 2007 G8 (before Russia's eviction from the G8) Summit in Heiligendamm, Germany, G8 Leaders called for terrorism financing and money laundering government experts to counter cash smuggling by identifying key transshipment and courier routes to maximize effective information exchange and enhance law enforcement investigations. The G8's interest at the time was building on the FATF's efforts to highlight the growing role played by cash couriers in moving terrorist funds. The FATF at this time encouraged countries to engage in cooperative agreements with other countries that would allow for bilateral customs information exchanges between customs on cross-border reports and the stopping or restraining of cash and bearer negotiable instruments. The objective of FATF was to focus on the 'moving' portion of the terrorist financing life cycle.

In response to the FATF call for action, in the 2007 G8 leaders' statement, the Roma group began focusing its CPSG subgroup's activities on countering cash couriers. In response to the CPSG's initiative, in 2009, seven of the eight G-8 countries[28] conducted a multilateral operational exercise, known as Operation Mantis, which targeted cash couriers at ports of entry. The result of that exercise was approximately $3.5 million seized in eighty-one separate cash seizures. During the three-day operation, authorities examined hundreds of flights at multiple international airports. For instance, an examination conducted by British authorities led to the arrest of a seventeen-year-old female who was apprehended as she attempted to leave the UK while carrying 380,000 British pounds in her checked luggage.[29] The G-8's Operation Mantis disrupted criminal and possibly terrorist finance and is illustrative of the ways the multilateral community can counter terrorism.

---

[28] Russia did not participate in the exercise.
[29] U.S. Department of Homeland Security. Morning roundup, July 9, 2009. www.dhs.gov/archive/news/2009/07/09/morning-roundup-july-9th

RECAP AND CONCLUDING THOUGHTS

A go-it-alone tact to tackling terrorist financing is destined to be incomplete. The importance of working within the multilateral constructs along with meeting the obligations of FATF and the United Nations Security Council Resolutions is a key component of crippling terrorists' capacity to raise funds. In addition to the broad remit of the UN and FATF, various multilateral institutions with regional and local approaches to cooperation, such as the FSRBs, OAS, OSCE, ARF, and ASEAN, among others, foster the sharing of information and skill-building that is necessary in countering terrorist financing.

The recommendations and resolutions that require countries to develop domestic laws and capacity to fight terrorism financing are the building blocks in the fight against illicit financing. To meet FATF compliance and UN obligations, however, member states require assistance. As this chapter outlined, a broad range of multilateral organizations are mindful of these needs and provide a range of assistance via trainings, workshops, tabletop exercises, software, and hardware needs to close gaps in regulatory, legal, and enforcement frameworks.

The underlying UN resolutions and FATF recommendations, however, are not only a public sector pursuit. The blocking of assets and denying services that can facilitate the flow of funds require private sector involvement. This need for private sector engagement also means that the government sector (also referred to as the public sector) must be a willing partner in providing useful guidance and information for the private sector to act upon as part of the whole of society's fight against illicit financing. The next chapter will explore the role of the private sector and how government–private sector interaction is working to thwart illicit financial activity.

9 The Role of the Private Sector in Countering Terrorist Financing and the Importance of Public–Private Partnerships

The private sector is on the front line in the battle against terrorist financing. Governments and intergovernmental bodies like FATF recognize the importance of the private sector, and as consequence, FATF has called upon it to align with its recommendations. Prior to the existence of FATF, the United States understood the vital role banks played in countering illicit crime. That's why the Bank Secrecy Act (BSA), discussed in Chapter 5, was passed in the 1970s. Criminal groups were using the formal financial system to store the proceeds of crime in banks and to further the money laundering process as part of an effort to give dollars made through violence look like legitimate greenbacks. Banks, however, are only a subset of the private sector actors that are critical to battling illicit finance. In this chapter, the role of banks will be examined, but other designated nonfinancial businesses and professions (DNFBPs) will be discussed. Professions like lawyers, accountants, and realtors make up a universe of professional enablers that allow for money to move for the benefit of terrorists and criminals. This chapter will examine how DNFBPs have become an increasing focus of attention of governments and bodies like the FATF. Additionally, the chapter will examine how governments are increasingly striking partnerships with private industry. The road of public-private (P2P) sector cooperation has been bumpy. Governments are often distrusting and wary about sharing information with the private sector. Fear of leak of sensitive information is often a key impediment to true cooperation, but for the private sector to be effective in its responsibilities to protect their systems from abuse it needs government information. When cooperation does not occur, or when bad actors operate within the private sector and knowingly facilitate financial crime or terrorist financing, the results can be catastrophic. Even when there are checks in place to guard against illicit use of finance, sophisticated terrorists or criminals can still stay under the radar and move or store money. As part of an effort to deal with this challenge, increasingly financial institutions are turning to technology to help identify suspicious transactions.

For large quantities to move throughout the financial system, people with specialized skills are needed to circumvent technology and human checks that have been adopted by the formal and informal financial systems to stem the flow of illicit finance. Investigative journalists have repeatedly illuminated how enablers have time and again foiled financial controls to move money for bad actors. The Panama Papers, Pandora Papers, and the FinCEN Files would all outline how money has been moved by white-collar professionals for the benefit of criminals, kleptocrats, and heads of state who are fleecing their citizens of their wealth.

The Panama Papers, as they would become known, were the results of a multiyear investigation conducted by the International Consortium of Investigative Journalists (ICIJ) that culminated in 2016. The ICIJ's work was based on millions of leaked documents that revealed how enablers, such as lawyers, provided their services to illicit actors so that they could move money to avoid financial controls. The funds would move to offshore accounts in bank secrecy tax havens, such as the British Virgin Islands, Panama, Bahamas, and the Seychelles.[1] These localities have long been, like Switzerland, seen by illicit actors, and licit actors, as safe places to park money away from the prying eyes of government regulation. Among the key actors in moving illicit funds was the Panama-based law firm Mossack Fonseca, according to the ICIJ 2016 investigation. The Attorney General of Panama explained that the law firm was responsible for the creation of offshore companies that were

---

[1] International Consortium of Investigative Journalists (ICIJ). "Explore the Panama Papers key figures," January 31, 2017. www.icij.org/investigations/panama-papers/explore-panama-papers-key-figures/.

used for "allegedly ... laundering millions of dollars from multiple illicit activities around the world."[2] Among Mossack Fonseca's clients were several Iranian sanctioned entities, including Petropars Ltd., an oil company that facilitated Iran's ballistic missile program.[3] The Panama Papers not only detailed Mossack and Fonseca's work on behalf of Iran, a US Department of State listed State Sponsor of Terrorism, but also detailed the facilitation of the movement of dirty money on behalf of North Korea, another State Department listed terrorist state. After the release of the Panama Papers, Europol discovered more than 3,500 individuals and companies that were probable matches for suspected criminals, including terrorists.[4] The Panama Papers release highlighted the key role reporters play in uncovering financial crimes, tax avoidance, and corruption – all of which create a fertile ground for terrorist financiers. Unfortunately, in the case of the Panama Papers, white-collar lawyers played an instrumental role in obfuscating wealth ownership by creating offshore companies to hide illicit wealth.

Four years later, the ICIJ would again release a tranche of documents that would highlight the important role enablers in the private sector play in facilitating the movement of dirty money. In what would be dubbed the FinCEN files, the ICIJ uncovered through the leaks of more than 2,500 documents how financial institutions like banks allowed for the movement of illicit funds. Among the key documents leaked were more than 2,000 bank-filed SARs. Among the transactions banks facilitated, according to the leaked documents,

---

[2] Fitzgibbon, W., Díaz-Struck, E., & Hudson, M. "Founders of Panama Papers Law Firm Arrested on Money Laundering Charges," *International Consortium of Investigative Journalists*, February 11, 2017. www.icij.org/investigations/panama-papers/20170210-mossfon-panama-arrests/.

[3] Garside, J., Pegg, D., Watt, H., & Bengtsson, H. "Mossack Fonseca Worked with Oil Firms Owned by Iranian State Despite Sanctions," *The Guardian*, April 6, 2016. www.theguardian.com/news/2016/apr/06/mossack-fonseca-oil-firms-petropars-iranian-state-sanctions-panama-papers.

[4] Pegg, D. "Panama Papers: Europol Links 3,500 Names to Suspected Criminals," *The Guardian*, December 1, 2016. www.theguardian.com/news/2016/dec/01/panama-papers-europol-links-3500-names-to-suspected-criminals.

were those carried out by Arab Bank, the world's largest Arab banking network with more than 600 branches spread across five continents, on behalf of Hamas, a US-designated Foreign Terrorist Organization (FTO) that would later carry out the deadliest terrorist attack in Israel's history on October 7, 2023.[5]

A year later, in 2021, another voluminous release of documents, nearly 12 million, by the ICIJ would again implicate the private sector in facilitating the movement of blood money. The ICIJ investigation, which would become known as the Pandora Papers, also documented how the uber wealthy and heads of state would fleece their populations and, in the case of Jordan's king, used enablers to move money to offshore accounts that would ultimately be used to purchase real estate in the United States.[6] Following the release of the Pandora Papers, FATF would issue a press release on October 2021 release explaining that,

> obscuring the true owners of corporate, trust, and other structures, and those who control them is a common technique to hide illicit profits ... recognizing the urgent need to take further action to combat the misuse of shell and front companies by illicit actors, the FATF has been leading work to update international requirements on the transparency of beneficial ownership.[7]

The FATF would also explain in its press release that enablers of financial crime benefit terrorist financing, and as a result of the weak controls on beneficial ownership by governments, it sought public comment on its intent to revise FATF Recommendation 24

---

[5] FinCEN Files reporting team. "FinCEN Files: UK Bank May Have Moved Money 'linked to terror activity'," *BBC News*, September 22, 2020. www.bbc.com/news/world-middle-east-54235202.

[6] Miller, G. "While His Country Struggles, Jordan's King Abdullah Secretly Splurges," *Washington Post*, October 3, 2021. www.washingtonpost.com/world/interactive/2021/jordan-abdullah-shell-companies-luxury-homes/?itid=lk_inline_manual_8.

[7] Financial Action Task Force. *Public Statement on Pandora Papers*. October 21, 2021. www.fatf-gafi.org/en/publications/Fatfgeneral/Pandora-papers.html.

to emphasize that DNFBPs provide regulatory authorities access to information that could shed light on possible abuses of beneficial ownership information.[8]

The various ICIJ investigations made clear that state sponsors of terrorism and designated FTOs benefitted from the services provided by white-collar professions. Whether a banker, lawyer, or realtor, services provided by banks, it is evident that DNFBPs are often instrumental in the movement of funds. This phenomenon predates the ICIJ set of investigative reports that detail the private sector's facilitation of illicit finance. In her excellent report on the Haqqani Network (HQN), Gretchen Peters details how HQN, a designated FTO by the State Department, was able to park its wealth in both commercial and residential real estate holdings.[9] Without the assistance of realtors, HQN would not be effective in storing its wealth in real estate – a common tactic and generally a prudent investment where real estate holdings can appreciate over time.

The roles played by bankers, accountants, lawyers, and realtors, among many other professions, are vitally important for the effective and efficient use of assets. An accountant or banker can hide the true source of funds by using their knowledge of regulatory, accounting, and auditing systems. A realtor can skip the process of determining who is the beneficial owner of a property. A law firm can create offshore companies, Limited Liability Companies (LLCs), and front organizations to obscure the identity of the criminal or terrorist benefiting from hiding money.

Knowing this, FATF has highlighted the importance of the private sector in battling terrorist finance by seeking government compliance on multiple recommendations related to the private sector's

---

[8] Financial Action Task Force. *Revisions to Recommendation 24 and Its Interpretive Note – Public Consultation*. www.fatf-gafi.org/en/publications/Fatfrecommendations/Public-consultation-r24.html.

[9] Peters, Gretchen. "Haqqani Network Financing: The Evolution of an Industry," *Combatting Terrorism Center at West Point*, July 2012. Page 1. https://ciaotest.cc.columbia.edu/wps/ctc/0025768/index.html.

responsibilities in countering illicit financial activity. Nearly every recommendation, in some fashion, can touch upon the role of the private sector. However, among the most important are those that are deemed preventative measures, which are contained within recommendations nine through twenty-three. Several of these recommendations speak specifically to the importance of banks, other depository institutions, and nonbanks facilitating the movement of funds, doing their customer due diligence (CDD, Recommendation 10), and keeping good records (Recommendation 11). FATF, in highlighting CDD and recording keeping is attempting to ensure that individuals cannot mask their identity while engaging in financial transactions. Collecting, verifying, and retaining customer information and information related to their transactions allows for regulators and law enforcement investigators to use those details to shape sanction measures or build cases. Information, such as date of birth, address, and the details of the receiver of funds, among other types of details that can be included on transaction forms, may ultimately be the missing information governments need to pursue measures against terrorist financiers.

FATF Recommendation 13 on correspondent banking is especially important for preventing countries that may be engaged in state-sponsored terrorism or proliferation financing activities related to the development of weapons of mass destruction programs. In implementing this recommendation, bankers at financial institutions are ensuring that cross-border correspondent banking relationships are also undergoing CDD. This is especially important for denying two US-listed state sponsor of terrorism countries, Iran and North Korea, from having their banks, often state-controlled, arrange for correspondent banking relations with overseas banks that could facilitate the movement of cash, which could benefit their terrorism-sponsoring or WMD proliferation regimes. Similarly, as terrorism financing expert Matthew Levitt pointed out in 2015, cutting off ISIS's access to the international financial system it could have gained through its access of the Bank of Mosul was critically important because, "scores of bank branches are located in areas of Syria and Iraq either controlled or contested by ISIS, including branches of international banks."[10] Ensuring that ISIS-controlled banks could not move wealth to sustain their operations or pay its external operatives plotting attacks in places like Europe was critically important in the fight against the group. However, the responsibility of literally turning off the access fell to bankers who are on the front lines of illicit financial battles.

In addition to the importance of the banking sector, the private sector's money value transfer services (MVTS) are highlighted for its importance by the FATF in recommendation 14. Among the most important aspects of this recommendation is the need for countries to license and register MVTS operating in their country and, like banks, MVTS carrying out sufficient CDD to ensure their services are not allowing for the movement of illicit finance. In 2002 testimony before Congress, Dennis Lormel, chief of the financial crimes section of the FBI, described al-Qa'ida's transaction profile, which included a "tendency to use Western Union to wire money."[11] As part of the private sector's response to al-Qa'ida and other terrorists using MVTS to move funds, groups like Western Union created its own in-house Financial Intelligence Unit and increased spending to ensure compliance with regulatory measures. In 2017 before the US House of Representatives Financial Services Subcommittee on Terrorism and Illicit Finance, Western Union's Duncan Deville explained it increased "overall compliance funding by more than 200 percent over the past five years, and now spends more than 200 million dollars annually on compliance. Approximately 2,400 full-time

---

[10] Levitt, M. "The Islamic State's Backdoor Banking," *The Washington Institute for Near East Policy*, March 24, 2015. www.washingtoninstitute.org/policy-analysis/islamic-states-backdoor-banking.

[11] Lormel, D. M. "Financing Patterns Associated with al-Qaeda and Global Terrorist Networks," *Federal Bureau of Investigation*, before the House Committee on Financial Services, Subcommittee on Oversight and Investigations, Washington, DC, February 12, 2002. https://archives.fbi.gov/archives/news/testimony/financing-patterns-associated-with-al-qaeda-and-global-terrorist-networks.

employees, over 20 percent of our workforce are exclusively dedicated to compliance functions."[12]

Within the world of financial services, in addition to behemoths in the private sector like Western Union and MoneyGram, there are more informal and geographic-specific service providers – in the world of terrorism financing, the best known is hawala. FATF in defining MVTS includes hawala,[13] hundi, and fei-chen as part of the universe value transfer service providers that can move large sums of "cash or other form of value to a beneficiary by means of communication ... that can involve final payment to a third party."[14] Hawalas have long been a staple of underground banking economies and pre-date the establishment of banks. A business, known as a hawaladar, may operate in a country and may provide services to a customer who wants to transfer money to a friend based overseas. The individual wants to move the money via the hawaladar because it will charge a lower percentage transaction fee than banks. The hawaladar may have a relationship with a hawaladar where his customer wants to send the money. The hawaladar will then call or communicate electronically with the other hawaladar about the transaction. At the same time, the customer will be given a remittance code that they will need to share with their friend overseas. For that friend to receive the cash, they will need to provide that code to the hawaladar in their country. In this exchange, no money physically moves, and the hawaladars may settle up later, at the end of the month or

---

[12] DeVille, D. "Testimony of Mr. Duncan DeVille, Global Head of Financial Crimes Compliance & US BSA Officer, The Western Union Company." *United States House of Representatives, Financial Services Subcommittee on Terrorism and Illicit Finance*, July 18, 2017. Page 3. www.congress.gov/115/meeting/house/106297/witnesses/HHRG-115-BA01-Wstate-DeVilleD-20170718.pdf.

[13] Hawala is an Arabic language term that means transfer or remittance. Hundi is the same type of financial instrument as hawala but created in medieval India. Fei-chen, which means flying cash, was created to serve the same purpose as hawala and hundi, but was created in China during the 800s during the Song dynasty.

[14] FATF. *International standards on combating money laundering and the financing of terrorism & proliferation. FATF*, Paris, France. Page 133. www.fatf-gafi.org/en/publications/Fatfrecommendations/Fatf-recommendations.html.

at the end of the week, by transferring goods, services, or cash. The hawala system is one that is based on trust and popular for its efficiency and cost-effectiveness. It is important to note, however, that hawala are not exclusively leveraged by illicit actors, like terrorists, to move funds. Expatriates, often moving for higher-paying jobs in places like the Persian Gulf, will send money back to family members who remained behind. Nonetheless, informal value transfer systems like hawalas have been abused by terrorists. Indeed, FATF in its typology report on abuse of hawalas by malign actors explains that even a decade after 9/11 the "globe has largely been ineffective in supervising HOSSPs."[15] More recently, in 2024, the US Department of the Treasury noted that a financier linked to al-Shabaab, a US State Department designated FTO, moved money using a hawala in support of al-Shabaab's money laundering activity.[16] Regulation of private sector entities, like hawala, has included licensing and registration as part of an effort to improve hawala reporting of potentially illicit financial activity. In 2009, FinCEN changed the added regulations for informal value transfer systems like hawalas, including the need for hawalas to register with the Treasury Department by filling out FinCEN form 107. The bulk of hawala-like structures in the United States are moving money in compliance with federal and state laws and, like banking institutions, must also file (and have done so) CTRs and SARs. Nonetheless, the 2024 Treasury Department's risk assessment illustrates that hawalas are still abused by terrorists despite regulations imposed upon the sector.

In addition to the frontline role played by banks, MVTS, and hawalas, FATF recommendations pointedly highlight the importance of DNFBPs. Two recommendations, 22 and 23, specifically

---

[15] HOSSPS stands for "hawala and other similar service providers"
FATF. "The Role of Hawala and Other Similar Service Providers in Money Laundering and Terrorist Financing." (2013, October). *FATF*. Page 9. www.fatf-gafi.org/en/publications/Methodsandtrends/Role-hawalas-in-ml-tf.html.

[16] U.S. Department of the Treasury. "Treasury Designates Transnational Al-Shabaab Money Laundering Network," *U.S. Department of the Treasury*, March 11, 2024. https://home.treasury.gov/news/press-releases/jy2168.

highlight the importance of DNFBPs. Recommendation 22 calls on DNFBPs to conduct CDD as banks would. Additionally, recommendation 22 details specifically the measures that relate to gem dealers, notaries, lawyers, casinos, real estate agents, accountants, and trust and company service providers, who should conduct business in a fashion that protects their communities from being abused by illicit actors. Recommendation 23 calls on DNFBPs to also file STRs, like banks. While banks play a role in ensuring that individuals and entities do not obfuscate the true source of their wealth, DNFBPs also play an important role in ensuring that beneficial ownership can be established – this has been particularly important in the wake of the Panama Papers, FinCEN Files, and Pandor Papers ICIJ investigations.

In highlighting the importance of beneficial ownership, the FATF produced a report that outlined its expectations for DNFBPs and banks. In the report, FATF defined the term beneficial owner "as the natural person(s) who ultimately owns or controls a customer and/or the natural person on whose behalf a transaction is being conducted. It also includes those persons who exercise ultimate effective control over a legal person or arrangement." In other words, the FATF definition focuses on the natural (not legal) persons who own and take advantage of capital or assets of the legal person; as well as on those who really exert effective control over it (whether or not they occupy formal positions within that legal person), rather than just the (natural or legal) persons who are legally (on paper) entitled to do so. For example, if a company is legally owned by a second company (according to its corporate registration information), the beneficial owners are actually the natural persons who are behind that second company or ultimate holding company in the chain of ownership and who are controlling it.[17] FATF's report and its recommendations 24 and 25 on beneficial ownership underscore the need for transparency which, if adhered to by DNFBPs and banks, would allow for law enforcement

---

[17] FATF. "Transparency and Beneficial Ownership," October 2014. *FATF*. www.fatf-gafi.org/content/dam/fatf-gafi/guidance/Guidance-transparency-beneficial-ownership.pdf.

and regulatory authorities to accrue insights that may help stop bad actors from secretly making money in schemes where ownership is difficult to determine. Economic powerhouse countries have fallen short in their FATF responsibilities in creating an environment for private sector entities to be held accountable for reporting on beneficial ownership. Indeed, in 2016, the FATF's mutual evaluation report (MER) determined the United States was deficient and did not meet its requirements as outlined in Recommendation 24.[18] Eight years later, the United States would finally receive a "largely compliant" rating from the FATF for Recommendation 24. In the Treasury Department's press release celebrating this finding, they explained, "the United States' upgraded rating is a result of a nearly decade of hard work by the Treasury Department, along with our interagency partners, to stop the flow of dirty money through anonymous companies."[19] While the United States was enmeshed in work to reform its own laws related to transparency of ownership, the various ICIJ investigations pointed to several US-based companies that were used by illicit actors and heads of state, such as the King of Jordan, to obscure the source of wealth and ownership over assets. Eventually, the key legislative vehicle for the United States to become compliant with the FATF recommendation was the adoption of the Corporate Transparency Act (CTA), which went into effect 2024. For the first time, DNFBPs, many of which are small businesses, as well as large corporations, would have to file reports detailing who a beneficial owner is and note to FinCEN anyone who may control 25 percent or more of a company.

Banks, MVTS, hawalas, and DNFBPs all possess critical information that can provide daylight to law enforcement and regulatory authorities on the illicit activities specific to their industry. Whether it is responding to new requirements like the CTA, or sending STRs

---

[18] FATF. "Anti-money Laundering and Counter-Terrorist Financing Measures – United States, Fourth Round Mutual Evaluation Report," 2016. *FATF*, Paris. www.fatf-gafi.org/publications/mutualevaluations/documents/mer-united-states-2016.html.

[19] U.S. Department of the Treasury. "Financial Action Task Force Highlights Treasury's Efforts to Counter Illicit Finance." https://home.treasury.gov/news/press-releases/jy2208.

to an FIU or filing CTRs, the private sector's information is critical to the success of stopping the flow if terrorist financing. The investigative reports of the ICIJ have highlighted that banks and nonbanks alike, however, have facilitated the movement of dirty money. While the CTA provides a tool to the government to gain insight, there are also time-honored approaches, such as fines and sanctions that have also been leveraged against private sector entities that have not carried out sufficient due diligence, or worse, have intentionally stored or moved money for terrorists.

The public–private sector dynamic can become adversarial, especially when governments identify private sector entities that have been facilitating terrorists' access to finance. Among the range of sticks that can be applied to these situations are sanctions and fines. Sanctions, often in the form of terrorist designations, have been used to shut down private sector businesses that have moved money on behalf of terrorists. For example, in 2012 the US Department of the Treasury, using its legal authorities under E.O. 13224 designated an Afghanistan-based hawala, Rahat Ltd., that facilitated the movement of millions of dollars on behalf of the Taliban. Noting Rahat Ltd.'s activities, the Treasury Department explained, "Rahat Ltd. has been used extensively by senior Taliban leadership to finance their violent activities."[20] In designating Rahat Ltd., the group's assets were subject to an asset freeze. In 2021, the US Treasury would designate an individual operating a hawala as a terrorist pursuant to E.O. 13224 due to his operation of a Turkey-based hawala. In the designation of Ismatullah Khalozai, the Treasury Department explained, "Khalozai has been an international financial facilitator for ISIS-K and … operated a Turkey-based hawala business to transfer funds for ISIS-K operations."[21]

---

[20] U.S. Department of the Treasury. "Treasury Imposes Sanctions on a Hawala and Two Individuals Linked to the Taliban." November 20, 2012. https://home.treasury.gov/news/press-releases/tg1777.

[21] U.S. Department of the Treasury. "Treasury Designates Key Financial Facilitator for the Islamic State's Afghanistan Branch." November 22, 2021. https://home.treasury.gov/news/press-releases/jy0502.

Like hawalas, the US Treasury has also designated DNFBPs as terrorist entities pursuant to E.O. 13224. For example, in 2019, the Treasury Department designated al-Hebo Jewelry Company for supporting ISIS's scheme to convert gold into cash. Treasury's press release explained how al-Hebo converted the gold into cash and then ISIS operatives could then secretly send the cash via hawalas based in Turkey to ISIS operatives in Syria and Iraq.[22] The al-Hebo case perfectly demonstrates how an informal value transfer system (like a hawala) linked to a DNFBP, in this case a jewelry company, can be leveraged by terrorists to convert an asset and then move the proceeds from a financial exchange to fund terrorism. In highlighting the roles played by DNFBPs, the Treasury Department's terrorist designations notify other government jurisdictions of the need to crack down on illicit financial activity of private sector entities that are actively aiding terrorist groups.

Like sanctions, another time-honored stick used against the private sector has been the levying of fines for lax implementation of regulations that have permitted for terrorist actors to use financial services. Fines have been imposed upon a broad range of private sector companies and banks that have permitted terrorists to use their services to move funds. The United Kingdom fined an MSB a record amount, nearly 8 million British Pounds, in 2019. In describing the fine, the UK noted the fine was levied as part of a broader crack down on MSBs for "money laundering to fund organized crime, such as drug trafficking, violent crime, and terrorism."[23] US-based MSBs, such as MoneyGram, have also been levied fines for not fulfilling their BSA and anti-money laundering responsibilities. In 2012, a Dallas-based MSB, MoneyGram, as part of a deferred prosecution agreement (DPA),

---

[22] U.S. Department of the Treasury. "Treasury Targets Wide Range of Terrorists and Their Supporters Using Enhanced Counterterrorism Sanctions Authorities." September 10, 2019. https://home.treasury.gov/news/press-releases/sm772.

[23] HM Revenue & Customs. "Money Sender Fined Record £7.8 Million in Money Laundering Crackdown," *Gov.UK*, September 4, 2019. www.gov.uk/government/news/money-sender-fined-record-78-million-in-money-laundering-crackdown.

with the Department of Justice admitted to anti-money laundering and wire-fraud violations. As part of the DPA, MoneyGram also agreed to forfeit $100 million. The Department of Justice press release announcing the DPA explained that "MoneyGram's involvement in this international fraud scheme resulted from a systematic, pervasive, and willful failure to meet its anti-money laundering (AML) obligations under the Bank Secrecy Act."[24] Several banks and private companies have also been on the losing side of large fines due to lax standards related to implementing AML/CFT regulatory provisions.

Among the major banks that have run afoul of US-based terrorism financing regulations is TD Bank. On October 10, 2024, FinCEN assessed the largest fine in its history. TD Bank was fined $1.3 billion for engaging its repeated violations of the BSA. The FinCEN press release painted a dark picture of TD Bank's transgressions, most notably a pattern of behavior that allowed its banking services to abet criminals and terrorists. As Treasury's Deputy Secretary Wally Adeyemo explained, "from fentanyl and narcotics trafficking to terrorist financing and human trafficking, TD Bank's chronic failures provided fertile ground for a host of illicit activity to penetrate our financial system."[25] TD Bank as part of its agreement with the US Treasury Department also agreed to undergo a four-year independent monitorship to ensure that the bank was credibly implementing AML/CFT safeguards. Other banks have been fined for allowing terrorist financiers to use their services, and some, like Lebanese Canadian Bank (LCB), have been identified as money launderers for designated FTOs, like Hizballah.

---

[24] U.S. Department of Justice. "Moneygram International Inc. Admits Anti-Money Laundering and Wire Fraud Violations, Forfeits $100 Million in Deferred Prosecution," *Department of Justice Archives*, November 9, 2012. www.justice.gov/archives/opa/pr/moneygram-international-inc-admits-anti-money-laundering-and-wire-fraud-violations-forfeits#:~:text=In%20addition%20to%20forfeiting%20%24100,regularly%20to%20the%20Justice%20Department.%E2%80%9D.

[25] Financial Crimes Enforcement Network (FinCEN). "FinCEN Assesses Record $1.3 Billion Penalty against TD Bank," *Financial Crimes Enforcement Network*, October 10, 2024. www.fincen.gov/news/news-releases/fincen-assesses-record-13-billion-penalty-against-td-bank.

In the case of the LCB, the United States Treasury Department used another tool, known as a 311 Action, to counter the bank's support for Hizballah. The Secretary of the Treasury under Section 311 of the USA Patriot Act can deem entire countries (like North Korea) or specific banks money laundering concerns. On February 10, 2011, the Treasury Department explained that it was protecting the US financial system from LCB because it was laundering the proceeds of Hizballah's criminal endeavors.[26] LCB and TD Bank represent extreme cases of where either direct support or willful ignorance have created opportunities for terrorists to store and move funds. Like DNFBPs, banks and MSBs are important nodes in the movement of legitimate commerce, but the sheer volume of personnel and assets moving makes regulatory, sanctions, and other government action imperfect solutions to prevent abuse of the private sector by malicious actors. The approach of using a cudgel to provoke private sector positive action against bad actors may result in an increase in STRs submitted to FIUs. The cudgel may also lead to technological improvements and the addition of new personnel to build compliance sections within banks and MSBs. ICIJ investigations that result in candid conversations in capitals, which can spark new regulation, may even create an aha moment for a realtor to file their suspicions with their regulator if they are worried about who is truly buying major commercial real estate. Nonetheless, for strong private–public partnerships (PPPs) to succeed, true collaboration is needed. Governments have been slow to recognize this, but increasingly new avenues for PPPs in the area of countering terrorist financing and illicit financial activity have been established.

The United States and the United Kingdom have both created structures to engage with private sector counterparts. In the United States, not long after 9/11, the FBI's Terrorist Financing

---

[26] U.S. Department of the Treasury (USDT). "Treasury Identifies Lebanese Canadian Bank Sal as a 'Primary Money Laundering Concern,'" *U.S. Department of the Treasury*, February 10, 2011. https://home.treasury.gov/news/press-releases/tg1057.

Operations Section (TFOS) would take the lead. In testimony before the House Committee on Financial Service Subcommittee on Oversight and Investigations, the FBI's Assistant Director for Counterterrorism would explain, "TFOS built upon these established mechanisms by developing a strong network within the private financial sector."[27] Shortly after 9/11, likely shaped by the 9/11 Committee's report on the mistakes made in the lead-up to al-Qa'ida's successful attack, the US government would invest personnel and resources to build relations with the private sector. In the area of terrorist financing, an existing group known as the Bank Secrecy Act Advisory Group (BSAAG) would play a greater role. The group would become an important forum for information exchange. As detailed in a Federal Register Notice on the BSAAG, FinCEN explained, "BSAAG is the means by which the Treasury receives advice on reporting requirements of the Bank Secrecy Act (BSA) and informs private sector representatives on how the information they provide is used."[28] BSAAG provides an opportunity for the private sector to give direct feedback to US government experts that can shape not only how interactions between the private sector and public sector take place but also allow for information exchange that provides both sectors a capacity to deal with illicit financing more effectively.

Often, it is the private sector that retains key information that would allow for law enforcement and regulators to unearth terrorist financing. In an interview with former Scotland Yard United Kingdom detective Shaun McLeary, he explains, "the private sector

---

[27] Pistole, J. S. *The Terrorist Financing Operations Section*. Testimony before the House Committee on Financial Services, Subcommittee on Oversight and Investigations, Federal Bureau of Investigation. September 24, 2003. https://archives.fbi.gov/archives/news/testimony/the-terrorist-financing-operations-section.

[28] Department of the Treasury, Financial Crimes Enforcement Network. *Bank Secrecy Act Advisory Group; Solicitation of Application for Membership*. Federal Register. December 5, 2024. www.federalregister.gov/documents/2024/12/05/2024-28451/bank-secrecy-act-advisory-group-solicitation-of-application-for-membership#:~:text=The%20BSAAG%20is%20the%20means,information%20they%20provide%20is%20used.

has information that can be vital to finding terrorists."[29] The information exchange must be a two-way street, however. As detailed in reporting by Valentina Pasquali, "TFOS gave bankers increasingly granular details from ongoing investigations ... including unclassified names, birthdates, and addresses of suspects."[30] This notion of a two-way street on collaboration between the private and public sectors was also emphasized by McLeary, who explained, "states cannot expect the private sector to have a better idea of what terrorist financing looks like than the states themselves. Providing the private sector with risk profiles, emerging trends, and typologies, both domestic and international, is essential."[31]

Like the United States, the United Kingdom sees the importance of the private sector and has created PPPs like the Joint Money Laundering Intelligence Taskforce (JMLIT) in 2015. The JMLIT, which is housed at the UK's National Economic Crime Centre, includes over forty financial institutions, the UK's Financial Conduct Authority, and five law enforcement agencies. The public–private sector cooperation at the JMLIT has resulted in more than 280 arrests and the seizure or restraint of assets totaling over 86 million British pounds.[32] The UK also established the Joint Fraud Task Force (JFT) in 2021 as a mechanism to hone cooperation between the private and public sectors. The JTF's engagement includes the insurance, accountancy, telecommunications, and banking sectors.[33] Like the JMLIT, the JFT may not tackle terrorist financing directly as a lead issue, but the overlap between money laundering

---

[29] Jason Blazakis Personal Interview with Shaun McLeary, former Scotland Yard financial investigator. February 20, 2025.
[30] Pasquali, V. "Exclusive: Fall of Afghanistan finds FBI without terrorist financing section," *ACAMS Money Laundering.com*, August 30, 2021. www.moneylaundering.com/news/exclusive-fall-of-afghanistan-finds-fbi-without-terrorist-financing-section/.
[31] Jason Blazakis Personal Interview of Shaun McLeary interview February 20, 2025.
[32] National Economic Crime Centre. "Improving the UK's response to economic crime." National Economic Crime Centre. *National Crime Agency*. www.nationalcrimeagency.gov.uk/what-we-do/national-economic-crime-centre.
[33] Home Office. "Joint Fraud Taskforce," *Gov.UK*, October 17, 2017. www.gov.uk/government/collections/joint-fraud-taskforce.

and fraudulent activities, such as ISIS's PPE scheme described in Chapter 10, and terrorist financing is evident. As such, like in the US case, the UK's establishment of multiple PPPs is indicative of the important role the private sector plays in countering illicit finance, including terrorism financing.

The US and UK models, however, are not necessarily role models for every country. As Tom Keatinge of the Royal United Services Institute (RUSI) has presciently observed, local context matters. A PPP structure in one country can differ from another. For instance, as Keatinge concluded in 2017, "partnership models that focus on developing typologies and better shared understanding of risk, such as those in Singapore, Canada, and Kenya, can be effective vehicles by which the private and public sectors come together to discuss mutual financial crime challenges, building trust and confidence in each other."[34] In layman's terms, a global cookie-cutter approach is not feasible because countries have different laws, regulatory regimes, and risk appetites for engagement with private sector colleagues. Nonetheless, there are, as a detailed 2017 report by RUSI on PPPs, best practices that can be followed to allow for effective private–public sector engagement. Among them, the need to adaptability to changing methods of illicit financing, establishing trust between sectors, a robust understanding of the parameters of the PPP relationship, investing in technology to foster cooperation, and getting buy-in from both public and private sector leadership figures is critical to an enduring relationship.[35] Without these basic features, a PPP will fail because the methods of exchange will be unclear and without a mooring that will keep all parties of the engagement on track.

---

[34] Keatinge, T. "Public–Private Partnerships and Financial Crime: Advancing an Inclusive Model," *RUSI*, December 1, 2017. www.rusi.org/explore-our-research/publications/commentary/public-private-partnerships-and-financial-crime-advancing-inclusive-model.

[35] Artingstall, D., & Maxwell, N. "The Role of Financial Information-Sharing Partnerships in the Disruption of Crime," *RUSI*, October 17, 2017. https://rusi.org/publication/occasional-papers/role-financial-information-sharing-partnerships-disruption-crime.

Private and public sector forms of engagement that center on information exchange also occur at intergovernmental levels. The FATF, for example, under the Private Sector Consultative Forum (PSCF), meets with the private sector once per year to discuss trends related to money laundering and terrorism financing. In 2024, the PSCF was hosted in Vienna, Austria, at the UN's Office of Drugs and Crime's headquarters. The meeting brought together nation states, multilateral bodies, and the private sector to specifically focus on challenges related to beneficial ownership, payment transparency, asset recovery, Central Bank Digital Currencies, and the importance of governments taking a risk-based approach to the abuse of the non-profit organizations by illicit actors.[36]

RECAP AND CONCLUDING THOUGHTS

Without the private sector, government capabilities to disrupt terrorism financing are less effective. The relationship between the public sector and the private sector can be adversarial, resulting in fines and sanctions. While banks, especially US-based ones, have been protecting their systems from abuse by criminal actors, they are imperfect. While the BSA was adopted in the 1970s, major banks like TD Bank still make major mistakes, resulting in significant penalties.

Banks are not the only game in town when it comes to moving or storing wealth. As this chapter explains, MSBs and DNFBPs also play a significant roles in obfuscating the source of wealth, or moving cash. As the ICIJ investigations, known as the Panama Papers, FinCEN files, and Pandora Papers make clear, white-collar law firms and other white-collar professionals can advance criminal, state sponsors of terrorism, and FTOs financial goals. As a result of these journalistic investigations, multiple countries, the United States among them, adopted new legislation with an eye toward improving transparency related to a range of transactions where ownership of

---

[36] FATF. "Private Sector Consultative Forum," *FATF*, April 2024. www.fatf-gafi.org/en/publications/Fatfgeneral/private-sector-consultative-forum-April-2024.html.

an asset has been previously unclear. In the United States, for example, the CTA was implemented in 2024. In the years ahead, whether the CTA sheds light on illicit transactions will become clearer when the first public reports examining implementation become public in 2025.

Cooperation, in the form of PPPs, at the national level is critical if criminal financing, including terrorist financing, is successfully countered. For the most part, these PPPs came into being post 9/11. As the 2017 RUSI report noted, implementation can be imperfect. More recently, the UN's Counterterrorism Executive Director (UN CTED) emphasized many of the same challenges identified by RUSI, such as one-way communication, unclear legal frameworks, not including nonbanks at forums, and a general lack of capacity. The UN CTED's 2023 report emphasized that the formation of PPPs can also result in unintended consequences, such as potentially harming human rights. The UN report explained, "PPPs necessarily must involve designing data systems and processes which provide access to and analysis of a wealth of information, often comprising sensitive information, which may result in human rights breaches if disclosed in an arbitrary or unlawful manner."[37] Potential access to banking information, addresses, dates of birth, among other personally identifiable information presents a challenge for enduring public–private sector exchanges. Governments, simply put, cannot run roughshod over the private sector in the pursuit of terrorist financiers. Respecting the need to protect data in accordance with international human rights law is critically important. To ensure this occurs, experts in the field who engage in capacity-building efforts to bolster banks, MSBs, and DNFBPs' responsiveness to government regulation and FATF recommendations must ensure that training modules incorporate the importance of privacy protections and human rights.

---

[37] United Nations. "Establishing Effective Public-Private Partnerships on Countering the Financing of Terrorism," *Security Council – Counter-Terrorism Committee (CTC)*, 2023. Page 17. www.un.org/securitycouncil/ctc/content/establishing-effective-public-private-partnerships-countering-financing-terrorism.

Capacity-building efforts that promote PPPs should also emphasize the importance of DNFBPs as stakeholders and, as such, should have a chair at the capacity-building meetings. This need is crystal clear, especially in the wake of the ICIJ's reports. And, of course, the consistent use of banking and nonbanking services by terrorist financiers, as this chapter has detailed, underscores the importance of the private sector's role in countering terrorist financing. The private sector continues to expand, however. Indeed, the expansion is often happening more quickly than governments can respond. The rise of cryptocurrency and other financial technology (FINTECH) developments further illuminate the importance of the private sector in battling terrorist financing. Chapter 10 will examine the burgeoning field of virtual assets, such as cryptocurrency, and what it may mean for those working in the AML/CFT field.

10 Cryptocurrency

Key Source of Terrorist Finance or Much Ado about Nothing?

Cryptocurrency is a form of digital currency and part of a broader ecosystem that the FATF deems a virtual asset. There are many different types of cryptocurrencies, but the most well-known is Bitcoin. Bitcoin was created in 2008 by the mysterious Satoshi Nakamoto, a nom de guerre for a yet-to-be-identified person who wanted to break the chains of government control over currency. This chapter focuses on terrorist use of cryptocurrency and how governments and the private sector are working, often together, against terrorist abuse of cryptocurrency and other virtual assets. First, this chapter will examine briefly what cryptocurrency is and how it works. Second, the chapter will examine briefly other examples of virtual assets, such as non-fungible tokens (NFTs). Finally, the bulk of this chapter will look out examples of terrorist use of cryptocurrency and NFTs and how governments are working with the private sector to trace the use of virtual currency – with the aim of blocking the movement of these assets and then ultimately freezing and seizing them.

Depending on the country, cryptocurrency can be a medium of exchange (like fiat currency), an asset class (like a commodity), and is a store of value (like an investment, such as gold, that could increase in value over time). For illicit actors like terrorist groups, because cryptocurrencies, like Bitcoin, have worth, they will be coveted. As detailed in this chapter, terrorist groups actively seek donations made in the form of cryptocurrency. That does not mean, however, that cryptocurrency is more prone to abuse than other mediums of exchange, like the US dollar. Many countries, like the United States and Japan, by way of examples, see cryptocurrency as a legal means of payment. In contrast, China has outlawed cryptocurrency as part of its fight against financial crime.[1] In reality, it is perhaps one of the key attributes of cryptocurrency that makes China nervous about its use. Cryptocurrency like Bitcoin is inherently decentralized, meaning that a central authority like a government or central bank does not have direct control over it. Simply put, China can't print Bitcoin, and because it is decentralized, it is thus harder to regulate. Because a large universe of cryptocurrencies is decentralized, illicit actors may find their use intriguing because the government's control over the medium of exchange is more limited. Second, another attribute of cryptocurrency is the fact that the transactions are pseudonymous, but there is a degree of transparency. While names of individuals involved in a Bitcoin exchange are not clearly listed in a public way, the transaction itself is detailed on a digital ledger.

Bitcoin (as well as other types of cryptocurrencies) transactions are recorded in a public ledger called the Blockchain, which Nakamoto invented when he created Bitcoin. The Blockchain is transparent to the public and this increases accountability and stands in contrast to fiat currency whereupon recording the movement of dollars, for example, is detailed privately by banks. The Blockchain detailing a Bitcoin transaction will contain a series of numbers and letters that may, upon the layperson's eye, look indecipherable. However, as will be detailed later in this chapter, multiple companies and governments can trace the transaction, at times back to an individual. Further, as will also be discussed, companies involved in facilitating cryptocurrency transactions also have a responsibility to document any suspicious use related to money laundering or terrorism financing. The FATF has worked closely with governments to ensure that virtual asset providers are fulfilling various FATF recommendations.

While the Blockchain and use of cryptocurrency can increase transparency and accountability, there are several limitations for

---

[1] Shin, F. "What's behind China's cryptocurrency ban?" *World Economic Forum*, January 31, 2022. www.weforum.org/stories/2022/01/what-s-behind-china-s-cryptocurrency-ban/#:~:text=The%20People's%20Bank%20of%20China,crime%20and%20prevent%20economic%20instability.

widespread adoption by terrorist groups and the average citizen alike. First, Bitcoin has a maximum supply of 21 million Bitcoins and as of December 2024, according to Investopedia, 19.9 million Bitcoins have already been minted.[2] Second, some cryptocurrencies, including Bitcoin, are volatile and the ups and downs of the market can discourage widespread use by users. The portability of cryptocurrency, because they exist only in digital form, however, is an added benefit, especially for terrorist groups who often must lug wads of cash across borders. Cryptocurrency can move with ease across borders and can be stored in digital wallets that are not subject to inspection by border patrol and customs officials at ports of entry.

There are numerous types of cryptocurrencies. Bitcoin is the most popular and it is followed by the Ethereum platform, which has the second-largest market capitalization as of February 2025.[3] While Ethereum is based on Blockchain technology like Bitcoin, what sets it apart from it is the fact that Ethereum supports smart contacts, which are self-executing contracts that contain terms of agreements between a buyer and seller. These smart contracts are written directly into the exchange as lines of code and can be used for a wide range of purposes, including, but not limited to, supply chain management or even voting systems. Ethereum's cryptocurrency is called 'Ether' and the broader Ethereum platform can also support a broad range of decentralized financial (DeFi) applications, which can be used for anything from gaming to social media. Arguably, Ethereum is more versatile than Bitcoin, but both represent a push toward decentralized finance. DeFi ultimately is a financial system that relies on Blockchain technology, which allows for permissionless and open exchange of finances without banks playing a prominent role. Banks represent the traditional system of centralized finance (CeFi), where

---

[2] Hayes, A. "What Happens to Bitcoin after All 21 Million Are Mined?" *Investopedia*, December 22, 2024. www.investopedia.com/tech/what-happens-bitcoin-after-21-million-mined/.

[3] CoinDesk. "Top cryptocurrency prices and market cap." *CoinDesk*. www.coindesk.com/price.

an intermediary like a lending institution, that is often highly regulated, will broker a transaction between parties. In contrast to DeFi within the world of CeFi, individuals, like a terrorist financer, will need to interact with a centralized institution, like a bank, if they want to move money from their account to someone within their terrorist orbit. The bank acts as a custodian of the funds and will enforce compliance and regulatory requirements before allowing the transaction to be processed. For illicit actors, cryptocurrency is intriguing because the middleman, like a bank, is removed.

While cryptocurrency use is an example of DeFi, it would be a mistake to assume that there isn't a universe of private sector entities needed to facilitate the effective use of virtual assets like cryptocurrency. But before exploring that universe, it is important to note that cryptocurrency is only one form of virtual asset. Stablecoins are another example of a virtual asset, and its chief distinguishing characteristic from other forms of cryptocurrency, like Bitcoin, is that a stablecoin is generally pegged against another asset, such as fiat currency. The largest stablecoin in terms of market capitalization as of February 2025 is the Tether USDT, which is linked to the Ethereum platform, and has a market cap of $141 billion.[4] The Tether USDT is pegged to the US dollar and has equivalent value to the dollar. Among the reasons for using a stablecoin as opposed to Bitcoin are smaller or no transaction fees for converting a stablecoin to fiat currency, passive income opportunities by earning interest, and less volatility.[5] Stablecoins, simply put, do not put its investors on the same roller-coaster ride as those who acquire Bitcoin. Another type of virtual asset is central bank digital currency (CBDC), which is digital form of central bank money. Unlike Bitcoin or stablecoins, governments play a leading role in CBDC development, use, and

---

[4] Kraken. "Top Stablecoins Coins by Carket cap." *Kraken*. www.kraken.com/categories/stablecoins.

[5] Christian, R. "World's 6 Largest Stablecoins: Top Cryptocurrencies that Maintain a Stable Price," *Bankrate*, November 22, 2024. www.bankrate.com/investing/worlds-largest-stablecoins/.

dissemination. According to the International Monetary Fund, as of 2022, more than 100 CBDCs were in development by countries.[6] Finally, another form of a virtual asset is NFTs. NFTs are different from cryptocurrency like Bitcoin in several ways. NFTs are non-fungible, and any potential value of an NFT is linked to the authenticity or novelty of the token. NFTs can take other types of digital forms, such as tweet, art, or music, and then mint them into an NFT for sale.[7] NFT use by terrorist groups will be examined in this chapter because they've been leveraged for financial purposes. While not the focus of this chapter, it is important to note that the Department of Treasury's 2024 report on risks associated with terrorist financing noted that terrorist groups, like ISIS, were moving toward using stablecoins, such as Tether USDT, to move or store funds.[8]

The constellation of private sector actors involved in the virtual asset space is increasingly becoming crowded, and with the growing popularity of virtual assets, such as Bitcoin, organizations like the FATF have taken notice. Indeed, FATF has highlighted the importance of virtual assets service providers (VASPs) to abide by AML/CFT recommendations. VASPs provide a service to its customers by facilitating an exchange between various types of virtual assets, such as converting Bitcoin to Dogecoin, or between a virtual asset and fiat currency when a customer may want to convert their Bitcoin to US dollars. VASP services converting a virtual currency into fiat currency are critically important because many purchases,

---

[6] Stanley, A. "Picture This: The Ascent of CBDCs." *Finance & Development Magazine*. *International Monetary Fund*. www.imf.org/en/Publications/fandd/issues/2022/09/Picture-this-The-ascent-of-CBDCs#:~:text=Central%20bank%20digital%20currencies%20(CBDCs,not%20volatile%2C%20unlike%20crypto%20assets.

[7] Blazakis, Jason. "Far-Right Online Financing and How to Counter It," *Global Center*, August 2022. https://globalcenter.org/resource/far-right-online-financing-and-how-to-counter-it/.

[8] U.S. Department of the Treasury, *2024 National Terrorist Financing Risk Assessment*, February 2024. https://home.treasury.gov/system/files/136/2024-National-Terrorist-Financing-Risk-Assessment.pdf.

such as the buying of a house, in multiple countries are dominated by the use of fiat. VASPs are diverse and include companies that: create digital wallets for the storage of virtual assets; businesses that pool the mining[9] of cryptocurrency for customers; custodians that hold cryptocurrency on behalf of their customer; brokerage services that trade or issue cryptocurrencies for their clients; and companies that maintain cryptocurrency, like Bitcoin ATMs that can convert Bitcoin into US dollars.

VASPs are involved at every stage of the virtual asset lifecycle, and this is why organizations like the FATF have increasingly focused their regulatory-related guidance on VASPs. Among recent policies developed by FATF that increase VASPs' and financial institutions' responsibilities related to documenting virtual asset usage is the broadening of FATF Recommendation 16 to cover VASPs. This policy shift of deploying the "Travel Rule" on VASPs has become a bone of contention within the virtual assets industry. The principal importance of the Travel Rule is not new in that it has been applied against banks and the 'movement' or 'travel' of fiat currency between individuals, entities, and organizations. FATF Recommendation 15 also sets forth a set of guidelines for countries to ensure that VASPs follow the same rules as financial institutions. FATF, by virtue of the travel rule and Recommendation 15, creates a regulatory framework that VASPs, like banks, must implement to ensure virtual currency is not being exploited by terrorist groups. For example, countries are required to require VASPs to secure a license to operate. The travel rule also requires VASPs to file suspicious transaction reports and other types of reports involving the movement of virtual currency between individuals. In the United States, FinCEN promulgates US-based reporting requirements on VASPs pursuant to guidance on Regulation FIN-2019-G001, which

---

[9] Cryptocurrencies like Bitcoin are 'mined' by solving complex cryptographic problems. This requires significant computer processing unit power and thus electricity. It is the only way, however, to create a new Bitcoin. Companies will assist 'miners' by facilitating the pooling of resources for the purposes of creating a new virtual asset.

was adopted in May 2019.[10] The FinCEN threshold for reporting on transactions involving virtual assets is much lower ($3,000) than the CTR threshold for financial institutions reporting on the movement of cash in excess of $10,000.

The application of the travel rule in the crypto world has resulted in pushback from the private sector. John Jefferies, the director of the private sector's Travel Rule Information Sharing Alliance (TRISA), is encouraging the Trump Administration to make changes to FIN-2019-G001. Among the key elements of the TRISA proposal is a call to eliminate the travel rule or establish a threshold at the same level as CTR's for fiat currency. TRISA also suggests combining blockchain analytics with curated crypto-crime databases to better identify risks associated with the movement of virtual currencies. TRISA also suggests more efficient use of AI tools and information sharing through prescribed mutually authenticated encrypted messaging for exchanges.[11]

FATF and various FIUs, such as FinCEN, have been clear about the possibility of virtual assets being used by terrorist groups, and as a consequence, FATF recommendations and government-specific regulations have been adopted to counter terrorist use of virtual currency. However, as detailed by Chainalysis's 2023 crypto crime report, during CY 2022, illicit transactions surpassed $20 billion for the first time.[12] Despite an increase in regulations, illicit actor interest in virtual assets is increasing. Nonetheless, in relative turns, the use of virtual assets to facilitate crime, much less terrorist financing, is very low compared to the use of cash or other types of assets to further misdeeds. Bad actors still rely on the formal financial

---

[10] Financial Crimes Enforcement Network (FinCEN). *Application of FinCEN's Regulations to Certain Business Models Involving Convertible Virtual Currencies*, May 9, 2019. www.fincen.gov/sites/default/files/2019-05/FinCEN%20Guidance%20on%20Virtual%20Currencies%20May%209%202019.pdf.

[11] Blazakis Interview of John Jeffries Director of TRISA, February 6, 2025.

[12] Chainalysis Team, "2023 Crypto Crime Trends: Illicit Cryptocurrency Volumes Reach All-Time Highs Amid Surge in Sanctions Designations and Hacking," *Chainalysis*, January 12, 2023. www.chainalysis.com/blog/2023-crypto-crime-report-introduction/.

system and the movement of cash to further their illegal activities, as detailed in the 2024 Nasdaq financial Crime Report. According to that report, more than $3.1 trillion in illicit flows moved through the global financial system, of which an estimated $11.5 billion related to terrorist financing.[13]

While the use of virtual assets to augment illicit financial activity, including terrorist financing, is a drop in the bucket in relative terms to the use of cash to facilitate illegal activity, there is no denying that multiple terrorist groups have solicited donations in the form of cryptocurrency from donors. As discussed in Chapter 4, Zoobia Shahnaz integrated cryptocurrency as part of her strategy to fund foreign fighters to join ISIS in Syria and Iraq. Shahnaz's activities were not an outlier for ISIS. More recently, between 2019 and 2022, Mohammed Azharuddin Chhipa of Fairfax County, Virginia, engaged in a fundraising effort via the use of social media to fundraise for those in need in shelter in the Middle East. In reality, Chhipa was actually raising funds to support ISIS members, some of whom were at the al-Hol camp in Syria.[14] During the three-year funding scheme, Chhipa would send along with his UK-based coconspirator, according to the US Department of Justice, more than $180,000 in cryptocurrency to support ISIS prison breaks, terrorist attacks, and ISIS foreign fighters.[15] According to the Justice Department, "Chhipa would receive electronic transfers of funds and travel hundreds of miles collect funds by hand. He would then covert the money to cryptocurrency and send it to Turkey, where it was smuggled to ISIS members in Syria."[16]

---

[13] AML Intelligence. "More than $3 Trillion in Illicit Funds Floored through Global Financial System in 2023; Banks Call for More Regulatory Guidance to Tackle Endemic," *Anti-Financial Crime & Financial Crime Compliance Regulatory Intelligence*, January 16, 2024. www.amlintelligence.com/2024/01/latest-more-than-3trillion-in-illicit-funds-flowed-thru-global-financial-system-in-2023-banks-call-for-more-regulatory-guidance-to-tackle-endemic/.

[14] Rizzo, S. "Va. Man Charged with Sending Money to ISIS Women Overseas," *The Washington Post*, May 5, 2023. www.washingtonpost.com/dc-md-va/2023/05/05/va-man-charged-isis-al-hol/.

[15] U.S. Department of Justice. "Virginia man convicted for crypto financing scheme to ISIS," *DOJ Archives*, December 16, 2024. www.justice.gov/archives/opa/pr/virginia-man-convicted-crypto-financing-scheme-isis.

[16] Ibid.

Chhipa's scheme was eerily similar to that of Shahnaz because the ultimate value of the cryptocurrency was its use in obscuring the ultimate source of the funds – and thus was more important as part of a terrorist financing cycle that allowed for the movement and storage of wealth.

ISIS is not the only group keen to benefit from accessing cryptocurrency. In 2020, the US Department of Justice announced how Hamas, al-Qa'ida, and ISIS engaged in broad schemes involving the use of cryptocurrency. In the case of Hamas, starting in 2019, its militant wing known as the al-Qassam Brigades started an online fundraising campaign where the group specifically called for Bitcoin donations. The Hamas campaign occurred over multiple webpages the group organized, and Hamas tried to reassure potential donors that all donations would be anonymous.[17] In the same press release, the Justice Department detailed that al-Qa'ida operated a "Bitcoin money laundering network using Telegram and other social media platforms to solicit cryptocurrency donations."[18] Al-Qa'ida during its multiyear campaign would use false charities and explicit calls for support to help the group purchase weapons so it could carry out terrorist attacks. Like al-Qa'ida, ISIS's scheme, which was also highlighted in the Department of Justice's press release, also tried to tug on the heartstrings of possible donors. ISIS's campaign was established under the guise of combatting COVID-19, and by using a fake website called "Face Mask Center," ISIS claimed that it was selling FDA-approved N95 masks that could help people remain healthy. The ISIS page accepted cryptocurrency as a form of payment.[19] Examples of terrorist groups raising, moving, and storing cryptocurrency remain a persistent challenge and these cases, and many others, utilize online

---

[17] U.S. Department of Justice. "Global Disruption of Three Terror Finance Cyber-enabled Campaigns," *DOJ Archives*, August 13, 2020. www.justice.gov/archives/opa/pr/global-disruption-three-terror-finance-cyber-enabled-campaigns.

[18] U.S. Department of Justice. "Virginia Man Convicted for Crypto Financing Scheme to ISIS." *DOJ Archives*. December 16, 2024. www.justice.gov/archives/opa/pr/virginia-man-convicted-crypto-financing-scheme-isis.

[19] US Department of Justice. "United States' Verified Complaint for Forfeiture in Rem." *DOJ Archives*. August 5, 2020. www.justice.gov/archives/opa/pr/global-disruption-three-terror-finance-cyber-enabled-campaigns.

fundraising often coupled with tales of woe. Playing on the heartstrings or health concerns of donor bases, groups like ISIS, al-Qa'ida, and Hamas is a common tactic. Similarly, groups telling donors that their donations cannot be tracked and that they are anonymous is another way to try and build faith with possible supporters.

As will be demonstrated in the next few pages, the concept of anonymity is a myth when it comes to the use of virtual assets to fund terrorism. Some terrorist groups, as part of an effort to circumvent law enforcement and private sector tracing of virtual assets transactions, have tried to use privacy coins, which are a type of cryptocurrency that are intentionally designed to prioritize the privacy and anonymity of users. Examples of these virtual assets include Monero, which has been gaining steam among illicit groups, like ISIS.

PUBLIC–PRIVATE SECTOR PARTNERSHIPS IN COUNTERING ILLICIT USE OF VIRTUAL ASSETS

Terrorist interest in cryptocurrency has not gone unnoticed, and public–private sector cooperation has been vital in combatting terrorist financing activity in the virtual asset space. Regulatory interest, such as FinCEN's advisory, and FATF recommendations provide important scaffolding for both private and public sector responses to illicit use of cryptocurrency. Multiple companies have dedicated efforts to trace illicit use of virtual currency and in some cases have directly partnered with governments to check terrorist use of these assets. Among the top companies that have engaged in tracking illicit use of virtual assets are CipherTrace,[20] TRM Labs, and Chainalysis. In some cases, the mere reporting of illicit activity in the form of publications can illuminate the untoward ways virtual assets can be leveraged. In other cases, the companies have worked directly with governments to stop terrorist groups and criminal organizations from doing the public harm by raising or moving cryptocurrency to fuel violent misdeeds.

---

[20] CipherTrace was purchased in 2021 by Mastercard. Later in 2024, various news services reported that many of the services provided by CipherTrace were discontinued by Mastercard.

CipherTrace, before it was purchased by MasterCard, was at the forefront of creating a capacity for tracing transactions involving privacy coins. In 2020, CipherTrace gained an ability to trace Monero and touted the ability to use its capability to combat illicit activities involving that privacy coin.[21] Also in November, CipherTrace filed two patents related to its proprietary technology that were critical to its Monero-tracing capability. The US government took notice of CipherTrace's capability to trace Monero and entered into multiple contracts with the organization, including a two-year project that CipherTrace announced in a press release touting its impending work with the Department of Homeland Security.[22] In CipherTrace's 2021 yearly report, it explained that it also played a role in the US Justice Department's 2020 action against Hamas, ISIS, and al-Qa'ida use of cryptocurrency. CipherTrace explained that its "analysts identified further movement of funds belonging to al Qassam Brigades – the military wing of Hamas ... and that CipherTrace reported on donations made to Syria terrorist organization al-Ikhwa, which were ultimately sent to al Qaeda."[23] The 2021 CipherTrace report detailing these tracing efforts also intimate coordination with the government of Israel in its seizing of cryptocurrency associated with Hamas's military wing. All this to say, CipherTrace's work with multiple governments is indicative of the importance of private–public sector coordination in the highly technical area of cryptocurrency tracing.

---

[21] de Candia, A. "CipherTrace: Two Patents for Tracking Monero (XMR)," *Cryptonomist*, November 23, 2020. https://en.cryptonomist.ch/2020/11/23/ciphertrace-patents-tracking-monero-xmr/.

[22] Savanović, D. "Can the IRS Track Monero? Not for Now, but They Are Trying," *PlasBit*, January 4, 2025. https://plasbit.com/anonymous/can-the-irs-track-monero#:~:text=In%20August%202020%2C%20a%20cryptocurrency,million%20from%20a%20government%20contract.

[23] CipherTrace. "Cryptocurrency Crime and Anti-money Laundering Report." *Cryptocurrency Intelligence*, August, 2021. Pages 28–30. https://info.ciphertrace.com/hubfs/CAML%20Reports/Cryptocurrency%20Crime%20and%20Anti-Money%20Laundering%20Report%2C%20August%202021.pdf.

CipherTrace's work is complex, as described in a 2020 interview with the former technical head of CipherTrace, Dave Jevans. Jevans describes on the show Monero Space that CipherTrace used a variety of tools, many of which were off of the blockchain, to identify the origin and destination addresses in Monero transactions. Jevans acknowledged, however, that Monero users can prevent certain types of identifying from being exposed by adopting strong operational security protocols.[24] The work to trace Monero is, according to the founding Chief Management Officer of CipherTrace, John Jefferies, difficult. Jeffries explained that tracing Monero is, "a game of cat and mouse and the Monero team issued patches immediately."[25] Monero took umbrage in firms like CipherTrace trying to break its privacy. This is unsurprising given the libertarian spirit behind the notion of cryptocurrency. Privacy coin companies like Monero especially prize deregulation, privacy, and protecting their users' identities. As such, developing patches that inhibit, even temporarily, blockchain analytic firms like CipherTrace from tracing transactions involving Monero is in keeping with the libertarian mindset that has made cryptocurrency popular among its enthusiasts.

Nonetheless, Monero being leveraged by terrorist actors is a deep concern, and other private sector companies have identified terrorist groups using the privacy coin. In a 2024 report by the Global Network on Extremism and Terrorism (GNET), ISIS's Khorasan Province (ISIS-K) based in Afghanistan was highlighted as a group heavily involved in acquiring Monero. GNET explained that ISIS-K had at one time identified Monero as its cryptocurrency of choice and that the group was intent on using the privacy coin as part of a diversification of financing and fundraising strategy.[26]

---

[24] Monero Space. "CipherTrace's Monero Tracing Tool – Chat with Dave Jevans, Dr. Sarang Noether, and Justin Ehrenhofer." August 31, 2020. www.youtube.com/watch?v=w5rtd3md11g. Accessed March 10, 2025.

[25] Blazakis interview of John Jefferies. February 4, 2025.

[26] Roul, A. "The Rise of Monero: ISKP's Preferred Cryptocurrency for Terror Financing." *Global Network on Extremism and Technology*, October 4, 2024. https://gnet-research.org/2024/10/04/the-rise-of-monero-iskps-preferred-cryptocurrency-for-terror-financing/.

The GNET report highlights underlying investigations by the blockchain analytic company, TRM Labs. Like CipherTrace, TRM Labs also has the capability to trace, to a certain extent, illicit activity involving the use of privacy coins like Monero. Like CipherTrace, TRM Labs explains in its October 2024 paper that Monero's intentional obscuring by using stealth addresses, ring confidential transactions, and ring signatures can make it difficult to understand the primary addresses and transaction amounts of those engaged in Monero transactions.[27]

Furthermore, in its July 2023 report, TRM Labs documented blockchain evidence that ISIS-K networks in multiple countries based in Southwest Asia and Central Asia between July 2022 and July 2023 controlled multiple cryptocurrency wallets and that the group received more than 2 million USD worth of the cryptocurrency Tether on the Tron network.[28] TRM Labs report would point to a moving trend of ISIS-K interest in the use of receiving Tether cryptocurrency via the Tron platform.[29] ISIS-K's interests in cryptocurrency have also brought multiple private sector companies together to battle against illicit use of cryptocurrency. In August 2024, TRM Labs along with TRON and Tether announced the formation of the T3 Financial Crime Unit (T3 FCU). The T3 FCU is a novel approach where three private sector entities are working collaboratively to ensure that the financial ecosystem surrounding the use of cryptocurrency is protected from illicit use. In a TRM Labs January 2025

---

[27] TRM Labs. "The Rise of Monero: Traceability, Challenges, and Research Review." *TRM Labs*, October, 2024. www.trmlabs.com/post/the-rise-of-monero-traceability-challenges-and-research-review#:~:text=While%20some%20traceability%20remains%20possible,asset%20fraud%20and%20financial%20crime.

[28] TRM Labs. "TRM Finds Mounting Evidence of Crypto Use by ISIS and Its Supporters in Asia." *TRM Labs*, July 2023. www.trmlabs.com/post/trm-finds-mounting-evidence-of-crypto-use-by-isis-and-its-supporters-in-asia.

[29] The Tron Network is decentralized blockchain operating platform that allows users to create, among many other things, decentralized applications. The Tron network, like Ethereum, relies on smart contracts for the implementation of peer-to-peer transactions. Tron's cryptocurrency is Tronix but users can also exchange/trade for other cryptocurrency, such as Tether, over its platform.

announcement, T3 FCU "froze more than 100 million in criminal assets globally ... across five continents."[30] The TRM Labs announcement noted among the activities identified were cases of terrorism financing. Private sector to private sector engagement, especially in the tracing of virtual assets, is critically important. In the case of T3 FCU, a blockchain analysis company (TRM Labs), a decentralized blockchain-based operating system (TRON), and a cryptocurrency company (Tether) that created the Tether stablecoin are pooling their distinct expertise and resources to combat illicit crime. In doing that, the troika can point to their adherence not only to underlying government regulations, such as FATF recommendations that push governments to regulate cryptocurrencies but also demonstrating to users that the companies are doing their level best to create a safe operating environment.

Another private firm well known in the blockchain forensics area is Chainalysis, founded in 2014, and is known as the first start-up company to engage in Bitcoin tracing. Chainalysis rose to prominence for its activities associated with partnership with US law enforcement that was engaged in taking down the infamous Silk Road darknet marketplace. The author Andy Greenberg detailed first in a Wired article and then later in more detail in his book Tracers in the Dark, outlined how Chainalysis analysts used their Bitcoin tracing capabilities to seize more than 1 billion dollars (in 2020 terms, but would grow significantly later, as discussed later in this chapter, with the rise of Bitcoin prices) from the various takedowns of the Silk Road marketplace.[31] The Silk Road marketplace was founded by Ross Ulbricht in 2011 and was immediately seen by US federal law enforcement as the most

---

[30] TRM Insights. "T3 Financial Crime Unit Marks Enforcement Victory: $100 Million in Criminal Assets Frozen Across Five Continents." *TRM Insights*, January 2, 2025. www.trmlabs.com/post/t3-financial-crime-unit-marks-enforcement-victory-100-million-in-criminal-assets-frozen-across-five-continents.

[31] Greenberg, A. "Inside the Bitcoin Bust That Took Down the Web's Biggest Child Abuse Site," *Wired*, April 7, 2022. www.wired.com/story/tracers-in-the-dark-welcome-to-video-crypto-anonymity-myth/.

sophisticated and extensive criminal marketplace on the internet. Silk Road was a black-market bazaar where criminals of all stripes could buy weapons, drugs, and, amongst many other things, traffic people. Silk Road represented a new wild-west internet frontier for both law enforcement and blockchain analytic companies like Chainalysis. Ulbricht aimed to provide anonymity for both buyers and sellers using his dark net marketplace. As part of an effort to do that, during Silk Road 1.0, users could only gain access using the Tor network, which hides both browser and internet service routes that often allow for easy identification of online activity. Unlike the surface web, where one can do a google search in plain site because of the user's Internet Protocol (IP) address, which serves as the equivalent of digital fingerprint, the darknet disguises a user's online activity. Digital fingerprints, in other words, are either difficult or impossible to trace. Another feature of Ulbricht's Silk Road marketplace was peer-to-peer transactions using Bitcoin. The combination of Tor and Bitcoin coupled with the sale of sins made Silk Road popular among criminal organizations and terrorist groups. Ulbricht was aware that Silk Road was abetting criminal and terrorist behavior, but he was making money on every transaction and reaped profits in the millions. Ultimately, Ulbricht, for allowing for a permissive environment for criminals to operate, when he was ultimately discovered due to the investigative work of US law enforcement and blockchain tracing by Chainalysis, would be prosecuted and sentenced to life in federal prison.[32] As Andy Greenberg extensively details in *Tracers in the Dark*, Chainalysis would not only collaborate with US federal law enforcement to take down Silk Road, but would also assist with investigations centering around AlphaBay.[33]

---

[32] U.S. Immigration and Customs Enforcement. "Ross Ulbricht, aka Dread Pirate Roberts, sentenced to life in federal prison for creating, operating 'Silk Road' website," *U.S. Immigration and Customs Enforcement*, May 29, 2015. www.ice.gov/news/releases/ross-ulbricht-aka-dread-pirate-roberts-sentenced-life-federal-prison-creating.

[33] Greenberg, A. *Tracers in the Dark: The Global Hunt for the Crime Lords of Cryptocurrency*. Doubleday. 2022.

AlphaBay was a darknet marketplace that facilitated wide-ranging criminal activity that was bought and sold using cryptocurrencies like Bitcoin, Monero, and Ethereum.[34]

The convergence of cryptocurrency and the darknet provides a permissive playground for illicit actors, including terrorists, to buy and sell material that can further their dangerous ambitions. The examples of taking down Silk Road and AlphaBay provide good examples of private–public sector partnerships. However, when a darknet marketplace is removed, it is often quickly replaced. Not long after the demise of Ulbricht's Silk Road, Silk Road 2.0 was created, and of course other marketplaces like AlphaBay continued the illicit darknet financing tradition that is devoid of regulation.

Chainalysis in a 2022 letter provided to the US Department of the Treasury documented a capacity to trace criminal use of NFTs and explained that illicit use of NFTs should be monitored closely by regulators.[35] In at least three occasions, designated terrorist groups have minted and attempted to sell NFTs (as art). In July 2022, the data analytics company, Kharon, founded by former US Department of the Treasury officials, detailed that the US Department of State designated terrorist group, the Russian Imperial Movement (RIM), was raising funds over the OpenSea NFT platform. In the Kharon report, RIM's NFT endeavor, dubbed the Terrircon Project, aimed to raise funds for use in Ukraine. RIM, according to Kharon's report, likely made less than $10,000 in sales, but the effort nonetheless illustrated the diversification of terrorist financing. NFTs are only bought and sold with cryptocurrency over platforms like OpenSeas. Later in 2022, the Wall Street Journal documented that another US and UN 1267 designated terrorist group, ISIS's Khorasan Province, minted an NFT that glorified ISIS's attack on a Taliban position

---

[34] U.S. Department of Justice. "AlphaBay, the Largest Online 'Dark Market,' Shut Down," *DOJ Archives*, July 20, 2017. www.justice.gov/opa/pr/alphabay-largest-online-dark-market-shut-down.

[35] Jonathan Levin, Letter to Jon Fishman, U.S. Department of the Treasury. November 3, 2022. Submitted via www.regulations.gov.

in Afghanistan.³⁶ Finally, the Russian private mercenary military company known the Wagner Group has also been active in the NFT space, according to March 2023 report by Elliptic, a blockchain analytics company.³⁷ The Wagner Group is treated as a terrorist group by the United Kingdom³⁸ and by the Parliamentary Assembly of the OSCE.³⁹

The private–public sector cooperation, especially by several blockchain analytic firms, is critical to countering terrorist use of virtual assets to further their illicit enterprises. The cooperation may take the form of side-by-side joint investigations, as exemplified by Chainalysis's work with various components of the US government, which were instrumental to removing dangerous darknet marketplaces. The work, as demonstrated by TRM Labs and Elliptic, could simply result in reports that notify the public of misuse of virtual assets, whether Bitcoin, NFTs, or something else, by terrorists. Finally, private sector collaboration, such as T3 FCU's work to identify illicit virtual currency transactions, is another powerful way to curtail behavior that seeks to exploit financial technology. These methods of detection and disabling terrorist use of virtual assets are also complemented often by government-led time-tested methods, like prosecutions and sanctions.

---

36 Talley, I. "Islamic State turns to NFTs to spread terror message." *The Wall Street Journal*, September 6, 2022. www.wsj.com/articles/islamic-state-turns-to-nfts-to-spread-terror-message-11662292800.

37 Elliptic. "How the Russia-Ukraine War Led to the Growth of NFT Fundraising." March 17, 2023. www.elliptic.co/blog/analysis/how-the-russia-ukraine-war-led-to-the-growth-of-nft-fundraising.

38 Home Office. "Wagner Group Proscribed," *Gov.UK*, September 15, 2023. www.gov.uk/government/news/wagner-group-proscribed#:~:text=The%20Russian%20mercenary%20organisation%2C%20Wagner,proscribed%20as%20a%20terrorist%20organisation.&text=Sunak%20Conservative%20government-,The%20Russian%20mercenary%20organisation%2C%20Wagner%20Group%2C%20has%20been%20proscribed%20as,on%20Wednesday%20(6th%20September).

39 OSCE Parliamentary Assembly. "Resolution on the Wagner Group's Terroristic Nature and Actions." OSCE PA. June 20–July 4, 2023. www.oscepa.org/en/documents/ad-hoc-committees-and-working-groups/ad-hoc-committee-on-countering-terrorism/4755-osce-pa-resolution-on-the-wagner-group-terroristic-nature-and-actions-30th-annual-session-2023/file.

SANCTIONS AND PROSECUTIONS IN RESPONSE TO ILLICIT VIRTUAL ASSET USE

There have been several US government direct responses to terrorists who have leveraged cryptocurrency to raise, move, or store assets for terrorist purposes, often at the benefit of a designated FTO. Interestingly, the Treasury Department has used its legal authorities pursuant to EO 13224 to designate in October 2023 the Hamas-linked Buy Cash Money and Money Transfer Company. Buy Cash, according to the Treasury Department, was designated for moving Bitcoin and storing Bitcoin in virtual wallets on behalf of Hamas. Further, the Treasury Department explained that the Israeli government seized a Bitcoin Wallet owned by Buy Cash.[40] Treasury's actions targeting individuals and groups involved in moving virtual currency are becoming more common. In addition to targeting crypto wallets, designating individuals and entities for moving cryptocurrency like Bitcoin on behalf of designated terrorist groups, cryptocurrency mixers, exchangers, and remitters have been sanctioned by the Treasury Department for augmenting illicit activities. Among the best examples is the Treasury Department's 2022 designation of Tornado Cash, a virtual currency mixer. Also known as tumblers, cryptocurrency mixers provide services to users of digital currency whereby the mixer can mix multiple types of virtual coins of several users and over a period of time as part of a process of obfuscating the original source of the funds. Tornado Cash, according to the Treasury Department's press release announcing the designation pursuant to EO 13694, provided services to a range of criminal groups. Among Tornado Cash's most significant misdeeds was facilitating the activity of North Korea's Lazarus Group. North Korea, sanctioned by the Department as a State Sponsor of Terrorism, has deployed a group of cyber hackers called the Lazarus Group to replenish North

---

[40] U.S. Department of the Treasury. "Following Terrorist Attack on Israel, Treasury Sanctions Hamas Operatives and Financial Facilitators," October 18, 2023. https://home.treasury.gov/news/press-releases/jy1816.

Korea's financial reserves by stealing cryptocurrency. Treasury specifically noted that Tornado Cash "laundered more than $7 billion worth of virtual currency since its creation in 2019. This includes over $455 million stolen by the Lazarus Group."[41] Increasingly, the use of sanction tools by governments will become prominent among the ways to counter terrorist group, states, and individual use of virtual assets to facilitate criminal endeavors. Every component in the virtual currency ecosystem could potentially be subject to terrorist designations – whether the specific person or group involved, the cryptocurrency stored in virtual wallets, the cryptocurrency mixers that obfuscate the sources of virtual wealth, or the actual seizing of the virtual assets. However, it will be incumbent upon governments to use its terrorist designation authorities responsibly in the virtual asset space because, as the Treasury Department also noted in its press release announcing the Tornado Cash designation, "most virtual currency activity is licit."[42]

The United States has also actively used prosecutions of individuals who have used virtual assets to benefit designated FTOs. The case of Shahnaz stands out as an example, but the Department of Justice also successfully prosecuted the aforementioned Mohammed Chhipa for his use of virtual currency to support ISIS. Chhipa would ultimately face the music of justice when he was finally convicted for providing material support to ISIS. In announcing his conviction in December 2024, nearly five years after Chhipa's support to ISIS began, the Department of Justice explained, "Chhipa faces a maximum penalty of 20 years in prison per count."[43] Exactly how many years Chhipa will spend behind bars is still to be determined as of

---

[41] U.S. Department of the Treasury. "U.S. Treasury Sanctions Notorious Virtual Currency Mixer Tornado Cash," August 8, 2022. https://home.treasury.gov/news/press-releases/jy0916#:~:text=Treasury%20will%20continue%20to%20aggressively,BSA)%20and%20its%20implementing%20regulations.

[42] Ibid.

[43] US Department of Justice. "Virginia Man Convicted for Crypto Financing Scheme to ISIS." *Department of Justice Archives*, December 16, 2024. www.justice.gov/archives/opa/pr/virginia-man-convicted-crypto-financing-scheme-isis.

early 2025, but frequently material supporters of designated FTOs will spend multiple decades in prison. The stories of Shahnaz and Chhipa using cryptocurrency to facilitate ISIS activity are not outliers and their prison stints serve as a reminder that the use of virtual currency will not inoculate terrorist financiers from the long arm of the law.

As important, however, as prosecutions related to the use of virtual currency is the seizing and forfeiture of assets associated with terrorist use of cryptocurrency. The Department of Justice's 2020 announcement of the dismantlement of Hamas, al-Qa'ida, and ISIS cyber-enabled fundraising schemes involving virtual assets was critically important because it resulted in the US government seizing millions of dollars scattered over multiple cryptocurrency accounts that were associated with the three designated FTOs.[44] At the time of the Department of Justice's action against the three terrorist groups, it was the largest ever cryptocurrency seizure connected to terrorist groups.[45]

In seizing the assets associated with the three terrorist groups, the US government was also complying with FATF Recommendation 38, which requires countries to seize assets to combat terrorist financing. Seizing assets is only one part of the asset management cycle, and it remains unclear whether the cryptocurrency seized in the 2020 case has been forfeited and sold by the US government. Asset forfeiture process is critical in that once it is completed, the US government can benefit from the proceeds of the sale associated with the forfeited asset. That process can be complex for various reasons, including determining who should have access to the stolen proceeds. The victims of terrorism, in this case those defrauded by

---

[44] U.S. Department of Justice. "Global Disruption of Three Terror Finance Cyber-Enabled Campaigns," *Department of Justice Archives*, August 13, 2020. www.justice.gov/opa/pr/global-disruption-three-terror-finance-cyber-enabled-campaigns.

[45] Farivar, C. "Feds Announce Largest Seizure of Cryptocurrency Connected to Terrorism," *NBC News*, August 13, 2020. www.nbcnews.com/tech/tech-news/feds-announce-largest-seizure-cryptocurrency-connected-terrorism-n1236610.

ISIS's COVID-19 scheme, would need to be possibly identified. In the case of Hamas, however, individuals may have been willingly providing support to Hamas and thus would have no legitimate claim to the asset. In fact, those individuals who provided support to Hamas could be potentially prosecuted for providing material support. It can take several years for the US government or the victims of terrorist financing schemes to benefit from the seizing and forfeiture of an asset associated with a terrorist or criminal group. There is no better example than the case of Silk Road, which Chainalysis, the blockchain analytic firm, worked on with the US government. In that case, more than $4 billion worth of Silk Road Bitcoin was tied up in a lengthy court process. In 2022, the US District Court for the Northern District of California ordered that the US government could liquidate (sell and profit from) the Bitcoin seized in the Silk Road case. Two years later, the US Supreme Court declined to hear the appeal, clearing the pathway for the US government to directly benefit from the Bitcoin seized in that case.[46] Keeping in mind that Silk Road was shut down by federal law enforcement in 2013, it has taken more than a decade for the US government to financially benefit from its work.

Taking assets from criminal groups, whether cryptocurrency, cars, real estate, or other high-value items, is one of the most important measures governments can take. Not only do governments take away an important source of terrorist financing, but it also denies groups the opportunity to benefit from the proceeds of crime. Hitting criminal groups in their wallets is crucial to countering the financing of terrorism and this is a reason why FATF Recommendation 38 has enshrined its importance. The messaging around these asset seizures is also important because it can signal to would-be terrorist financiers that your profits can be taken by the government. This can have

---

[46] Gomez, E. "Supreme Court Clears Path for US to Sell $4.4 Billion in Seized Silk Road Bitcoin," *Crypto Briefing*, October 7, 2024. https://cryptobriefing.com/supreme-court-silk-road-bitcoin/.

a deterrent effect and is noted as a key reason why the FBI pursues asset forfeiture in its effort to dismantle terrorist networks.[47]

CONCLUDING THOUGHTS AND RECAP

Efforts to counter the misuse of virtual assets, such as cryptocurrency, are broad, but nascent in their development. In particular, measures to regulate innovative and emerging financial technology like virtual assets have resulted in tension between the cryptocurrency world and governments and intergovernmental organizations like the FATF. FATF's travel rule, as well as FinCEN's implementation, has been a source of constant friction. The industry, through groups like TRISA, has pushed back and may have an opening to see modifications to the US-based implementation with the incoming Trump Administration, which is going to be much more crypto-friendly and will likely alter stringent regulations that the Biden Administration. Critics of the Biden Administration, including Republican lawmakers, dubbed Biden's policies "Operation Choke Point 2.0." In fact, in February 2025, the House of Representatives Financial Services Committee convened a hearing on regulation in the digital asset ecosystem and entitled the hearing "Operation Choke Point 2.0: The Biden Administration's effort to put Crypto in the Crosshairs."[48] Three of the four witnesses lamented that the banking sector was de-banking crypto and crypto-adjacent companies, resulting it a stifling of innovation in the industry.

The Trump Administration's appointment of David Sacks to serve as the "crypto czar" will ease some of the concerns within the crypto industry. Sacks, in his first press conference, hosted on

---

[47] FBI. "Asset forfeiture." *Federal Bureau of Investigations*. www.fbi.gov/investigate/white-collar-crime/asset-forfeiture.

[48] US House Committee on Financial Services. "Meuser: The Biden Administration's Operation Choke Point 2.0 Was Carried Out by the Prudential Regulators to Target and Debank the Digital Asset Ecosystem." *Financial Services House.Gov*. February 6, 2025. https://financialservices.house.gov/news/documentsingle.aspx?DocumentID=409457#:~:text=Meuser%3A%20The%20Biden%20Administration's%20Operation,Asset%20Ecosystem%20%7C%20Financial%20Services%20Committee.

February 5, 2025, emphasized the importance of innovation with the crypto industry, creating easy-to-understand regulations and emphasized President Trump's desire to see growth and US leadership in the crypto space.[49] Sacks and Trump's push to innovate further in the crypto industry is reasonable and potentially important for mainstreaming the use of digital assets. However, as demonstrated in this chapter, illicit actors, such as ISIS and Hamas, are leveraging digital assets to further their deadly causes. As such, complete deregulation of the industry should be a nonstarter. There are some problematic signs that the Trump Administration may err too far in taking a lenient position against those who would abuse the digital asset space for their own selfish purposes. For example, President Trump on January 22, 2025, pardoned the notorious founder of the Silk Road marketplace, Ross Ulbricht, who conducted more than $200 million in illicit trades involving Bitcoin.[50] President Trump later would release Alexander Vinnick from US prison as part of a prisoner swap with the Russian Federation. Vinnick was behind bars due to his involvement in an extensive money laundering scheme that centered around the use of Bitcoin.[51] The dual releases of Ulbricht and Vinnick are especially disconcerting under the backdrop of President Trump's creation of his own cryptocurrency just months before the 2024 Presidential election.[52]

While President Trump's light-touch cryptocurrency regulation may have some undeterminable negative effects that can result in an increase of digital assets for criminal or terrorist purposes, decreasing regulation is unlikely to stifle the work of private sector companies

---

[49] Sacks, D. "David Sacks on Creating Regulatory Clarity for Crypto," *YouTube*, February 5, 2025. www.youtube.com/watch?v=pAiBxfFunbE.
[50] Raymond, N. "Trump pardons Silk Road founder Ross Ulbricht for Online Drug Scheme," *Reuters*, January 22, 2025. www.reuters.com/world/us/trump-pardons-silk-road-founder-ulbricht-online-drug-scheme-2025-01-22/.
[51] Ilyushina, M. "Who Is Alexander Vinnik, the Russian Cybercriminal Swapped for Marc Fogel?" *The Washington Post*, February 12, 2025. www.washingtonpost.com/world/2025/02/12/alexander-vinnik-crypto-marc-fogel-exchange/.
[52] Bladt, C., Kaufman, K., & Mahtani, M. "Trump's Big Cryptocurrency Bet," *CBS News*, August 1, 2024. www.cbsnews.com/news/trump-cryptocurrency-campaign-nashville/.

that are carrying out important forensic work to unearth, often with law enforcement, bad actor use of cryptocurrency. Further, prosecutions of terrorists who increase their wealth by securing, transferring, or storing cryptocurrency are likely to continue unabated. The game of cat and mouse between governments, private industry, and terrorist financiers and money launderers will continue in the virtual asset space just as it has with the use of fiat currency for decades. Thus, continued vigilance is going to be critical over the next few years if cryptocurrency can make the jump from fad to mainstream use. To do that successfully, the financial technology industry will need to ensure to continue to take positive steps by preventing terrorists from gaining a digital foothold in the cryptocurrency space. If they do, virtual asset service providers' reputations will only be further tarnished.

11 Conclusion

With the rise of virtual assets and President Donald J. Trump's strategic interest in seeing cryptocurrency become more mainstream, there are significant risks to US national security interests, to include the effectiveness of terrorist designations. In offering an alternative to the US dollar that encourages wider use of virtual assets, there runs the risk that the power the United States has over international commerce becomes less significant. Banks derisk from doing business in countries that are labeled SSTs, such as Iran and North Korea, by the United States because they want to be able to have access to the dollar. If the importance of the dollar is deemphasized, could the power of US SST listings, and FTO designations for that matter, diminish? There is not a straightforward answer to this question, but it is one that policymakers, law enforcement officials, and financial regulators need to consider. A silver lining, as discussed throughout Chapter 10, is that governments, working with blockchain analytical firms, retain an ability to crack down on illicit use of virtual assets. While reforms, such as interrogating the travel rule to determine whether revisions would be useful to promote creativity in the cryptocurrency industry, are worthy of examination, there are also significant risks to allowing the virtual asset field to run amok with moves to deregulate. A balance will be important to strike given that criminals and terrorists, as well as state sponsors of terrorism, have leveraged cryptocurrency to further their deadly desires.

Nonetheless, while the rise of financial technology allows for legitimate and illicit consumers to move assets at the click of a button, the private sector is not completely helpless in warding off terrorist financiers. In response, a robust regulatory technology

(RegTech) industry has blossomed as part of an effort to assist the private sector in ensuring compliance with regulatory requirements, such as the implementation of terrorist designations. In fact, the RegTech industry is expected to grow on an annual basis between 2024 and 2029 by nearly 25 percent.[1] Technology has long been a key component of banking compliance, including the use of fuzzy logic tools that allows compliance specialists to better identify records associated with designated actors, like terrorists. Now, Artificial Intelligence (AI) is increasingly becoming important for the private sector to carry out CDD, KYC, and sanctions implementation. As AI continues to develop, banks, MSBs, and DNFBPs will improve their capabilities to stop transactions associated with designated terrorists. Just as important, these tools will also improve the consistent challenge banks have related to false positive hits – essentially when someone that may have a similar name to a designated terrorist and has their assets inappropriately frozen. Minimizing false positives will advance human rights. Simply put, people should not be incorrectly deprived of their assets.

During a February 2025 "No Money For Terror" conference convened in Munich, Germany, and organized by the German Finance Ministry, the chair, Dr. Jörge Kukies, of the meeting not only emphasized the importance of human rights consideration when countering the financing of terrorism but also emphasized concerns regarding how FATF recommendations could be weaponized. Dr. Kukies noted, "the need to remain vigilant against the misuse of FATF standards to suppress civil society ... and ensure counter-terrorist financing measures are applied in line with FATF

---

[1] "Global RegTech Business Report 2024–2029: Key Trends, Recent Launches, Partnerships and Collaborations Influencing the Rapidly Growing Multi-Billion Dollar Market." Fintech Futures. *Globe Newswire*, October 31, 2024. www.fintechfutures.com/techwire/global-regtech-business-report-2024-2029-key-trends-recent-launches-partnerships-and-collaborations-influencing-the-rapidly-growing-multi-billion-dollar-market/.

guidance and international law on human rights, and are not politically weaponized."[2] Terrorist designations are ultimately about labeling an individual for carrying out terrorist acts, but there is continued future risk that countries will leverage targeted financial sanctions to go after enemies. As discussed in Chapter 6, China was keen to leverage a possible US FTO designation of Uighurs as part of a policy to crackdown on political enemies and dissidents in Xinjiang Province. When governments push for a terrorist designation, evidence of terrorism must be provided. Otherwise, the private sector could be placed in a position to inappropriately freeze assets or limit access to the financial system – and in doing that, an individual's human rights have been eroded.

While there are limitations in how the private sector can push back against government action, for the most part, the western application of terrorist designations has been appropriately designed, albeit far from perfect. As discussed in Chapters 9 and 10, the private sector is on the front line in the battle against terrorist financing. The filing of STRs/SARs and CTRs are among the most important ways the private sector fights against illicit financing. As former Scotland Yard Investigator Shaun McLeary described, "STRs/SARs are another tool to create a hostile environment in which terrorists operate."[3] STRs filed by investigators allow regulators and investigators to look backwards, forward, and sideways during an investigation. In the aftermath of an attack, the financial data gleaned from private sector filings can allow for an investigator to determine how the terrorist attack developed and better understand the timeline for the attack. Examining STRs can provide peripheral new views of the case where new identities and associations are linked to the

---

[2] Federal Ministry of Finance. *Ministerial Conference on Counter-Terrorism Financing.* February 13, 2025. www.bundesfinanzministerium.de/Content/EN/Downloads/Financial-Markets/no-money-for-terror-chairs-summary.pdf?__blob=publicationFile&v=6.

[3] Blazakis personal interview of Shaun McLeary February 20, 2025.

criminal conspiracy. In doing that, the private sector is opening new avenues for inquiries. Finally, STRs can provide the warning signs of the preparation of a terrorist attack. That forewarning can help governments stop an attack from occurring. Without the private sector, financial investigations into terrorist activity become harder to disrupt. For these reasons, and many more discussed in Chapters 9 and 10, it is incumbent that the public–private sector lines of communications remain open. The government has more work to do to establish trust with the private sector. As the UN CTED and RUSI have identified, PPPs remain imperfect.

Arguably, the most significant tool used to fight against terrorist financing is the use of terrorist designations, the focus of Chapter 6. The United States, the chief purveyor of terrorist designations, has a process to designate a group or individual that is time-consuming. Classified intelligence and open-source information, the twin topics discussed in Chapter 5, are critical in the development of the underlying case for sanctioning a terrorist. The use of targeted financial sanctions will not always result in a panacea in the fight against terrorist financing. Designating terrorists can only be effective if the tool is deployed and as discussed in Chapter 3, it has been sparingly utilized by the United States against violent far-right individuals and groups. Against ISIS, the use of designations, as discussed in Chapter 4, had limitations. Instead, using military force to target ISIS critical infrastructure, resulting in crippling the group's finances and leadership, was more effective. Nonetheless, FTO designations are an especially powerful tool that has resulted, as discussed in Chapter 6, assets frozen and material support prosecutions of ISIS supporters, such as Zoobia Shahnaz, who was discussed in Chapters 4 and 10.

In the early days of the Trump Administration, it was evident that the FTO tool would remain popular. On the first day of the new Administration, Donald Trump issued an Executive Order calling on the State Department to designate Mexican drug cartels and two gangs as FTOs.[4] A month later, the State Department would announce the FTO designations of six Mexican drug cartels, a Venezuelan gang, and an El Salvador-based gang. Eight designations in a month's time are unprecedented, especially when considering the process, outlined in detail in Chapter 6, for designating terrorists pursuant to US law. This begs the question: what types of corners did the State Department cut to fulfill President Trump's desire to poke a finger in the eye of the Mexican government, which was opposed to the FTO designations?[5] The decision to label criminal groups is also unprecedented, likely unwise, and risks conflating terrorism and crime groups, the latter of course, which is solely motivated by financial considerations, not ideological, a hallmark of what motivates terrorist groups. The cartel and gang FTO designations by the United States may also increase the number of STR filings by the private sector, which could further overwhelm regulatory authorities that already have a difficult time sifting through the thousands of STRs/SARs that financial and nonfinancial institution submit per day. The result could make it harder to recognize real terrorist financing, such as adaptations made by groups like ISIS and al-Qa'ida, typologies, and trends.

Early decisions by the Trump Administration are not promising for creating an environment that is inhospitable to terrorists, criminal, and corrupt leaders keen to profit or move money to further their objectives. On February 10, the Trump Administration issued an executive order to pause the enforcement of the Foreign Corrupt Practices Act (FCPA). The decision to suspend FCPA enforcement possibly presents a challenge for countering terrorism financing. In a May 2024 empirical study by Meierrieks and Auer, which was

---

[4] The White House. *Designating Cartels and Other Organizations as Foreign Terrorist Organizations and Specially Designated Global Terrorists*, January 20, 2025. www.whitehouse.gov/presidential-actions/2025/01/designating-cartels-and-other-organizations-as-foreign-terrorist-organizations-and-specially-designated-global-terrorists/.

[5] Blazakis, J. M. "The Case against Designating Cartels as Terrorists: It Risks Diluting the Term into Meaninglessness while Proving Little or No Benefit to Law Enforcement," *The Wall Street Journal*, February 19, 2025. www.wsj.com/opinion/the-case-against-designating-cartels-as-terrorists-90c6c44f.

published by Cambridge University Press, there is a statistical association between political corruption and terrorism.[6] Rooting out corrupt practices is critical given that terrorist groups have long pointed to government corruption as a rallying call for new members and financial support. The underlying conditions that allow for corruption to thrive, insufficient laws, poorly constructed economic policies, and a permissive environment for bribery allow for terrorist groups to build support, and thus finance. Two core aspects of the FCPA are to counter bribery and to ensure that accounting principles are in place to ensure that public officials are doing public good. In removing enforcement, even temporarily, of the FCPA, it creates a problematic signal to the world that the United States no longer cares about fighting against conditions that provide a more fertile ground for terrorists to act. In looking at Transparency International's Corruption Perceptions Index (CPI), it is no surprise that multiple states that have significant challenges in countering terrorism, and its financing, are also rated at the bottom of the CPI. For example, out of 180 rated countries, Syria, a US State Sponsor of Terrorism and led, as of early 2025, by a State Department designated terrorist, sits at 177. Other State Department State Sponsors of Terrorism, North Korea, Iran, and Cuba rank poorly, checking in at 170, 151, and 81 on the CPI. Countries like Nigeria, which is battling FTOs like Boko Haram and ISIS's Province in West Africa rank 140.[7]

Looser enforcement of FCPA will create more welcoming conditions for financial sectors and DNFBPs to be abused by terrorist groups. Improvements made by the private sector to improve transparency around difficult issues like beneficial ownership, a topic discussed in Chapter 9, is now at risk. The ICIJ's investigations found that corrupt politicians, criminals, and terrorists have tried to hide their wealth by

---

[6] Meierriiks, D., & Auer, D. "Bribes and Bombs: The Effect of Corruption on Terrorism," *American Political Science Review*, 2024. https://doi.org/10.1017/S0003055424000418.

[7] Transparency International. *Corruption Perceptions Index*. www.transparency.org/en/cpi/2024/index/cod. Accessed March 1, 2025.

obscuring their true source of ownership. In President Trump's first term, he vetoed the Corporate Transparency Act, which would later be adopted by Congress to ensure US compliance with FATF recommendations. During Trump's second term, Republicans have been more outspoken in their opposition to the CTA.[8] There are also signs that the Trump Administration may want to make modifications to the implementation of the CTA. If so, this would create a more maneuverability in the US commercial and financial systems for bad actors to disguise their activities. In fact, in a discouraging sign, the US Department of the Treasury announced on March 2, 2025, that it would not "enforce any penalties or fines associated with the beneficial information rule under the existing regulatory deadlines."[9] The Treasury Department press release also explained that it would be proposing additional rules related to beneficial information. Very likely, these rules will further loosen efforts that increased transparency of beneficial ownership.

Among the most important ways of countering terrorist financing is through the work of the United Nations and the FATF. Chapter 8 examined the myriad of ways international cooperation plays a role in fighting against terrorist groups, including the use of sanctions by the UN's 1267 Sanctions Committee and implementation of FATF's recommendations. President Trump's view of multilateralism is pessimistic, and the UN has raised his hackles on several occasions. During President Trump's first term, the United States significantly cut back its funding of the UN.[10]

---

[8] Navera, T. "Trump Suggests Corporate Transparency Act Tweaks Amid Support," *Bloomberg Tax*, February 10, 2025. https://news.bloombergtax.com/daily-tax-report/trump-suggests-corporate-transparency-act-tweaks-amid-support; https://news.bloombergtax.com/daily-tax-report/trump-suggests-corporate-transparency-act-tweaks-amid-support.

[9] U.S. Department of the Treasury. "Treasury Department Announces Suspension of Enforcement of Corporate Transparency Act against U.S. Citizens and Domestic Reporting Companies," *US Treasury*, March 2, 2025. https://home.treasury.gov/news/press-releases/sb0038.

[10] Wamsley, L. "Trump Administration Touts A Smaller U.N. Budget (And Takes Credit For It)," *NPR*, December 26, 2017. www.npr.org/sections/thetwo-way/2017/12/26/573483336/trump-administration-touts-a-smaller-u-n-budget-and-takes-credit-for-it.

At the beginning of Trump's second term, his animus for the UN was clear when he said the UN must "get its act together."[11] President Trump's interest in focusing on issues closer to home, such as immigration on the US southern border, has also resulted in significant cuts in US foreign assistance during the start of his second term. For example, several US anti-terror programs, especially in Africa, where there is a significant uptick in terrorism, have been left in limbo because of the foreign aid freeze.[12] The impact of these freezes and cuts will inevitably affect the deployment of multilateral and unilateral capacity-building programs, to include the area of counterterrorism financing training.

In the wake of 9/11, the United States led global efforts to disrupt terrorist financing. However, given the global nature of commerce and the transnational connections terrorist groups have developed, countering the financing of terrorism increasingly required international cooperation and coordination. Systems of cooperation and coordination, such as through the sharing of financial intelligence through FIU channels of communication, became more robust. Nonetheless, there are significant changes on the horizon, and it is likely recent decisions surrounding issues like the FCPA are a harbinger of less regulation and enforcement. Thus, the years ahead may be rocky, resulting in less cooperation and less effectiveness in countering illicit financing. President Trump's lighter regulatory touch will create more avenues for bad actors to exploit. As a result of laxer laws and less enthusiasm for multilateralism, it becomes much more likely that terror will be financed. Consequently, more than ever, terrorist financing will become harder to disrupt.

---

[11] Mason, J., & Nichols, M. "Trump Says UN Has to 'Get Its Act Together,' UN Pushes Back," *Reuters*, February 4, 2025. www.reuters.com/world/us/trump-signs-orders-iran-withdrawing-us-un-human-rights-council-unrwa-2025-02-04/.

[12] Houreld, K., Chason, R., George, S., & Salim, M. "Trump's Global Funding Freeze Leaves Anti-Terror Programs in Limbo," *The Washington Post*, February 16, 2025. www.washingtonpost.com/world/2025/02/16/trump-funding-freeze-terrorism-africa/.

Bibliography

ACADEMIC JOURNAL ARTICLES AND REPORTS

Blazakis, J. Far-right online financing and how to counter It. Global Center. August 2022. https://globalcenter.org/resource/far-right-online-financing-and-how-to-counter-it/.

Furtell, R., Simi, P., & Gottschalk, S. (2006). Understanding music in movements: The white power music scene. *The Sociological Quarterly*, 47(4), 465–494.

Hamm, M. S. (2005). Crimes committed by terrorist groups: Theory, research, and prevention (Final report). U.S. Department of Justice. www.ojp.gov/pdffiles1/nij/grants/211203.pdf.

Jamshidi, M. (2022). The world of private terrorism litigation. *Michigan Journal of Race & Law*. University of Florida Levin College of Law Research Paper No. 22-25. https://papers.ssrn.com/sol3/papers.cfm?abstract_id=4138659.

Lormel, D. M. (2008, March). Combating terrorist financing at the agency and interagency levels. *Combating Terrorism Center at West Point*, 1(4), 5–7. https://ctc.westpoint.edu/combating-terrorist-financing-at-the-agency-and-interagency-levels/.

National Commission on Terrorist Attacks upon the United States. (2004). *Monograph on terrorist financing*. https://9-11commission.gov/staff_statements/911_TerrFin_Monograph.pdf.

Roul, A. (2024, October 4). The rise of Monero: ISKP's preferred cryptocurrency for terror financing. Global Network on Extremism and Technology. https://gnet-research.org/2024/10/04/the-rise-of-monero-iskps-preferred-cryptocurrency-for-terror-financing/.

Sanford, M. (2020). "This is a game": A history of the Foreign Terrorist Organization and State Sponsors of Terrorism lists and their applications. *History in the Making*, 13(1), Article 10. https://web.archive.org/web/20220619225117/https:/scholarworks.lib.csusb.edu/cgi/viewcontent.cgi?article=1140&context=history-in-the-making.

BOOKS

Adams, J. (1986). *The financing of terror* (pp. 135–187). Simon and Schuster.

Biersteker, T. J., & Eckert, S. T. (2008). *Countering the financing of terrorism* (1st ed.). Routledge.

Blazakis, J. (2019). *White supremacy extremism: The transnational rise of the violent white supremacist movement*. The Soufan Center.

Blazakis, J., & Rennebaum, M. (2022, July). *Deterrence and denial: The impact of sanctions and designations on violent far-right groups: Comparing violent far-right terrorist designations among Five Eyes countries*. The Soufan Center.

Byman, D. (2005). *Deadly connections: States that sponsor terrorism* (pp. 259–273). Cambridge University Press.

Chaliand, G., & Blin, A. (2007). *The history of terrorism: From antiquity to al Qaeda* (1st ed.). University of California Press.

Douglas, F. (2004). *Blood from Stones: The Secret Financial Network of Terror*. Broadway Books.

Greenberg, A. (2022). *Tracers in the dark: The global hunt for the crime lords of cryptocurrency*. Doubleday.

Gretchen, P. (2012, July). *Haqqani Network financing: The evolution of an industry*. Combating Terrorism Center at West Point.

Hoffman, B. (2017). *Inside terrorism*. Columbia University Press.

Keatinge, T., & Izenman, K. (2019, May). *Fundraising for right-wing extremist movements*. Royal United Services Institute.

Laqueur, W. (1977). *A history of terrorism* (1st ed.). Little, Brown and Company.

Melzer, R., & Serafin, S. (Eds.). (2013). *Right-wing extremism in Europe: Country analyses, counter-strategies and labor-market oriented exit strategies* (p. 194). Friedrich-Ebert-Stiftung. https://library.fes.de/pdf-files/dialog/10031.pdf

Miller-Idriss, C. (2020). *Hate in the homeland: The new global far right* (1st ed.). Princeton University Press.

Worley, M., & Copsey, N. (2007). White youth. In: Nigel Copsey and Matthew Worley eds., *Tomorrow belongs to us: The British far right since 1967* (pp. 112–131). Routledge.

Yarmolinsky, A. (1962). *Road to revolution: A century of Russian radicalism*. Collier Books.

LEGAL TEXT

Bender's Immigration and Nationality Act Pamphlet. (2011). Immigration and Nationality Act, at Section 219(a)(1).

Blocking property and prohibiting transactions with persons who commit, threaten to commit, or support terrorism; 66, Fed. Reg. 186. (2001, September 23). www.gpo.gov/fdsys/pkg/FR-2001-09-25/pdf/01-24205.pdf

Financial Action Task Force. (2013, October). The Role of Hawala and Other Similar Service Providers in Money Laundering and Terrorist Financing. FATF. Page 9. www.fatf-gafi.org/en/publications/Methodsandtrends/Role-hawalas-in-ml-tf.html.

Financial Action Task Force. (2013, June). International Best Practices: Targeted Financial Sanctions Related to Terrorism and Terrorist Financing (Recommendation 6). Page 7. www.fatf-gafi.org/en/publications/Fatfrecommendations/Bpp-finsanctions-tf-r6.html#:~:text=FATF%20Recommendation%206%20requires%20countries,accordance%20with%20the%20relevant%20UNSCRs.

U.S. Department of Justice. (2023, May 5). Virginia man charged with sending money to ISIS women overseas. *The Washington Post*. www.washingtonpost.com/dc-md-va/2023/05/05/va-man-charged-isis-al-hol/.

U.S. Department of Justice. (2017, July 20). AlphaBay, the Largest Online "Dark Market," Shut Down. *DOJ Archives*. www.justice.gov/archives/opa/pr/alphabay-largest-online-dark-market-shut-down.

U.S. Immigration and Customs Enforcement. (2015, May 29). Ross Ulbricht, aka Dread Pirate Roberts, sentenced to life in federal prison for creating, operating "Silk Road" website. U.S. Immigration and Customs Enforcement. www.ice.gov/news/releases/ross-ulbricht-aka-dread-pirate-roberts-sentenced-life-federal-prison-creating.

United Nations. (2024, July 22). Letter Dated 19 July 2024 from the Chair of the Security Council Committee Pursuant to Resolutions 1267 (1999), 1989 (2011), and 2253 (2015) Concerning Islamic State in Iraq and the Levant (Da'esh), Al-Qaida and Associated Individuals, Groups, Undertakings and Entities Addressed to the President of the Security Council. https://docs.un.org/en/S/2024/556

United Nations. (2024, June 10). *Resolution 2734 (2024) Adopted by the Security Council at Its 9649th Meeting*. https://docs.un.org/en/S/RES/2734(2024)

United Nations. (2001, September 28). *Resolution 1373 (2001) Adopted by the Security Council at Its 4385th Meeting* (p. 2). www.unodc.org/pdf/crime/terrorism/res_1373_english.pdf

United Nations. (1999, October 15). *Security Council Meeting Record S/PV.4051*. https://docs.un.org/en/S/PV.4051

United States V. Tawhedi. (2025, October 8). W. D. of Okla., United States District Court. Criminal Complaint (p. 21).

PERSONAL INTERVIEWS

Blazakis Interview of John Jeffries. February 4, 2025.
Jason Blazakis Personal Interview of Shaun McLeary interview February 20, 2025.
Jason Blazakis Personal Interview with Shaun McLeary, former Scotland Yard financial investigator. February 20, 2025.

ONLINE ARTICLES AND REPORTS

Artingstall, D., & Maxwell, N. (2017, October 17). The role of financial information-sharing partnerships in the disruption of crime. *RUSI*. https://rusi.org/publication/occasional-papers/role-financial-information-sharing-partnerships-disruption-crime.

ASEAN Regional Forum. (2024). Work plan for counter terrorism and transnational crime 2024–2026. Page 13. https://aseanregionalforum.asean.org/wp-content/uploads/2024/07/6.-ARF-2024-2026-CTTC-Work-Plan_26-July_FINAL-CONSENSUS.pdf.

Asia-Pacific Economic Cooperation (APEC). (2014). Secure finance workshop on countering the financing of terrorism with new payment systems. https://aimp2.apec.org/sites/PDB/Lists/Proposals/DispForm.aspx?ID=1525.

Blazakis, J. M. (2022, January 26). U.S. has taken FARC off its terrorist list, giving insight into Biden's foreign policy. *The Conversation*. https://theconversation.com/us-has-taken-farc-off-its-terrorist-list-giving-insight-into-bidens-foreign-policy-174667.

Blazakis, J. M. (2020, May 31). Using a terrorism list to squeeze Cuba and Venezuela. *Lawfare*. www.lawfaremedia.org/article/using-terrorism-list-squeeze-cuba-and-venezuela.

Blazakis, J. M., & Tankel, S. (2020, June 4). The growing irrelevance of State's list of countries not cooperating on counterterrorism. *Just Security*. www.justsecurity.org/70529/the-growing-irrelevance-of-of-states-list-of-countries-not-cooperating-on-counterterrorism/.

Borges, E. (2024, June 24). What is open source intelligence (OSINT)? *Recorded Future*. www.recordedfuture.com/blog/open-source-intelligence-definition.

Chainalysis Team. (2023). Crypto crime trends: Illicit cryptocurrency volumes reach all-time highs amid surge in sanctions designations and hacking. www.chainalysis.com/blog/2023-crypto-crime-report-introduction/.

Christian, R. World's 6 largest stablecoins: Top cryptocurrencies that maintain a stable price. www.bankrate.com/investing/worlds-largest-stablecoins/.

CoinDesk. Top cryptocurrency prices and market cap. www.coindesk.com/price.

de Candia, A. (2020, November 23). CipherTrace: Two patents for tracking Monero (XMR). *Cryptonomist*, https://en.cryptonomist.ch/2020/11/23/ciphertrace-patents-tracking-monero-xmr/.

Dodge, W. S. (2016, September 30). Does JASTA violate international law? *Just Security*. www.justsecurity.org/33325/jasta-violate-international-law-2/.

Egmont Group of Financial Intelligence Units. (n.d.). About the Egmont Group. https://egmontgroup.org/about/.

Egmont Group of Financial Intelligence Units. (n.d.). IEWG – Information exchange working group. https://egmontgroup.org/working-groups/iewg/.

Elliptic. (2023, March 17). How the Russia-Ukraine war led to the growth of NFT fundraising. www.elliptic.co/blog/analysis/how-the-russia-ukraine-war-led-to-the-growth-of-nft-fundraising.

Financial Action Task Force. (2024, April). Private sector consultative forum. www.fatf-gafi.org/en/publications/Fatfgeneral/private-sector-consultative-forum-April-2024.html.

Financial Action Task Force. (2025, February). International standards on combating money laundering and the financing of terrorism & proliferation, 2012–2025. www.fatf-gafi.org/en/publications/Fatfrecommendations/Fatf-recommendations.html.

Financial Action Task Force. (2025, January 25). Countries under FATF's Black and Grey Lists. www.fatf-gafi.org/en/countries/black-and-grey-lists.html.

Financial Action Task Force. (2024, October). Call for action: High-risk and other monitored Jurisdictions. www.fatf-gafi.org/en/publications/High-risk-and-other-monitored-jurisdictions/Call-for-action-october-2024.html.

Financial Action Task Force. (2021, October 21). Public Statement on Pandora Papers. www.fatf-gafi.org/en/publications/Fatfgeneral/Pandora-papers.html.

Financial Action Task Force. Revisions to recommendation 24 and its interpretive note – Public Consultation. www.fatf-gafi.org/en/publications/Fatfrecommendations/Public-consultation-r24.html.

FinCEN Files reporting team. (2020, September 22). FinCEN Files: UK bank may have moved money "linked to terror activity." *BBC News*. www.bbc.com/news/world-middle-east-54235202.

Garside, J., Pegg, D., Watt, H., & Bengtsson, H. (2016, April 6). Mossack Fonseca worked with oil firms owned by Iranian state despite sanctions. *The Guardian*. www.theguardian.com/news/2016/apr/06/mossack-fonseca-oil-firms-petropars-iranian-state-sanctions-panama-papers.

Global Center on Cooperative Security. (2022, June 28). Global Center on cooperative security: June 28, 2022. https://x.com/GlobalCtr/status/1541758566440255496.

Hardy, P. D., & Danch, S. (2024, June 10). FinCEN releases year-in-review for FY 2023: SARs, CTRs, and information sharing. Ballard Spahr LLP. www.moneylaunderingnews.com/2024/06/fincen-releases-year-in-review-for-fy-2023-sars-ctrs-and-information-sharing/#:~:text=Collectively%2C%20they%20filed%20during%20FY,received%20in%20a%20trade%20or.

Hayes, A. (2024, December 22). What happens to Bitcoin after all 21 million are mined? *Investopedia*. www.investopedia.com/tech/what-happens-bitcoin-after-21-million-mined/.

How the SWIFT system works. Investopedia. www.investopedia.com/articles/personal-finance/050515/how-swift-system-works.asp.

Jamshidi, M. (2023, July 24). Iran's ICJ case against Canada tests the terrorism exception to sovereign immunity. *Just Security*. www.justsecurity.org/87357/irans-icj-case-against-canada-tests-the-terrorism-exception-to-sovereign-immunity/.

Keatinge, T. (2017, December 1). Public–private partnerships and financial crime: Advancing an inclusive model. *RUSI*. www.rusi.org/explore-our-research/publications/commentary/public-private-partnerships-and-financial-crime-advancing-inclusive-model.

Kraken. Top Stablecoins Coins by Carket cap. Kraken. www.kraken.com/categories/stablecoins.

Levitt, M. (2015, March 24). The Islamic State's backdoor banking. *The Washington Institute for Near East Policy*. www.washingtoninstitute.org/policy-analysis/islamic-states-backdoor-banking.

Lormel, D. M. (2002, February 12). *Financing patterns associated with al-Qaeda and global terrorist networks*. Federal Bureau of Investigation, before the House Committee on Financial Services, Subcommittee on Oversight and Investigations, Washington, DC. https://archives.fbi.gov/archives/news/testimony/financing-patterns-associated-with-al-qaeda-and-global-terrorist-networks.

Maltego Team. (2024, June 18). OSINT cybercrime investigations investigator know-how: Everything about social media intelligence (SOCMINT) and investigations. *Maltego*. www.maltego.com/blog/everything-about-social-media-intelligence-socmint-and-investigations/.

Meierriiks, D., & Auer, D. (2024). Bribes and bombs: The effect of corruption on terrorism. *American Political Science Review*. https://doi.org/10.1017/S0003055424000418.

Miller, G. (2021, October 3). While his country struggles, Jordan's King Abdullah secretly splurges. *The Washington Post*. www.washingtonpost.com/world/interactive/2021/jordan-abdullah-shell-companies-luxury-homes/?itid=lk_inline_manual_8.

Monero Space (2020, August 31). CipherTrace's Monero Tracing Tool – Chat with Dave Jevans, Dr. Sarang Noether, and Justin Ehrenhofer. www.youtube.com/watch?v=w5rtd3md11g.

Navera, T. (2025, February 10). Trump suggests corporate transparency act tweaks amid support. *Bloomberg Tax*. https://news.bloombergtax.com/daily-tax-report/trump-suggests-corporate-transparency-act-tweaks-amid-support.

Organization for Security and Co-operation in Europe (OSCE). (2024). The role of the OSCE in countering the financing of terrorism. www.osce.org/secretariat/482445.

OSCE Parliamentary Assembly. (2023). Resolution on the Wagner Group's Terroristic Nature and Actions. *OSCE PA*. June 20–July 4. www.oscepa.org/en/documents/ad-hoc-committees-and-working-groups/ad-hoc-committee-on-countering-terrorism/4755-osce-pa-resolution-on-the-wagner-group-terroristic-nature-and-actions-30th-annual-session-2023/file.

Pasquali, V. (2021, August 30). Exclusive: Fall of Afghanistan finds FBI without terrorist financing section. *ACAMS Money*. Laundering.com. www.moneylaundering.com/news/exclusive-fall-of-afghanistan-finds-fbi-without-terrorist-financing-section/.

Pegg, D. (2016, December 1). Panama Papers: Europol links 3,500 names to suspected criminals. *The Guardian*. www.theguardian.com/news/2016/dec/01/panama-papers-europol-links-3500-names-to-suspected-criminals.

Roggio, B. (2013, July 17). AQAP confirms deputy emir killed in US drone strike. *FDD's Long War Journal*. www.longwarjournal.org/archives/2013/07/aqap_confirms_deputy.php 7.

Roth, J., Greenburg, D., & Wille, S. B. (2004, August 21). Monograph on terrorist financing, National Commission on terrorist attacks upon the United States, Staff Report to the Commission. Page 30. https://govinfo.library.unt.edu/911/staff_statements/911_TerrFin_Monograph.pdf.

Roth, J., Greenburg, D., & Wille, S. B. (2004, August 21). Monograph on terrorist financing: Staff Report to the Commission, National Commission on terrorist attacks upon the United States. Page 10. https://govinfo.library.unt.edu/911/staff_statements/911_TerrFin_Monograph.pdf.

Roth, J., Greenburg, D., & Wille, S. B. (2004). Monograph on terrorist financing: Staff Report to the Commission, National Commission on terrorist attacks upon the United States. Page 13.

Sacks, D. (2025, February 5). David Sacks on creating regulatory clarity for crypto. *YouTube*. www.youtube.com/watch?v=pAiBxfFunbE.

Savanović, D. (2025, January 4). Can the IRS track Monero? Not for now, but they are trying. *PlasBit*. https://plasbit.com/anonymous/can-the-irs-track-monero#:~:text=In%20August%202020%2C%20a%20cryptocurrency,million%20from%20a%20government%20contract.

Schanzer, J. (2019, March 22). Why the U.S. still designates terrorist groups. *Foreign Policy*. https://foreignpolicy.com/2019/03/22/why-the-u-s-still-designates-terrorist-groups/.

Sheff, D. (2014, April 1). Nigeria's Boko Haram: A new terrorist group. *The Atlantic.* www.theatlantic.com/international/archive/2014/04/nigerias-boko-haram-a-new-terrorist-group/359337/.

Shin, F. (2022, January 31). What's behind China's cryptocurrency ban? *World Economic Forum.* www.weforum.org/stories/2022/01/what-s-behind-china-s-cryptocurrency-ban/#:~:text=The%20People's%20Bank%20of%20China,crime%20and%20prevent%20economic%20instability.

Sossman, N. A short history of terrorist designations. *National Security Archive.* https://nsarchive.gwu.edu/briefing-book/terrorism/2020-01-09/short-history-terrorist-designations.

Stanley, A. Picture this: The ascent of CBDCs. *Finance & Development Magazine. International Monetary Fund.* www.imf.org/en/Publications/fandd/issues/2022/09/Picture-this-The-ascent-of-CBDCs#:~:text=Central%20bank%20digital%20currencies%20(CBDCs,not%20volatile%2C%20unlike%20crypto%20assets.

The Daily Show with Trevor Noah. (2016, July 21). Boko Haram RNC viewing party. www.cc.com/video-clips/ewuqz6/the-daily-show-with-trevor-noah-boko-haram-rnc-viewing-party.

The Lawfare Institute. (2017, January 13). Designating terrorists and terrorist groups. *Lawfare.* www.lawfaremedia.org/article/designating-terrorists-and-terrorist-groups.

Transparency International. Corruption perceptions index. www.transparency.org/en/cpi/2024/index/cod.

TRM Labs. (2024, October). The rise of Monero: Traceability, challenges, and research review. *TRM Labs.* www.trmlabs.com/resources/blog/the-rise-of-monero-traceability-challenges-and-research-review.

TRM Labs. (2023, July). TRM finds mounting evidence of crypto use by ISIS and its supporters in Asia. TRM Labs. www.trmlabs.com/post/trm-finds-mounting-evidence-of-crypto-use-by-isis-and-its-supporters-in-asia.

United Nations Office of Counter-Terrorism. (2024, June 25). Soft Launch of the GoFintel Software. www.un.org/counterterrorism/events/soft-launch-gofintel-software.

United Nations Office of Counter-Terrorism. (2022). New avenues to address terrorist financing. UN Counter-Terrorism Centre (UNCCT). www.un.org/counterterrorism/cct/countering-the-financing-of-terrorism.

United Nations Office on Drugs and Crime. Training & Tools. www.unodc.org/unodc/en/money-laundering/global-programme-against-money-laundering/training-and-tools.html.

United Nations Office on Drugs and Crime. (2024). UNODC Supports Jordan to Implement UN Security Council Sanctions. www.unodc.org/unodc/en/terrorism/latest-news/2024_unodc_-unodc-supports-jordan-to-implement-un-security-council-sanctions.html.

United Nations Security Council Counter-Terrorism Committee Executive Directorate (CTED). (2024, November). Trends tracker: Evolving trends in the financing of foreign terrorist fighters' activity: 2014–2024. www.un.org/securitycouncil/ctc/sites/www.un.org.securitycouncil.ctc/files/cted_trends_tracker_evolving_trends_in_the_financing_of_foreign_terrorist_fighters_activity_2014_-_2024.pdf.

NEWS ARTICLES AND REPORTS

Bacon, T., & Doctor, A. C. (2023, March 2). The death of Bilal al-Sudani and its impact on Islamic State operations. George Washington University. https://extremism.gwu.edu/death-of-bilal-al-sudani.

BBC News. (2017, May 8). Nigeria Chibok abductions: What we know. *BBC News*. www.bbc.com/news/world-africa-32299943.

Bell, B., & Kirby, P. (2023, February 1). Vienna murders: Four guilty of helping jihadist in terror attack. *BBC News*. www.bbc.com/news/world-europe-64482080.

Bladt, C., Kaufman, K., & Mahtani, M. (2024, August 1). Trump's big cryptocurrency bet. *CBS News*. www.cbsnews.com/news/trump-cryptocurrency-campaign-nashville/.

Blazakis, J. M. (2018, December 3). Labeling Venezuela a terror-supporting state doesn't fit. *The Hill*. https://thehill.com/opinion/international/418984-labeling-venezuela-a-terror-supporting-state-doesnt-fit.

Blazakis, J. M. (2025, February 19). The case against designating cartels as terrorists: It risks diluting the term into meaninglessness while proving little or no benefit to law enforcement. *The Wall Street Journal*. www.wsj.com/opinion/the-case-against-designating-cartels-as-terrorists-90c6c44f.

Bond, G., Thompson, A. C., & Winston, A. (2017, October 19). Racist, violent, unpunished: A white hate group's campaign of menace. *ProPublica*. www.propublica.org/article/white-hate-group-campaign-of-menace-rise-above-movement.

CipherTrace. (2021, August). Cryptocurrency crime and anti-money laundering report. *Cryptocurrency Intelligence*. Pages 28–30. https://info.ciphertrace.com/hubfs/CAML%20Reports/Cryptocurrency%20Crime%20and%20Anti-Money%20Laundering%20Report%2C%20August%202021.pdf.

Connor, T., & Arkin, D. (2017, July 8). Hobby Lobby has bought tons of antiquities. Where do they come from? *NBC News*. www.nbcnews.com/news/us-news/spotlight-hobby-lobby-s-biblical-collection-after-smuggle-case-n780286.

Farivar, C. (2020, August 13). Feds announce largest seizure of cryptocurrency connected to terrorism. *NBC News*. www.nbcnews.com/tech/tech-news/feds-announce-largest-seizure-cryptocurrency-connected-terrorism-n1236610.

Fintech Futures. (2024, October 31). Global RegTech Business Report 2024–2029: Key trends, recent launches, partnerships and collaborations influencing the rapidly growing multi-billion dollar market. *Globe Newswire*. www.globenewswire.com/news-release/2024/10/31/2357344/0/en/Global-RegTech-Business-Report-2024-2029-Key-Trends-Recent-Launches-Partnerships-and-Collaborations-Influencing-the-Rapidly-Growing-Multi-Billion-Dollar-Market.html.

Fitzgibbon, W., Díaz-Struck, E., & Hudson, M. (2017, February 11). Founders of Panama Papers law firm arrested on money laundering charges. International Consortium of Investigative Journalists. www.icij.org/investigations/panama-papers/20170210-mossfon-panama-arrests/.

Gomez, E. (2024, October 7). Supreme Court clears path for US to sell $4.4 billion in seized Silk Road Bitcoin. *Crypto Briefing*. https://cryptobriefing.com/supreme-court-silk-road-bitcoin/.

Gartenstein-Ross, D. (2010, November 23). Death by a thousand cuts. *Foreign Policy*. https://foreignpolicy.com/2010/11/23/death-by-a-thousand-cuts-2/.

Gordon, M. R. (2015, November 17). U.S. strikes Syria oil fields used by ISIS. *The New York Times*. www.nytimes.com/2015/11/17/world/middleeast/us-strikes-syria-oil.html.

Greenberg, A. (2022, April 7). Inside the Bitcoin Bust That Took Down the Web's Biggest Child Abuse Site. *Wired*. www.wired.com/story/tracers-in-the-dark-welcome-to-video-crypto-anonymity-myth/.

Home Office. (2023, September 15). Wagner group proscribed. *Gov.UK*. www.gov.uk/government/news/wagner-group-proscribed#:~:text=The%20Russian%20mercenary%20organisation%2C%20Wagner,proscribed%20as%20a%20terrorist%20organisation.&text=Sunak%20Conservative%20government-,The%20Russian%20mercenary%20organisation%2C%20Wagner%20Group%2C%20has%20been%20proscribed%20as,on%20Wednesday%20(6th%20September).

Hosenball, M., & Shiffman, J. (2012, May 17). U.S. Justice Dept urges terror label for Nigerian militants. *Chicago Tribune*. http://articles.chicagotribune.com/2012-05-17/news/sns-rt-us-usa-security-bokoharambre84h01i-20120517_1_haqqani-network-militant-group-terrorist-group.

Houreld, K., Chason, R., George, S., & Salim, M. (2025, February 16). Trump's global funding freeze leaves anti-terror programs in Limbo. *The Washington Post*. www.washingtonpost.com/world/2025/02/16/trump-funding-freeze-terrorism-africa/.

Ilyushina, M. (2025, February 12). Who is Alexander Vinnik, the Russian cybercriminal swapped for Marc Fogel? *The Washington Post*. www.washingtonpost.com/world/2025/02/12/alexander-vinnik-crypto-marc-fogel-exchange/.

International Consortium of Investigative Journalists (ICIJ). (2017, January 31). Explore the Panama Papers key figures. www.icij.org/investigations/panama-papers/explore-panama-papers-key-figures/.

Kerry, J. (2014, September 22). Remarks at threats to cultural heritage in Iraq and Syria event. U.S. Department of State. https://2009-2017.state.gov/secretary/remarks/2014/09/231992.htm.

Kessler, G. (2014, May 18). "Boko Haram": Inside the State Department debate over the 'terrorist' label. *The Washington Post*. www.washingtonpost.com/world/national-security/boko-haram-inside-the-state-department-debate-over-the-terrorist-label/2014/05/18/2fe89778-dbf6-11e3-9f37-7b1a11b5b3a1_story.html.

King, W. (1985, April 12). Indictment of 24 neo-Nazis expected under U.S. racketeering law. *The New York Times*. www.nytimes.com/1985/04/12/us/indictment-of-24-neo-nazis-expected-under-u-s-racketeering-law.html.

King, W. (1985, September 29). 1983 arrest an elusive clue to neo-Nazi group's plans. *The New York Times*. www.nytimes.com/1985/09/29/us/1983-arrest-an-elusive-clue-to-neo-nazi-group-s-plans.html.

Macaulay, C. (2023, January 27). Bilal al-Sudani: U.S. forces kill Islamic State Somalia leader in cave complex. *BBC News*. www.bbc.com/news/world-africa-64423598.

Macnair, L. (2023, June 28). Understanding Fashwave: The alt-right's ever-evolving media strategy. *GNET*. https://gnet-research.org/2023/06/28/understanding-fashwave-the-alt-rights-ever-evolving-media-strategy/.

Madruga, I. (2024, April 12). An incel's fantasy: Into the world of tradwives. *The Johns Hopkins News-Letter*. www.jhunewsletter.com/article/2024/04/an-incels-fantasy-into-the-world-of-tradwives.

Mason, J., & Nichols, M. (2025, February 4). Trump says UN has to 'Get Its Act Together,' UN Pushes Back. *Reuters*. www.reuters.com/world/us/trump-signs-orders-iran-withdrawing-us-un-human-rights-council-unrwa-2025-02-04/.

Mazzetti, M. (2013, January 24). No. 2 leader of Al Qaeda in Yemen is killed. *The New York Times*. www.nytimes.com/2013/01/25/world/middleeast/said-ali-al-shihri-qaeda-leader-in-yemen-is-dead.html.

Minder, R. (2018, May 2). Basque group ETA disbands, after terrorist campaign spanning generations. *The New York Times*. www.nytimes.com/2018/05/02/world/europe/spain-eta-disbands-basque.html.

Murray, S., & Nossiter, A. (2011, August 26). Suicide bomber attacks U.N. bomber in Nigeria. *The New York Times.* www.nytimes.com/2011/08/27/world/africa/27nigeria.html.

Otis, J. (2016, September 24). The American diplomat who helped bring an end to Colombia's war. NPR Parallels (Audio). www.npr.org/sections/parallels/2016/09/24/495185560/the-american-diplomat-who-helped-bring-an-end-to-colombias-war.

Raymond, N. (2025, January 22). Trump pardons Silk Road founder Ross Ulbricht for online drug scheme. *Reuters.* www.reuters.com/world/us/trump-pardons-silk-road-founder-ulbricht-online-drug-scheme-2025-01-22/

Reilly, K. (2016, July 22). Read Chris Christie's convention speech attacking Hillary Clinton. *TIME.* http://time.com/4419974/chris-christie-republican-convention-speech/.

Rosenberg, M., & Weiser, M. (2021, September 5). How a Nazi rally in Whitefish led to a deadly attack in Charlottesville. *The New York Times.* www.nytimes.com/2021/09/05/us/politics/nazi-whitefish-charlottesville.html.

Sahimi, M. (2009, October 22). Who supports Jundallah? PBS (KQED). www.pbs.org/wgbh/pages/frontline/tehranbureau/2009/10/jundallah.html.

Shear, M. D., & Sanger, D. E. (2017, November 20). Trump returns North Korea to list of state sponsors of terrorism. *The New York Times.* www.nytimes.com/2017/11/20/us/politics/north-korea-trump-terror.html.

Talley, I. (2022, September 6). Islamic State turns to NFTs to spread terror message. *The Wall Street Journal.* www.wsj.com/articles/islamic-state-turns-to-nfts-to-spread-terror-message-11662292800.

Taylor, M. (2011, July 25). Norway gunman claims he had nine-year plan to finance attacks. *The Guardian.* www.theguardian.com/world/2011/jul/25/norway-gunman-attack-funding-claim.

Taylor, M., & Wainwright, M. (2010, August 28). English Defence League supporters attack police at Bradford rally. *The Guardian.* www.theguardian.com/uk/2010/aug/28/english-defence-league-bradford-demonstrations.

The Associated Press. (2011, August 31). Pakistani fertilizer fuels Afghan bombs. *Dawn News.* www.dawn.com/news/655920/pakistani-fertilizer-fuels-afghan-bombs.

The Washington Post. (2016, October 25). What terrorist labels mean and how they are applied. *Washington Post.* www.washingtonpost.com/world/national-security/what-terrorist-labels-mean-and-how-they-are-applied/2016/10/25/dec53130-96f1-11e6-a6c1-6b29e8e08a68_story.html.

U.S. Department of Justice. (2020, August 13). Global disruption of three terror finance cyber-enabled campaigns. *DOJ Archives.* www.justice.gov/archives/opa/pr/global-disruption-three-terror-finance-cyber-enabled-campaigns.

U.S. Department of Justice. (2020, August 5). *United States' verified complaint for Forfeiture in Rem. DOJ Archives.* www.justice.gov/archives/opa/pr/global-disruption-three-terror-finance-cyber-enabled-campaigns.

U.S. Department of Justice. (2024, December 16). Virginia man convicted for crypto financing scheme to ISIS. *DOJ Archives.* www.justice.gov/archives/opa/pr/virginia-man-convicted-crypto-financing-scheme-isis.

U.S. Department of the Treasury. (2023, October 18). Following terrorist attack on Israel, treasury sanctions Hamas operatives and financial facilitators. https://home.treasury.gov/news/press-releases/jy1816.

Wamsley, L. (2017, December 26). Trump administration touts a smaller U.N. budget (and takes credit for it). *NPR.* www.npr.org/sections/thetwo-way/2017/12/26/573483336/trump-administration-touts-a-smaller-u-n-budget-and-takes-credit-for-it.

Weiner, R., & Silverman, E. (2017, October 27). He joined the Islamic State, then fled. Now, he's been sentenced to prison for 20 years. *The Washington Post.* www.washingtonpost.com/local/public-safety/he-joined-the-islamic-state--then-fled-now-he-will-go-to-prison-for-20-years/2017/10/27/9c8a34c2-b813-11e7-9e58-e6288544af98_story.html?noredirect=on&utm_term=.4230c93b9aa1.

GOVERNMENT REPORTS

CJTF-OIR Public Affairs. (2018, March 26). Coalition forces kill ISIS financial facilitator. Combined Joint Task Force – Operation Inherent Resolve. www.inherentresolve.mil/NEWSROOM/News-Releases/Article/1227052/coalition-forces-kill-isis-financial-facilitator/.

Department of Justice. (2016, November 18). Illinois man sentenced to 40 months in federal prison attempting to provide material support to ISIL. Justice News, Office of Public Affairs. www.justice.gov/opa/pr/illinois-man-sentenced-40-months-federal-prison-attempting-provide-material-support-isil.

Department of the Treasury, Financial Crimes Enforcement Network. (2024, December 5). *Bank Secrecy Act Advisory Group; Solicitation of Application for Membership.* Federal Register. www.federalregister.gov/documents/2024/12/05/2024-28451/bank-secrecy-act-advisory-group-solicitation-of-application-for-membership#:~:text=The%20BSAAG%20is%20the%20means,information%20they%20provide%20is%20used.

DeVille, D. (2017, July 18). *Testimony of Mr. Duncan DeVille, Global Head of Financial Crimes Compliance & US BSA Officer, The Western Union Company.* United States House of Representatives, Financial Services Subcommittee on Terrorism and Illicit Finance. www.congress.gov/115/meeting/house/106297/witnesses/HHRG-115-BA01-Wstate-DeVilleD-20170718.pdf.

European Commission. (2022, November 11). Report from the Commission to the European Parliament and the Council on the joint review of the implementation of the Agreement between the European Union and the United States of America on the processing and transfer of financial messaging data from the European Union to the United States for the purposes of the Terrorist Finance Tracking Program. European Commission. https://eur-lex.europa.eu/legal-content/EN/TXT/PDF/?uri=CELEX:52022DC0585.

Executive Order 13224. (2001, September 23). Blocking property and prohibiting transactions with persons who commit, threaten to commit, or support terrorism; 66, Fed. Reg. 186. U.S. Government Printing Office. www.gpo.gov/fdsys/pkg/FR-2001-09-25/pdf/01-24205.pdf.

FATF. (2001, October). FATF IX Special Recommendations. FATF. www.fatf-gafi.org.

FATF. (2014, October). Transparency and Beneficial Ownership. FATF. www.fatf-gafi.org/content/dam/fatf-gafi/guidance/Guidance-transparency-beneficial-ownership.pdf.

FATF. (2015, February). Financing of the Terrorist Organisation Islamic State in Iraq and the Levant (ISIL). FATF. www.fatf-gafi.org.

FATF. (2016). *Anti-money Laundering and Counter-Terrorist Financing Measures – United States, Fourth Round Mutual Evaluation Report*. FATF, Paris. www.fatf-gafi.org/publications/mutualevaluations/documents/mer-united-states-2016.html.

FATF. (2021). Ethnically or racially motivated terrorism financing. FATF. www.fatf-gafi.org.

FATF. (2024, November 20). Treasury imposes sanctions on a Hawala and two individuals linked to the Taliban. U.S. Department of the Treasury. https://home.treasury.gov/news/press-releases/tg1777.

Federal Bureau of Investigation. (n.d.). How we investigate: Intelligence. Federal Bureau of Investigation. www.fbi.gov/how-we-investigate/intelligence.

Federal Bureau of Investigation. (n.d.). Joe Pistone: Undercover agent. Federal Bureau of Investigation. www.fbi.gov/history/famous-cases/joe-pistone-undercover-agent.

Federal Bureau of Investigation. Asset forfeiture. Federal Bureau of Investigations. www.fbi.gov/investigate/white-collar-crime/asset-forfeiture.

Federal Deposit Insurance Corporation. (2007). Connecting the dots: The importance of timely and effective suspicious activity reports. Federal Deposit Insurance Corporation. www.fdic.gov/bank-examinations/connecting-dotsthe-importance-timely-and-effective-suspicious-activity-reports.

Federal Ministry of Finance. (2025, February 13). Ministerial conference on counter-terrorism financing. www.bundesfinanzministerium.de/Content/EN/

Downloads/Financial-Markets/no-money-for-terror-chairs-summary.pdf?_ blob=publicationFile&v=6.

Financial Crimes Enforcement Network (FinCEN). (2019, May 9). Application of FinCEN's regulations to certain business models involving convertible virtual currencies. www.fincen.gov/sites/default/files/2019-05/FinCEN%20 Guidance%20on%20Virtual%20Currencies%20May%209%202019.pdf.

Financial Crimes Enforcement Network. (2005, April 8). Suspicious activity report initiates material support investigation. U.S. Department of the Treasury. www.fincen.gov/resources/law-enforcement/case-examples/suspicious-activity-report-initiates-material-support.

Financial Crimes Enforcement Network (FinCEN). (2024, October 10). FinCEN assesses record $1.3 billion penalty against TD Bank. www.fincen.gov/news/ news-releases/fincen-assesses-record-13-billion-penalty-against-td-bank.

HM Revenue & Customs. (2019, September 4). Money sender fined record £7.8 million in money laundering crackdown. *Gov.UK*. www.gov.uk/government/ news/money-sender-fined-record-78-million-in-money-laundering-crackdown.

Home Office. (2017, October 17). Joint Fraud Taskforce. *Gov.UK*. www.gov.uk/ government/collections/joint-fraud-taskforce.

IMF. Anti-money Laundering/Combatting the Financing of Terrorism (AML/ CFT). IMF. www.imf.org/external/np/leg/amlcft/eng/aml1.htm.

Intelligence and Security Committee. Could 7/7 have been prevented? Review of the intelligence on the London terrorist attacks on 7 July 2005. UK Parliament. https://fas.org/irp/world/uk/july7review.pdf.

Internal Revenue Service. Bank Secrecy Act. U.S. Department of the Treasury. www.irs.gov/businesses/small-businesses-self-employed/bank-secrecy-act#:~:text=Congress%20passed%20the%20Bank%20Secrecy,%2C%20 tax%2C%20and%20regulatory%20matters

Klein, A. (2020, November 19). Statement by Chairman Adam Klein on the Terrorist Finance Tracking Program. U.S. Privacy and Civil Liberties Oversight Board. https://documents.pclob.gov/prod/DynamicImages/Generic/e426b076-928d-4a79-ac0c-9ed9efe9e4cf/TFTP%20Chairman%20Statement%2011_19_20.pdf.

National Economic Crime Centre. Improving the UK's response to economic crime. National Economic Crime Centre. National Crime Agency. www .nationalcrimeagency.gov.uk/what-we-do/national-economic-crime-centre.

Office of the Director of National Intelligence. (n.d.). Counterterrorism guide: Terrorist groups. Office of the Director of National Intelligence. www.dni.gov/ nctc/groups.html#:~:text=To%20designate%20a%20country%20as%20a%20 State%20Sponsor,designation%20is%20rescinded%20in%20accordance%20 with%20statutory%20criteria.

Office of the Press Secretary. (2001, September 24). President freezes terrorists' assets. George W. Bush Whitehouse Archives. https://georgewbush-whitehouse.archives.gov/news/releases/2001/09/text/20010924-4.html.

Pistole, J. S. (2003, September 24). Testimony before the House Committee on Financial Services Subcommittee on Oversight and Investigations. Federal Bureau of Investigation. https://archives.fbi.gov/archives/news/testimony/the-terrorist-financing-operations-section.

Roth, J., Greenburg, D., & Wille, S. B. (2004). Monograph on terrorist financing: Staff report to the Commission. National Commission on Terrorist Attacks upon the United States. https://9-11commission.gov/staff_statements/.

State Sponsors of Terrorism Designations. U.S. Department of State. www.state.gov/terrorist-designations-and-state-sponsors-of-terrorism/state-sponsors-of-terrorism/.

Temple, C. (2005, July 28). Financing of insurgency operations in Iraq. House Armed Services Subcommittee on Terrorism, Unconventional Threats, and Capabilities and House Financial Services Subcommittee on Oversight and Investigations (p. 2). https://financialservices.house.gov/media/pdf/072805ct.pdf.

The Commission on the Intelligence Capabilities of the United States Regarding Weapons of Mass Destruction. (2005, March 31). Report to the President of the United States (pp. 378–379). www.govinfo.gov/content/pkg/GPO-WMD/pdf/GPO-WMD.pdf

The White House. (2025, January 20). Designating cartels and other organizations as foreign terrorist organizations and specially designated global terrorists. www.whitehouse.gov/presidential-actions/2025/01/designating-cartels-and-other-organizations-as-foreign-terrorist-organizations-and-specially-designated-global-terrorists/.

The White House. (2016, September 23). Veto message from the president – S.2040. Office of the Press Secretary. https://obamawhitehouse.archives.gov/the-press-office/2016/09/23/veto-message-president-s2040.

U.S. Department of Homeland Security. (2009, July 9). Morning roundup. www.dhs.gov/archive/news/2009/07/09/morning-roundup-july-9th.

U.S. Department of Justice. (2020, March 13). Long Island woman sentenced to 13 years' imprisonment for providing material support to ISIS. U.S. Department of Justice. www.justice.gov/usao-edny/pr/long-island-woman-sentenced-13-years-imprisonment-providing-material-support-isis.

U.S. Department of Justice. (2012, November 9). *Moneygram International Inc. Admits Anti-Money Laundering and Wire Fraud Violations, Forfeits $100 Million in Deferred Prosecution*. www.justice.gov/archives/opa/pr/moneygram-international-inc-admits-anti-money-laundering-and-wire-fraud-violations-forfeits#:~:text=In%20addition%20to%20forfeiting%20%24100,regularly%20to%20the%20Justice%20Department.%E2%80%9D.

U.S. Department of Justice. (2010, September 1). Pakistani Taliban leader charged in terrorism conspiracy resulting in murder of seven Americans in Afghanistan. FBI. https://archives.fbi.gov/archives/washingtondc/press-releases/2010/wfo090110.htm.

U.S. Department of State. (2022). AML/CFT Capacity Building in the Federal Republic of Nigeria. Winter. www.grants.gov/search-results-detail/341352.

U.S. Department of State. (2021). Country reports on terrorism. Bureau of Counterterrorism. www.state.gov/reports/country-reports-on-terrorism-2021/.

U.S. Department of State. (2017, January 10). State Department terrorist designation of Alexanda Amon Kotey. Bureau of Counterterrorism and Countering Violent Extremism. www.state.gov/j/ct/rls/other/des/266771.htm.

U.S. Department of State. (2016, December 28). Amendment to the terrorist designations of Lashkar e-Tayyiba. Bureau of Counterterrorism and Countering Violent Extremism. www.state.gov/j/ct/rls/other/des/266629.htm.

U.S. Department of State. (2013, November 13). Terrorist designations of Boko Haram and Ansaru. Bureau of Counterterrorism and Countering Violent Extremism. www.state.gov/j/ct/rls/other/des/266565.htm.

U.S. Department of State. (2012, September 28). Delisting of the Mujahedin-e Khalq. Bureau of Counterterrorism and Countering Violent Extremism. www.state.gov/j/ct/rls/other/des/266607.htm.

U.S. Department of State. (2012, September 21). Department of State: Public notice 8050; 77, Fed. Reg. 193. U.S. Government Printing Office. www.gpo.gov/fdsys/pkg/FR-2012-10-04/pdf/2012-24505.pdf.

U.S. Department of State. (2011, March 24). Department of State's terrorist designation of Ibrahim Hassan Tali Al-Asiri. Bureau of Counterterrorism and Countering Violent Extremism. www.state.gov/j/ct/rls/other/des/266641.htm.

U.S. Department of State. (2011, October 4). Terrorist designation of Ibrahim Awwad Ibrahim Ali al-Badri. Bureau of Counterterrorism and Countering Violent Extremism. www.state.gov/j/ct/rls/other/des/266629.htm.

U.S. Department of State. (2010, November 3). Secretary of State's terrorist designation of Jundallah. Bureau of Counterterrorism and Countering Violent Extremism. www.state.gov/j/ct/rls/other/des/266649.htm.

U.S. Department of State. (2010, September 1). Designations of Tehrik-e Taliban Pakistan and two senior leaders. Bureau of Counterterrorism and Countering Violent Extremism. www.state.gov/j/ct/rls/other/des/266652.htm.

U.S. Department of State. (n.d.). Individuals and entities designated by the State Department under E.O. 13224. Bureau of Counterterrorism and Countering Violent Extremism. www.state.gov/j/ct/rls/other/des/143210.htm.

U.S. Department of the Treasury. (2025, March 2). Treasury department announces suspension of enforcement of Corporate Transparency Act against U.S. citizens and domestic reporting companies. *US Treasury*. https://home.treasury.gov/news/press-releases/sb0038.

U.S. Department of the Treasury. (2024, February 27). Counter ISIS Finance Group Leaders Issue Joint Statement. U.S. Department of the Treasury. https://home.treasury.gov/news/press-releases/jy2131.

U.S. Department of the Treasury. (2024, February). 2024 National terrorist financing risk assessment. U.S. Department of the Treasury. https://home.treasury.gov/system/files/136/2024-National-Terrorist-Financing-Risk-Assessment.pdf.

U.S. Department of the Treasury. (2024, March 11). Treasury designates transnational Al-Shabaab money laundering network. U.S. Department of the Treasury. https://home.treasury.gov/news/press-releases/jy2168.

U.S. Department of the Treasury. (2022, August 8). U.S. Treasury Sanctions Notorious Virtual Currency Mixer Tornado Cash. https://home.treasury.gov/news/press-releases/jy0916#:~:text=Treasury%20will%20continue%20to%20aggressively,BSA)%20and%20its%20implementing%20regulations.

U.S. Department of the Treasury. (2021, February 10). Treasury targets designations on terrorist networks. U.S. Department of the Treasury. https://home.treasury.gov/news/press-releases/jy0012.

U.S. Department of the Treasury. (2021, November 22). Treasury designates key financial facilitator for the Islamic State's Afghanistan Branch. https://home.treasury.gov/news/press-releases/jy0502.

U.S. Department of the Treasury. (2019, September 10). Treasury targets wide range of terrorists and their supporters using enhanced counterterrorism sanctions authorities. https://home.treasury.gov/news/press-releases/sm772.

U.S. Department of the Treasury. (2016). Terrorist assets report: Calendar year 2016. Office of Foreign Assets Control. www.treasury.gov/resource-center/sanctions/Programs/Documents/tar2016.pdf.

U.S. Department of the Treasury. (2014, August 6). Treasury designates three key supporters of terrorists in Syria and Iraq. U.S. Department of the Treasury. https://home.treasury.gov/news/press-releases/jl2605.

U.S. Department of the Treasury. (2011, February 10). Treasury identifies Lebanese Canadian Bank Sal as a 'Primary Money Laundering Concern.' https://home.treasury.gov/news/press-releases/tg1057.

U.S. Department of the Treasury. (2005, July 28). Testimony of Acting A/S Glaser on financing for the Iraqi insurgency. U.S. Department of the Treasury. https://home.treasury.gov/news/press-releases/js2658.

U.S. Department of the Treasury. (n.d.). Terrorist finance tracking program: Questions and answers. U.S. Department of the Treasury. https://home.treasury.gov/system/files/246/Terrorist-Finance-Tracking-Program-Questions-and-Answers.pdf.

U.S. Department of the Treasury. (n.d.). Terrorist finance tracking program (TFTP). U.S. Department of the Treasury. https://home.treasury.gov/policy-issues/terrorism-and-illicit-finance/terrorist-finance-tracking-program-tftp.

U.S. Department of the Treasury. Financial Action Task Force highlights treasury's efforts to counter illicit finance. https://home.treasury.gov/news/press-releases/jy2208.

U.S. Government Accountability Office. (2016, August). Report to Congressional Requesters (pp. 7–8). www.gao.gov/assets/gao-16-673.pdf.

U.S. House Committee on Financial Services. (2025, February 6). Meuser: The Biden administration's Operation Choke Point 2.0 was carried out by the prudential regulators to target and debank the digital asset ecosystem. Financial Services. *House.Gov*. https://financialservices.house.gov/news/documentsingle.aspx?DocumentID=409457#:~:text=Meuser%3A%20The%20Biden%20Administration's%20Operation,Asset%20Ecosystem%20%7C%20Financial%20Services%20Committee.

U.S. Immigration and Customs Enforcement. (2011, September 11). 3 plead guilty to conspiracy to provide support to the Pakistani Taliban. *ICE Newsroom*. www.ice.gov/news/releases/3-plead-guilty-conspiracy-provide-material-support-pakistani-taliban.

United Nations Office on Drugs and Crime. Combating Terrorist Financing. UNODC. www.unodc.org/unodc/en/terrorism/expertise/combating-terrorist-financing.html.

United Nations Security Council. (2017, December 11). Hajjaj bin Fahd al-Ajmi. United Nations. main.un.org/securitycouncil/en/sanctions/1267/aq_sanctions_list/summaries/individual/hajjaj-bin-fahd-al-ajmi.

UN Security Council. (2017, July 20). Security Council ISIL (Da'esh) and Al-Qaida sanctions committee adds two names to its sanctions list. UN Security Council. www.un.org/press/en/2017/sc12919.doc.htm.

Index

9/11, 6–8, 24–26, 42, 59–63, 79–81, 85, 109, 128, 130, 137, 140, 158, 160, 175, 181, 186, 219
2024 Nasdaq financial Crime Report, 195

Active Clubs, 35
Adeyemo, Wally, 180
Afghanistan, 24, 87, 100, 109, 111, 113, 132, 178, 183, 199, 204
Africa, 22, 48, 51, 57–58, 78, 94, 103–107, 146, 148–149, 219
Africa Bureau, 103–107
AI, 194, 213
al-Asiri, Ibrahim, 89, 110
al-Badri, Ibrahim Awwad Ibahim Ali, 89
al-Barnawi, Abu Musab, 94
Alexander II, 2–3
al-Farouq, 87
al-Gama'a al-Islamiyya, 4
Algeria, 97, 122
al-Hebo Jewelry Company, 179
al-Hol camp, 195
Ali, Qasim, 103
al-Mansur, Salim, 48
Al-Muhammadia Students, 92
AlphaBay, 202–203
al-Qa'ida, 5–7, 16, 24, 41–43, 45, 48, 60–64, 79, 85, 87, 89, 96, 106, 109–110, 113, 118, 128, 141–142, 151–152, 154, 156–158, 173, 182, 196, 198, 207, 216
al-Qassam Brigades, 196
al-Shabaab, 175
al-Shihri, Said Ali, 123
al-Sudani, Bilal, 51
al-Zawahiri, Ayman, 87
AML/CFT, 12, 24, 141, 149, 180, 187, 192
AMS, 92
Anglin, Andrew, 32–33
Animal Liberation Front, 87
APG, 148
AQAP, 7–8, 89, 110, 123–124

Arab Bank, 170
Arabs, 95
Arafat, Yasir, 150
ARF/CTTC, 162
ASEAN, 162–163, 166
Asia, 22, 45, 78, 147, 162–164, 200
assassinate, 2, 133
assassination, 3, 110–111, 115
assets, 13, 16, 23, 25, 48, 86, 90, 120, 124, 197, 201
ATM, 6, 85
Atomwaffen Division, 1
attacks, 3–8, 16, 21, 25, 28, 37–38, 43, 47, 68–69, 79, 81, 87–88, 92, 97, 106, 108, 110, 112–113, 116, 118, 130, 137, 158, 173, 195–196
Aum Shinrikyo, 88
Australia, 41

Bahamas, 168
Bank of Mosul, 172
Bank Secrecy Act, 18, 23, 73, 167, 180, 182
Basque Fatherland and Liberty, 88
Bates, John D., 103
beneficial ownership, 170, 176, 185, 217
Benjamin, Daniel, 100, 104
BH, 100, 103–104
Biden, Joe, 131, 135, 209
bin Laden, Usama, 7, 66, 86–87, 109, 153
bin Nayif, Muhammad, 110
Bitcoin, 32–33, 52, 144, 188–193, 196, 201, 204–205, 208, 210
Black September, 150
black-market, 202
Blinken, Anthony, 135
Blood & Honor, 34
Boko Haram, 87, 100, 103–107, 149, 217
bomb, 1–2, 4–5, 7, 89, 100, 110
bombing, 4, 14, 27, 51, 104, 111
Boogaloo, 29
border patrol, 113, 142, 190
Bowers, Robert, 27

239

Breivik, Anders, 28, 37
British Virgin Islands, 168
Brussels, 47, 82
BSA, 23, 25, 73–74, 174, 179–180, 182, 185, 206
BSAAG, 182
Byman, Daniel, 138–139

Cambridge University Press, 139, 217
Camp Ashraf, 122
Canada, 41, 135–136, 138, 184
Carson, Johnnie, 104–105
CBDC, 191
CDD, 172–173, 175, 213
CeFi, 190
CFATF, 148
Chainalysis, 194, 197, 201, 203–204, 208
charities, 6, 16, 62, 92, 109, 196
Chhipa, Mohammed Azharuddin, 195
China, 92, 95, 119, 174, 188–189, 214
Chinese, 95–96
Christie, Chris, 106–107
CHS, 64
CIA, 61–62, 99
CICTE, 164
CIFG, 56–57
CipherTrace, 197–200
Clinton, Hillary, 100–102, 104–106, 117, 122
COMINT, 66
compliance, 21, 23–24, 78, 90, 134, 141, 144, 147–148, 154, 158, 163, 166, 171, 173, 175, 181, 191, 213, 218
Congress, 40, 63, 73, 95, 105, 109, 117, 120, 126, 173, 218
counterfeiting, 39–40
counterterrorism, 3, 8–9, 58, 66, 71, 82, 84, 86, 100–101, 123, 132, 135–137, 144, 151, 156, 159–160, 163, 219
Counterterrorism Bureau, 55, 86, 93, 105, 149
Counterterrorism Bureau and Treasury, 93
COVID-19, 196, 208
CPI, 217
CPSG, 165
Crimea, 118
crowdfunding, 30
cryptocurrency, 10, 29, 32–33, 52, 65, 70, 80, 144, 157, 163, 187–191, 193–200, 202–203, 205, 207–210, 212
CSIS, 27

CT, 93–96, 98–100, 102–103, 116, 118, 120, 123, 125
CTA, 177, 186, 218
CTC, 62, 160, 186
CT/CTFD, 93–94, 96, 98–100, 116, 118, 120, 123, 125
CTED, 160–161, 186, 215
CTITF, 159
CTRs, 18, 74–77, 175, 178, 214
Cuba, 131–132, 137, 217
currency, 17, 23, 32, 52, 55, 73–74, 142, 144, 188–189, 191–194, 197, 204–207, 211
mixer, 205
Cuspert, Denis, 91
Cynthia Miller-Idriss, 30

Daily Stormer, 32, 34
Dark Net, 47
darknet marketplace, 201, 203
DEA, 22
DeFi, 190–191
deficiencies, 145–149
delistings, 124
Department of Defense, 50, 60–61, 99
Department of Justice, 39, 51, 53, 64, 90, 94, 101, 104, 112–113, 116, 124, 180, 195–196, 203, 206–207
deregulation, 199, 210
derisk, 145, 212
diamonds, 24
digital wallets, 190, 193
DNFBPs, 24, 74, 142, 167, 171, 175–177, 179, 181, 185–186, 213, 217
Dodge, William, 137
DOJ, 94, 195–196, 203
DPA, 179
drug, 7, 16, 22, 24, 179, 210, 215
due diligence, 23, 97, 141, 172, 178
Duncan Deville, 173
Durra Europos, 67

EAG, 148
East Turkestan Islamic Movement, 95
ECG, 144
ECJ, 153
economy, 88, 112, 130, 145
EEC, 17
Egmont Group, 77–79
Egypt, 109, 118
El Salvador, 216

El Shafee Sheikh, 96
El Sheikh, 96
Elliptic, 204
Environmental Liberation Front, 87
E.O., 48, 85–86, 88, 90, 92–94, 96, 98, 102, 108, 110, 112–114, 116–117, 120–121, 123, 125–126, 178–179, 205
equity check, 97–99, 103, 107, 111, 121
ESAAMLG, 148
ETA, 88, 122
Ethereum, 190–191, 200, 203
ETIM, 95
EU, 81–82, 153–154
Europe, 22, 28, 39, 45, 78, 82, 92, 152, 154, 164, 173
European Court of Justice, 153
European Union, 81, 83, 132, 153
Europol, 169
Expatriates, 15, 175
extortion, 7, 14, 16, 44

Facebook, 59, 71, 92, 108, 115, 126
Faisal Shahzad, 100, 111
FARC, 102, 122, 135
far-right groups, 28–29, 35, 38, 40, 43, 49
fashwave, 33–34
FATF, 9, 11, 21, 24–25, 37–39, 41–42, 44, 46, 57, 77–80, 140–149, 151, 155, 158–159, 162, 165–167, 170–177, 185–186, 188–189, 192–194, 197, 201, 207–209, 213, 218
FBI, 16, 53, 60, 62–67, 71, 75, 80, 90, 94, 99, 112–113, 173, 181, 183, 209
FCPA, 216–217, 219
fei-chen, 174
financing terms
    front companies, 21
FinCEN Files, 168, 170, 176
FININT, 59, 75–80, 82
FINTECH, 187
FIU, 74, 76–78, 80, 164, 178, 194, 219
Five-Eye, 41
Flannery, Michael, 14
formal financial system, 6, 13, 23, 85, 101, 107, 124, 167, 195
Forza Nuova, 35
France, 37–39, 92, 97, 129, 174
freezing, 124, 143, 147, 188
FRN, 117, 120, 123
FSIA, 136

FSRBs, 144, 147, 149, 166
FTOs, 48, 51–53, 65, 84–87, 89–90, 92–95, 99–108, 110–114, 116–117, 120–124, 126, 133–135, 170–171, 175, 180, 185, 205–207, 212, 214–217
fundraising, 9, 12–13, 38, 48, 65, 72, 195–196, 199, 204, 207

G7, 140, 164
G8, 165
GABAC, 148
GAFILAT, 148
gang, 216
General Court, 153
GEOINT, 66–67
Germany, 6, 38, 50, 97, 165, 213
GIABA, 148
GNET, 34, 199
gold, 19, 24, 179, 188
GPML, 161, 164
Greenberg, Andy, 201

Haiti, 146
Hammerskins, 34
Haqqani Network, 24, 100, 102, 119, 171
hawala, 157, 174–175, 178–179
hawaladar, 174
Hizballah, 22–23, 79, 147, 159, 180–181
Holbrooke, 100–103
Holbrooke, Richard, 100
House of Commons, 5
HQN, 24, 119–120, 171
human right, 153–154
human trafficking, 47, 180
HUMINT, 59, 61, 63–67, 69–70, 72, 108
hundi, 174
Hussein, Saddam, 43, 134

ICIJ, 168–171, 176–178, 181, 185, 187, 217
ICRG, 145
IEEPA, 88
illicit finance, 16, 72, 140, 142, 167–168, 171, 173, 184
IMF, 12
IMINT, 65–67, 72, 108
immigration, 52, 84, 87, 90, 103, 109, 111, 117, 202
INA, 87–88, 111, 121
income streams, 6, 9, 43

International Court of Justice, 136
international law, 135–137, 153, 214
investigations, 39, 62, 69, 73, 90, 94, 143, 165, 168–169, 171, 176–177, 181, 183, 185, 200, 202, 204, 215, 217
IRA, 13–15, 17, 22
Iran, 113, 131, 134–136, 138, 146–147, 169, 172, 212, 217
Iran's Islamic Revolutionary Guard, 113
Iraq, 40, 42–51, 54–56, 58, 60–61, 64, 67, 72, 90, 122, 130, 157, 161, 173, 179, 195
Ireland, 14–17
Irfan Ul Haq, 103
ISIL, 44, 46, 57, 90, 96, 152, 154, 157
ISIS, 1, 9, 26, 40–58, 63–65, 67–69, 71–72, 77–79, 82, 88, 90–91, 94, 96, 118, 125, 127, 142–143, 149, 152, 154, 156–157, 159, 161, 172, 178–179, 184, 192, 195–200, 203, 206–208, 210, 215–217
Israel, 97, 129, 150, 170, 198, 205
Israel–Palestinian conflict, 150

Jabhat al-Nusrah, 64, 72, 91, 95
Jamaat al Dawa al Quran, 94
Jamshidi, 133–134, 136
Japan, 88, 188
JASTA, 136–137
JDQ, 94
Jefferies, John, 194, 199
Jemaah Islamiyah, 5
Jevans, Dave, 199
JFT, 183
JMLIT, 183
Joint Comprehensive Plan of Action, 134
Jundallah, 113
JVTA, 136–137

Kadeer, Rebiya, 95
Kadi, Yassin, 153
Kayani, Ashfaq Parvez, 101
Kazakhstan, 97
Keatinge, Tom, 184
Kenya, 4, 184
Kerry, John, 54, 107
KFR, 160
Khalozai, Ismatullah, 178
Khan, Mohammad Hamzah, 90
Kharon, 203
Khweis, Mohamad, 124

kidnapping, 7, 16, 21, 44, 107, 110, 160, 163
Kim Jong Un, 133
KKK, 28
kleptocrats, 168
Kotey, Alexanda, 96
Ku Klux Klan, 87
Kukies, Jörge, 213
Kyrgyzstan, 164

Laden, Bin, 7, 61, 66, 128
Laqueur, Walter, 1
Lashkar-e Tayyiba, 92
Latin America, 22, 148, 164
Laura Southern, 31
laws, 10, 21, 40, 42, 67, 72, 84, 133, 136–137, 145–146, 148, 162, 166, 175, 177, 184, 217, 219
Lazarus Group, 205
LCB, 22, 180–181
Lebanese Canadian Bank, 22–23, 180–181
Lebanese Hizballah, 22
Lebanon, 109
LeT, 92, 119–120, 126
Levitt, Matthew, 172
LH, 22
licit, 9, 13, 16, 28, 37–40, 43, 168, 206
LLCs, 171
LOC, 116, 125
London, 5, 47, 133
lone wolf, 37
looting, 55, 67
Lubeck, Paul, 105
Lyon group, 165

Maduro, 133
Maghreb, 106
Malaysia, 133, 163
manifesto, 37
martyrdom, 3
MasterCard, 198
McLeary, Shaun, 182–183, 214
McRaven, Admiral, 104
McRaven, William H., 104
Mehsud, 113
Mehsud, Hakimullah, 112
MEK, 122, 134
MENAFATF, 148
MER, 145, 177
mercenary, 204
MERs, 144, 148

methods of terrorist financing
    legitimate businesses, 7
    placement, 17
Middle East, 45, 75, 78, 85, 148, 161, 195
military, 7, 15, 21, 42, 49, 51, 60, 68, 99,
    130, 198, 204, 215
Milli Muslim League, 126
MML, 126
Monaco, Lisa, 104
Monero, 197–200, 203
money laundering, 10–11, 17–19, 21–23,
    52, 73–74, 76, 78–80, 140–146, 149,
    160–161, 163–165, 167, 169, 174–175,
    179, 181, 183, 185, 189, 196, 198, 210
MoneyGram, 174, 179
MONEYVAL, 148
monitoring, 24, 145
Mossack Fonseca, 168–169
movement, 16–17, 29–31, 34–37, 39,
    55, 68, 81, 87, 95, 113, 119, 142,
    169–173, 178, 181, 188–189,
    193–196, 198
MSB, 179
MT, 157
Murphy, Thomas, 17
MVTS, 173–175, 177

Nakamoto, Satoshi, 188
narco state, 133
Narodnaya Volya, 2
Nasir Tawhedi, 64
national security, 88, 92–93, 97–98, 105,
    108, 112, 122–123, 125, 212
National Security Council, 125
neo-Nazi, 1, 32, 34, 38–39
New York City, 16, 54, 100, 111
New Zealand, 38, 41
NFCC, 84, 131–134, 137
NFTs, 188, 192, 203–204
Nigeria, 78, 87, 104–107, 146, 149, 217
Nigerian, 104–105, 107
Noah, Trevor, 107
NOFO, 149
NORAID, 14–16
Nordic Resistance, 28
North Korea, 131, 133, 139, 146–147, 169,
    172, 181, 205, 212, 217
Norway, 28, 37–38, 77
Noting Rahat Ltd., 178
NPOs, 141, 149

NPS, 163
NSA, 66, 99
NSC, 125

OAS, 164, 166
Oathkeepers, 32
Obama, Barack, 106–107, 137
OFAC, 48, 75, 93, 116, 120
Office of Counterterrorism Finance and
    Designations, 93
OIC, 150
oil, 1, 43–44, 46, 48–50, 55, 57, 67–68, 169
Ombudsperson, 153
OpenSeas, 203
Operation Choke Point 2.0., 209
Operation Mantis, 165
Operation Pegasus, 22
operations, 2, 6, 16, 37, 39, 42, 44–45, 49,
    55–56, 64, 69, 73, 85, 87, 90, 95,
    98–99, 109, 140, 142, 161, 173,
    178, 182
Order, 39, 85, 156, 158, 215
organized crime, 40, 64, 73, 140, 179
OSCE, 164, 166, 204
Owaye Azazi, 105

P2P, 167
Pakistan, 1, 24, 52, 87, 94, 98, 100–102,
    111–112, 119, 132
Palestinian, 3, 150
Panama Papers, 168–169, 176, 185
Pandora Papers, 168, 170, 185
pariah state, 147
Paris, 37–39, 47, 82, 174, 177
Patriot Act, 181
Patterson, Anne, 100–103
PDG, 144
People's Will, 2–3
Persian Gulf, 6, 24, 109, 175
Peters, Gretchen, 24, 171
Petropars Ltd., 169
PIJ, 3
Pistone, Joe, 64
PLO, 150
PPPs, 181, 183–184, 186, 215
private sector, 8, 12, 16, 53–54, 59, 67, 72,
    77, 89, 141, 144–145, 156, 166–167,
    169–171, 173–174, 177–179,
    181–186, 188, 191–192, 194, 197,
    199–200, 204, 210, 212, 214, 216–217

propaganda, 32, 34, 43–44, 127
prosecutions, 6, 31, 53, 70, 90, 107, 143, 204, 206–207, 211, 215
Proud Boys, 29, 32, 41
PSCF, 185
Putin, Vladimir, 155

QAnon, 29

ransom, 7, 16, 45, 160, 163
recommendations, 11, 24–25, 57, 78–80, 140–149, 158–159, 166–167, 170–172, 174–177, 186, 189, 192–194, 197, 201, 207–208, 213, 218
RegTech, 213
report, 6, 24, 31, 37–39, 41, 44–45, 57, 62, 67, 70, 73–75, 79–80, 85, 124, 143, 157–158, 161, 171, 175–176, 182, 184, 186, 192, 194, 198–200, 203, 213, 218
Revolutionary Armed Forces of Colombia, 102
RFJ, 55
RICO, 40
right wing, 27
RIM, 28, 203
Rise Above Movement (RAM), 36
robbery, 38, 40
Robinson, Tommy, 31
Roma group, 164–165
RTMG, 143
Rundo, Robert, 35
RUSI, 31, 184, 186, 215
Russia, 2–3, 36, 48, 92, 97, 118, 132–133, 148, 155, 165, 204
Russian Federation, 118, 148, 210

Sacks, David, 209–210
sanctions, 9, 41–42, 48, 57–58, 72, 85–86, 93–94, 98, 101, 118–119, 124, 128, 131–132, 139, 144, 151–155, 158, 160, 162, 169, 178–179, 181, 185, 204, 213–215, 218
Sanctions Committee. UN 1267, 154
SARs, 18, 74–77, 169, 175, 214, 216
Saudi Arabia, 45, 56, 94, 109, 118, 133, 153
Sayyaf, Abu, 46, 51, 53–54
Scandinavian, 91
Scotland Yard, 182–183, 214
SDGTs, 84, 88, 96, 121, 124

SDN, 120
Security Council resolution 1822, 152
Security Council resolution 1904, 153
Security Council Resolution 1989, 154
Security Council Resolution 2734, 152
Security Resolution 1988, 154
seizing, 111, 188, 198, 206–207
Senegal, 118
sentenced, 53, 90, 125, 202
Seychelles, 168
Shahnaz, Zoobia, 52–53, 63, 66, 195, 206, 215
Shahzad, Faisal, 100–101
SIGINT, 65–67, 72, 108
Silicon Valley, 91–92, 126
Silk Road, 201–203, 208, 210
Skinhead, 34
Skirpal, Sergei, 133
Slab, 17
smuggling, 7–8, 18, 43, 49, 55, 165
SOCMINT, 69–72
Somalia, 51, 161
Soufan Center, 31, 36, 41
South Sudan, 146
Spain, 88
Spencer, Richard, 32
SRAP, 100, 102
SSTs, 84, 130–137, 139, 212
stablecoins, 191
State Department, 9, 55, 60, 84, 86–87, 89, 91–100, 102, 104, 107–108, 110–114, 120, 123, 125, 130, 149, 169, 171, 175, 215, 217
the State Department, 84, 99, 123, 126, 149
Strait of Malacca, 162
suicide, 4, 88, 104, 110–111, 113
Switzerland, 18, 168
Syria, 40, 42–51, 54–56, 64, 67, 72, 90, 95, 130–131, 136, 161, 173, 179, 195, 198, 217

T3 FCU, 200, 204
tactics, 3, 28, 64, 105, 141, 148
Taliban, 87, 100, 102–103, 111–113, 129, 151, 154, 178, 203
Tankel, Stephen, 132
Tanya Gersh, 32
Tanzania, 4
tax, 17, 21, 44, 73, 168, 218
Tehrik-e, 87, 100, 111–112

TEL, 85
Terrircon Project, 203
terrorism, 1, 8–9, 11, 13, 25, 27–28, 37–40, 49, 60, 66, 70, 72, 75, 79–81, 84, 86–88, 92, 96, 100, 102, 106, 109–112, 115, 118, 124, 129, 131–132, 134–138, 141–144, 146–147, 149–150, 152–153, 155, 158–166, 171–172, 174, 179–180, 184–186, 189, 197, 201, 204, 207–208, 212–213, 216, 219
terrorist, 1–3, 5–8, 11–13, 16–21, 23, 25, 28, 33–34, 37, 40–42, 44, 47–48, 51–53, 55, 57–64, 66, 68–70, 72–74, 76–83, 85–102, 104, 106–107, 109–111, 113–114, 116–121, 124, 126, 128–132, 135, 137–147, 149, 151–153, 155–163, 165–167, 169–171, 173, 177–183, 186, 188, 190–199, 202–205, 207–208, 210, 212–219
  attack, 2, 5, 25, 61, 66, 71, 81, 83, 128, 170, 214
  designations, 9, 28, 40, 48, 53, 60, 72, 85–86, 93–94, 97–101, 106–107, 114, 116–117, 120–121, 124, 126, 158, 178–179, 206, 212–215
  group, 1, 9, 13, 17, 34, 41–42, 44, 47, 49, 52, 55, 59, 62, 78, 86–87, 91, 94–95, 107, 109, 113, 121, 126, 139, 203, 206
  organizations, 129–130
terrorist financing terms
  armed robbery, 39
  crowdfunding, 31, 56
  donations, 31, 45, 91, 188, 195–198
Tether, 191, 200
TFEU, 60
TFOS, 64, 66, 182–183
TFTP, 81–82
the Order, 38–39
theft, 7, 15, 54
Three Percenters, 32
Tidal Wave II, 50, 67–68
Tillerson, Rex, 117
Tornado Cash, 205–206
TPB, 162
tradwife, 36
training camp, 87
TRISA, 194, 209
TRM Labs, 197, 200, 204

Tron network, 200
Trump, Donald, 10, 33, 131, 133, 194, 209–210, 212, 215–216, 218–219
Tsarnaev Brothers, 82
TTP, 100–103, 111–112
Turkey, 43, 52, 161, 178–179, 195
Twitter, 59, 72, 108, 115
typologies, 143, 148, 183–184, 216

UAE, 109
UCO, 64
Uighurs, 95, 214
Ukraine, 36, 148, 155, 203–204
Ulbricht, Ross, 201–202, 210
UN 1267, 41, 57, 96, 118, 151–157, 159, 203
UN Security Council Resolutions, 141, 147
UN Terrorist Financing Convention, 147
Unite the Right Rally, 35
United Kingdom, 5, 17, 35, 41, 92, 96, 179, 181–183, 204
United Nations, 8, 11, 41–42, 45, 56, 58, 72, 96, 104, 117–118, 140, 143, 150–153, 157–162, 166, 186, 218
United Nations Convention for the Suppression of the Financing of Terrorism, 143
United States, 1, 4, 6–8, 14, 16, 22, 27–29, 34–35, 38, 40–42, 46, 48–49, 51–53, 55–57, 60–62, 65, 67, 70–72, 74, 81, 83–93, 95–96, 98, 100–101, 103, 107, 109, 112–114, 117–122, 125, 127–132, 134–136, 138–139, 148, 150, 153–154, 156, 158, 162–164, 167, 170, 174–175, 177, 181, 183, 185, 188, 193, 196, 206, 212, 215–219
United States Court of Appeals, 114
University of California in Santa Cruz, 105
UNOCT, 159–161
UNODC, 11, 160–162, 164
UNSC, 153–154
UNSCR, 151–152, 158, 162–163
UNSCR 1267, 152, 158–159, 163
UNSCR 1373, 158, 162
UNSCR 2734, 152
US House of Representatives Financial Services Subcommittee on Terrorism and Illicit Finance, 173

Valentina Pasquali, 183
VASPs, 192–193

Venezuela, 131–133, 137
Vinnick, Alexander, 210

Wagner Group, 204
Wall Street Journal, 203–204, 216
wearable hate, 30
Weather Underground, 87
website, 29–30, 32, 34, 56, 64, 156, 196, 202
West Africa, 22, 78, 94, 148–149, 217
Western Union, 173–174

White House, 99, 126, 137, 216
white-power, 34
WMD, 70, 146–147, 172
WUC, 95

Yemen, 118, 123, 130
Yousaf, Zahid, 103

Zardani, Asif Ali, 101
Zarif, Mohammed Javad, 134

For EU product safety concerns, contact us at Calle de José Abascal, 56–1°, 28003 Madrid, Spain or eugpsr@cambridge.org.

www.ingramcontent.com/pod-product-compliance
Ingram Content Group UK Ltd.
Pitfield, Milton Keynes, MK11 3LW, UK
UKHW021619130126
466887UK00019B/324